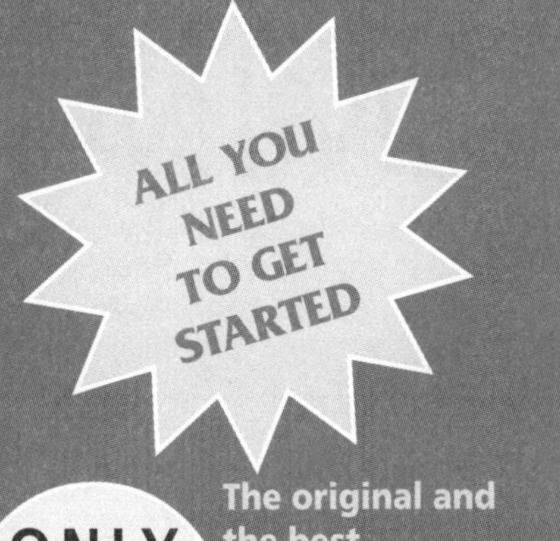
ALL YOU
NEED
TO GET
STARTED

The original and the best.

**ONLY £8.99** except where priced

WORD 2000
MADE SIMPLE
PHOTOSHOP 5
MADE SIMPLE
MARTIN EVENING &
WINDOWS 98
MADE SIMPLE
P.K. McBRIDE
THE INTERNET
MADE SIMPLE
FULL COLOUR EDITION

These books explain the basics of software packages and computer topics in a clear and simple manner, providing just enough information to get started. They are ideal for users who want an insight into software packages and computers without being overwhelmed by technical jargon

- **Easy to Follow**
- **Task Based**
- **Jargon Free**
- **Easy Steps**
- **Practical**
- **Excellent Value**

MADE SIMPLE
BOOKS
An imprint of
Butterworth-Heinemann
http://www.bh.com

t forget to visit our website **http://www.madesimple.co.uk**

# COMP
# MADE

CW01483702

NEW
**AOL 4.0**
Keith Brindley
0 7506 4626 8 1999

NEW
**Access 2000**
Moira Stephen
0 7506 4182 7 1999

NEW
**Access 2000 in Business**
Moira Stephen 1999
7506 4611 X £11.99

**Access 97 for Windows**
Moira Stephen
0 7506 3800 1 1997

**Access for Windows 95 (V.7)**
Moira Stephen
0 7506 2818 9 1996

**Access for Windows 3.1 (V.2)**
Moira Stephen
0 7506 2309 8 1995

NEW
**Adobe Acrobat & PDF**
Graham Douglas
0 7506 4220 3 1999

NEW
**Compuserve 2000**
Keith Brindley
0 7506 4524 5 1999

**Compuserve (V.3)**
Keith Brindley
0 7506 3512 6 1998

NEW
**Designing Internet Home Pages** *Second Edition*
Lilian Hobbs
0 7506 4476 1 1999

NEW
**Excel 2000**
Stephen Morris
0 7506 4180 0 1999

NEW
**Excel 2000 in Business**
Stephen Morris 1999
0 7506 4609 8 £11.99

**Excel 97 for Windows**
Stephen Morris
0 7506 3802 8 1997

**Excel for Windows 95 (V.7)**
Stephen Morris
0 7506 2816 2 1996

**Excel for Windows 3.1 (V.5)**
Stephen Morris
0 7506 2070 6 1994

NEW
**Explorer 5.0**
P K McBride
0 7506 4627 6 1999

**Explorer 4.0**
Sam Kennington
0 7506 3796 X 1998

**Explorer 3.0**
Sam Kennington
0 7506 3513 4 1997

NEW
**Internet In Colour** *2nd Edition*
P K McBride 1999
0 7506 4576 8 £14.99

NEW
**Internet for Windows 98**
P K McBride
0 7506 4563 6 1999

**Internet for Windows 95**
P K McBride
0 7506 3846 X 1997

NEW
**FrontPage 2000**
Nat McBride
0 7506 4598 9 1999

**FrontPage 97**
Nat McBride
0 7506 3941 5 1998

NEW
**The iMac Made Simple**
Keith Brindley
0 7506 4608 X 1999

NEW
**Microsoft Money 99**
Moira Stephen
0 7506 4305 6 1999

NEW
**Publisher 2000**
Moira Stephen
0 7506 4597 0 1999

**Publisher 97**
Moira Stephen
0 7506 3943 1 1998

**MS-DOS**
Ian Sinclair
0 7506 2069 2 1994

**Multimedia for Windows 95**
Simon Collin
0 7506 3397 2 1997

**Netscape Communicator 4.0**
Sam Kennington
0 7506 4040 5 1998

**Netscape Navigator (V.3)**
P K McBride
0 7506 3514 2 1997

NEW
**Office 2000**
P K McBride
0 7506 4179 7 1999

**Office 97**
P K McBride
0 7506 3798 6 1997

NEW
**Outlook 2000**
P K McBride
0 7506 4414 1 1999

NEW
**Pagemaker (V.6.5)**
Steve Heath
0 7506 4050 2 1999

NEW
**Photoshop 5**
Martin Evening
Rod Wynne-Powell
0 7506 4334 X 1999

**Powerpoint 2000**
Moira Stephen
0 7506 4177 0 1999

**Powerpoint 97 for Windows**
Moira Stephen
0 7506 3799 4 1997

**Powerpoint for Windows 95 (V.7)**
Moira Stephen
0 7506 2817 0 1996

NEW
**Sage Accounts**
P K McBride
0 7506 4413 3 1999

**Searching the Internet**
P K McBride
0 7506 3794 3 1998

**Windows 98**
P K McBride
0 7506 4039 1 1998

**Windows 95**
P K McBride
0 7506 2306 3 1995

**Windows 3.1**
P K McBride
0 7506 2072 2 1994

NEW
**Windows CE**
Craig Peacock
0 7506 4335 8 1999

**Windows NT (V4.0)**
Lilian Hobbs
0 7506 3511 8 1997

NEW
**Word 2000**
Keith Brindley
0 7506 4181 9 1999

NEW
**Word 2000 in Business**
Keith Brindley 1999
0 7506 4610 1 £11.99

**Word 97 for Windows**
Keith Brindley
0 7506 3801 X 1997

**Word for Windows 95 (V.7)**
Keith Brindley
0 7506 2815 4 1996

**Word for Windows 3.1 (V.6)**
Keith Brindley
0 7506 2071 4 1994

**Word Pro (4.0) for Windows 3.1**
Moira Stephen
0 7506 2626 7 1995

**Works for Windows 95 (V.4)**
P K McBride
0 7506 3396 4 1996

**Works for Windows 3.1 (V.3)**
P K McBride
0 7506 2065 X 1994

Includes New Titles for 1999

# FrontPage 2000 Made Simple

Nat McBride

MADE SIMPLE
BOOKS

OXFORD AUCKLAND BOSTON JOHANNESBURG MELBOURNE NEW DELHI

Made Simple
An imprint of Butterworth-Heinemann
Linacre House, Jordan Hill, Oxford OX2 8DP
225 Wildwood Avenue, Woburn MA 01801-2041
A division of Reed Educational and Professional Publishing Ltd

A member of the Reed Elsevier plc group

First published 1999


**British Library Cataloguing in Publication Data**
A catalogue record for this book is available from the British Library

ISBN 0 7506 4598 9

Typeset by Elle and P.K.McBride, Southampton
Icons designed by Sarah Ward © 1994
Printed and bound in Great Britain

PLANT A TREE
BTCV
British Trust for Conservation Volunteers
FOR EVERY TITLE THAT WE PUBLISH, BUTTERWORTH-HEINEMANN WILL PAY FOR BTCV TO PLANT AND CARE FOR A TREE.

# Contents

# Preface

HTML – HyperText Markup Language – is the language used to construct pages on the World Wide Web. These pages, and also different parts of the same page, are connected by hypertext links, which guide Web browsers such as Netscape and Explorer through the Internet.

HTML is not a complicated programming language, but it still takes a while to learn, and even experienced users will admit that it is slow and fiddly to work with at times. Since most computer users are not programmers, but are familiar with systems like Microsoft Windows or the Macintosh Operating System, it made sense for the software companies to develop programs which act as HTML translators. You tell the program what you want, using its toolbar and menu commands, and it translates that into HTML so that Web browsers can read it.

There are a number of HTML editing packages available now, all of which do the same sort of job, but some of which do it much better than others. FrontPage 2000 is the latest version from Microsoft and it is probably the most powerful package you can get at the moment. It is comfortable to use, and very thorough – you can chop and change things as much as you like, and FrontPage will run around after you, tidying up all the loose ends.

FrontPage also makes use of a number of mini-programs called 'Components' which allow you to equip your web site with facilities which would normally require the help of an experienced programmer. The Components not only save time when constructing your site, but also make it easy to collect and organise feedback from your visitors; you can even add a search function to help visitors find what they want.

You don't need to know any HTML or have any technical experience to create a professional-looking web site using FrontPage – it is far more a question of letting your creative side loose on the machine! It is useful to have some knowledge of how computer networks work, if you want to set up a complicated site with password-restricted areas, for example, but other than that, all you need is a copy of FrontPage, a little imagination – and this book!

The first few pages will give you a general idea of how FrontPage works, and show you around the screen layout; after that you can jump straight into constructing a web site. The following chapters will explain what you can do with FrontPage, and more importantly, how to do it with a minimum of fussing, head-scratching and hair-tearing! Finally, I have included a 'Links and resources' page to point you in the direction of some helpful sources of tips and advice. Keep an eye out when you're surfing the Web, too – there's a whole world of ideas out there, and often, people who have used FrontPage to construct their sites will display a FrontPage icon somewhere. SITE CREATED WITH Microsoft® FrontPage™

So, put on your construction hat and read on – the World Wide Web is your oyster!

# 1 Getting started

# What is a web?

Most HTML editors help you create Web pages which can then be linked together into a Web site. FrontPage 2000 takes a more interconnected approach by prompting you to create fully linked sets of pages called 'webs'.

At its most basic, a web could be a single page, to which you might add a couple of hyperlinks to your favourite Web sites. The upper limit on the size of a web is determined only by the amount of space you have on your Web server, and might include hundreds of pages. Most webs will fall somewhere comfortably between the two – the FrontPage Web templates give a fair idea of typical webs.

## Creating a new web

Before you sit down to work on your masterpiece of web design, it's not a bad idea to build a practice site, just to get the hang of it. FrontPage has a number of web templates and wizards which give you a basis to work on, so let's start with one of these.

The wizards will ask you to set various options before it creates the web – what kind of information to include, how a search function is to work, and so on.

For now, choose **Personal Web** from the list, as we just want a simple web with a few pages so that you can master the basics of web work – formatting pages, previewing the web in a browser, organising your files and keeping track of your work.

## Basic steps

1. Open the File menu.
2. Choose New, then Web...
3. Click on a template to see its description.
4. Select Personal Web.
5. Type a filename for the web. This goes after the "\" where it says "My Webs\".
6. Click OK.
7. Double-click on one of the files.
8. Type "Hey, that wasn't so hard!" in the main window.

### Installation

**If you have not already installed FrontPage, run setup.exe from the CD to start the installation program. If you are prompted to install a Personal Web Server, select Yes; this allows webs to run on your machine as they would on the World Wide Web.**

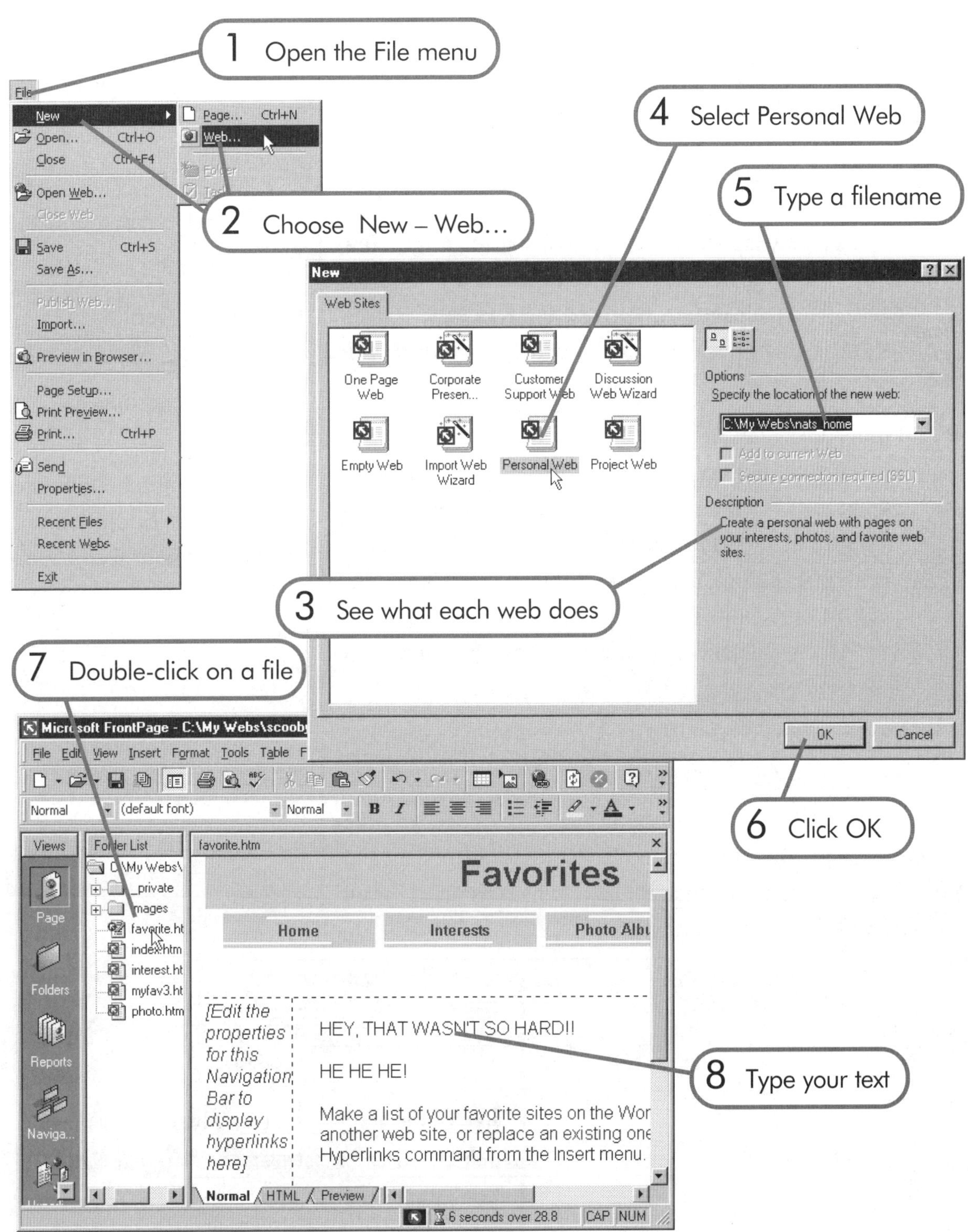
1 Open the File menu
2 Choose New – Web…
3 See what each web does
4 Select Personal Web
5 Type a filename
6 Click OK
7 Double-click on a file
8 Type your text
New
Web Sites
One Page Web
Corporate Presen...
Customer Support Web
Discussion Web Wizard
Empty Web
Import Web Wizard
Personal Web
Project Web
Options
Specify the location of the new web:
C:\My Webs\nats_home
Add to current Web
Secure connection required (SSL)
Description
Create a personal web with pages on your interests, photos, and favorite web sites.
OK
Cancel
Favorites
Home
Interests
HEY, THAT WASN'T SO HARD!!
HE HE HE!

# The FrontPage Window

When you open a web in FrontPage, the window is split into three areas:

- **Views Bar** – on the left-hand side there is a bar with six buttons on it. This is used to switch between the different ways of viewing your web. For instance, **Page view** shows you your web one page at a time, and is used for working on the pages themselves. **Folders view** is used for organising your web, and so on. We will deal with each view separately in a moment.
- **Folder List** – next to the **Views bar** there is a list of files in your web, arranged in the same way as in Windows Explorer. This view is available in **Page**, **Navigation**, and **Hyperlink views**, and can be turned off to give you more working space by clicking the **Folder List** button. This list is used to move between pages when you're working: double-clicking on a file opens it in the main area as a **Page view**.
- The main area in the window is your working space, and what you see here depends on which **View** you are using.

Across the top of the window you have the menu and the standard toolbar. Below that is the Text formatting toolbar, and along the bottom is another toolbar, which is used when working with images.

## Basic steps

1 Create a new web.

*Or if you have created one or two test webs:*

2 Open the File menu.

3 Choose Recent Webs.

4 Select a web.

5 Double-click on a filename to open a page.

6 Click on the buttons on the Views bar to look around your web.

## Tip

**Before you start work, have a look around a new web by switching between the different Views, just to get used to them.**

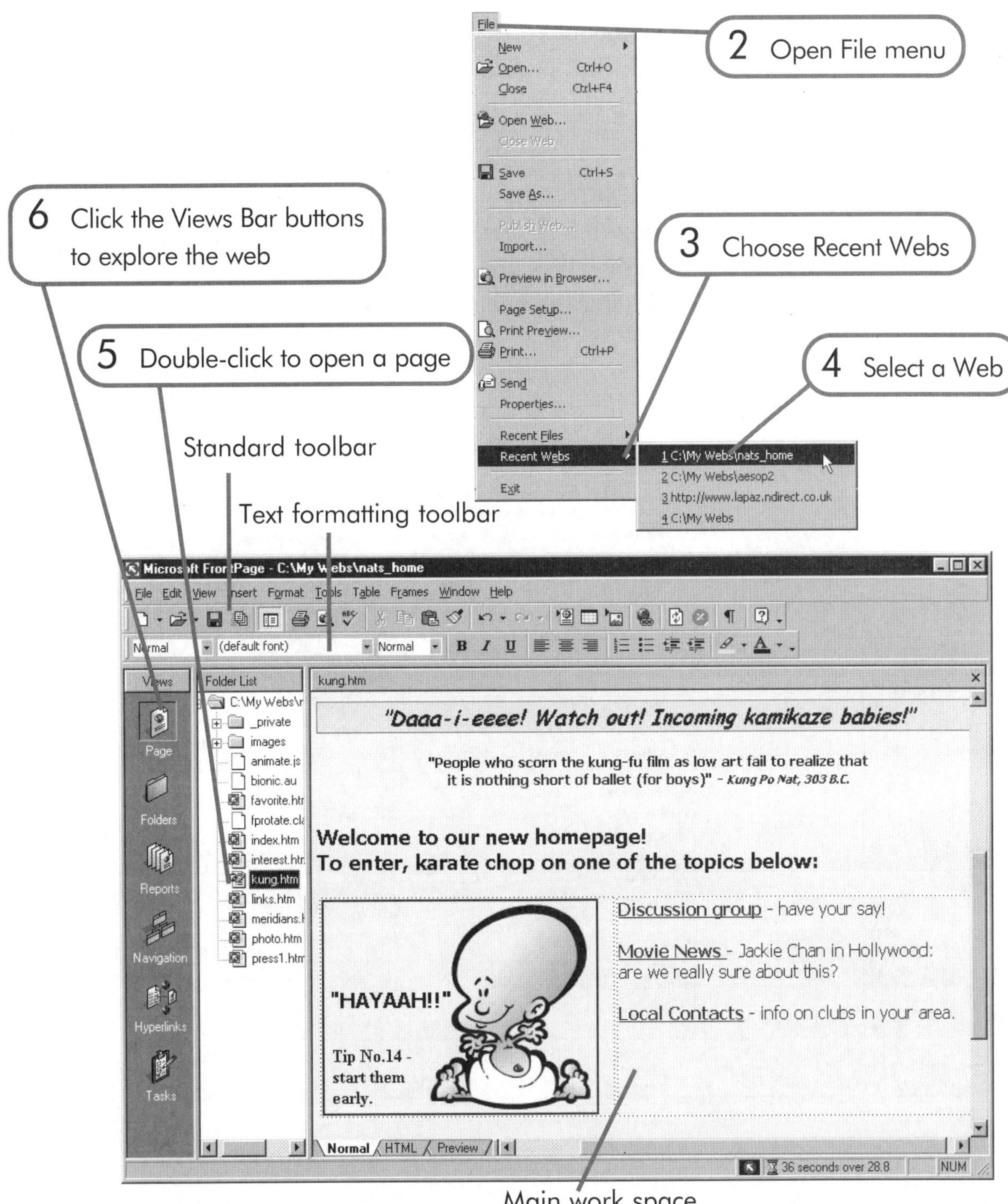
2 Open File menu
3 Choose Recent Webs
4 Select a Web
5 Double-click to open a page
6 Click the Views Bar buttons to explore the web
Standard toolbar
Text formatting toolbar
Main work space
File
New
Open... Ctrl+O
Close Ctrl+F4
Open Web...
Close Web
Save Ctrl+S
Save As...
Publish Web...
Import...
Preview in Browser...
Page Setup...
Print Preview...
Print... Ctrl+P
Send
Properties...
Recent Files
Recent Webs
Exit
1 C:\My Webs\nats_home
2 C:\My Webs\aesop2
3 http://www.lapaz.ndirect.co.uk
4 C:\My Webs
"Daaa-i-eeee! Watch out! Incoming kamikaze babies!"
"People who scorn the kung-fu film as low art fail to realize that it is nothing short of ballet (for boys)" - Kung Po Nat, 303 B.C.
Welcome to our new homepage!
To enter, karate chop on one of the topics below:
"HAYAAH!!"
Tip No.14 - start them early.
Discussion group - have your say!
Movie News - Jackie Chan in Hollywood: are we really sure about this?
Local Contacts - info on clubs in your area.

# Folders view

## Basic steps

Use the **Folders view** to work with your files – if you have a lot of files and want to find a specific one, click on one of the headers in the main window to list files in order by **Name**, page **Title**, file **Size**, etc.

FrontPage also needs to switch between views to stay organised – whenever you save a file to your web from another program (e.g. an image editor such as PaintShop Pro), you will need to go into **Folders view** and click the **Refresh** button before you can use the file in **Page view**.

1 Click on the Folders button.

2 Click on a header to list files by Name, Type, etc.

3 Double-click on a file to open it in Page view.

4 Click on Folders to return to Folders view.

5 Click the Refresh button to update the list of files.

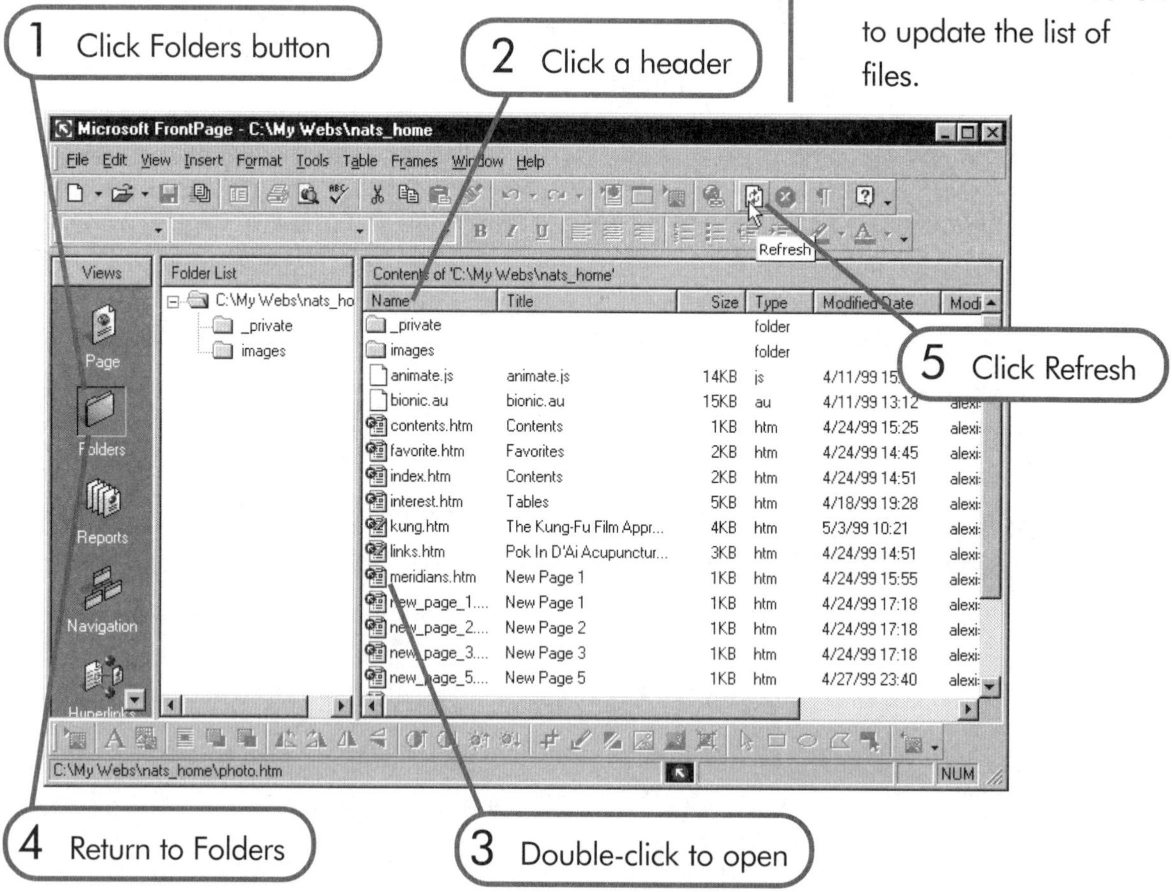

1 Click Folders button

2 Click a header

5 Click Refresh

4 Return to Folders

3 Double-click to open

Microsoft FrontPage - C:\My Webs\nats_home

File Edit View Insert Format Tools Table Frames Window Help

Refresh

| Views | Folder List | Contents of 'C:\My Webs\nats_home' | | | | | |
|---|---|---|---|---|---|---|---|
| | C:\My Webs\nats_ho | Name | Title | Size | Type | Modified Date | Modi |
| Page | _private | _private | | | folder | | |
| | images | images | | | folder | | |
| Folders | | animate.js | animate.js | 14KB | js | 4/11/99 15: | |
| | | bionic.au | bionic.au | 15KB | au | 4/11/99 13:12 | alexi |
| Reports | | contents.htm | Contents | 1KB | htm | 4/24/99 15:25 | alexi |
| | | favorite.htm | Favorites | 2KB | htm | 4/24/99 14:45 | alexi |
| Navigation | | index.htm | Contents | 2KB | htm | 4/24/99 14:51 | alexi |
| | | interest.htm | Tables | 5KB | htm | 4/18/99 19:28 | alexi |
| | | kung.htm | The Kung-Fu Film Appr... | 4KB | htm | 5/3/99 10:21 | alexi |
| | | links.htm | Pok In D'Ai Acupunctur... | 3KB | htm | 4/24/99 14:51 | alexi |
| | | meridians.htm | New Page 1 | 1KB | htm | 4/24/99 15:55 | alexi |
| Hyperlink | | new_page_1.... | New Page 1 | 1KB | htm | 4/24/99 17:18 | alexi |
| | | new_page_2.... | New Page 2 | 1KB | htm | 4/24/99 17:18 | alexi |
| | | new_page_3.... | New Page 3 | 1KB | htm | 4/24/99 17:18 | alexi |
| | | new_page_5.... | New Page 5 | 1KB | htm | 4/27/99 23:40 | alexi |

C:\My Webs\nats_home\photo.htm

NUM

## Basic steps

1. Click on the Hyperlinks button.
2. Click ⊞ on a page to show its hyperlinks.
3. Click ⊟ to hide them.
4. Click on a page in the Folder List.

*Or*

5. Right-click on a page and choose Move to Center to see the links in and out of this page.

# Hyperlinks view

This shows the hyperlink structure of your web. An arrow pointing from one page to another shows that there is a hyperlink between them. A plus sign on a page shows that there are more hyperlinks leading from it; click once on the page to show them.

If you just browse through the links in your web, you may find this view more confusing than helpful! It is more useful to take a particular page and look at the links coming into and out of it.

### Take note

**Hyperlinks only go in one direction (shown by the arrow) – to be able to go back and forth between two pages you need a link on each.**

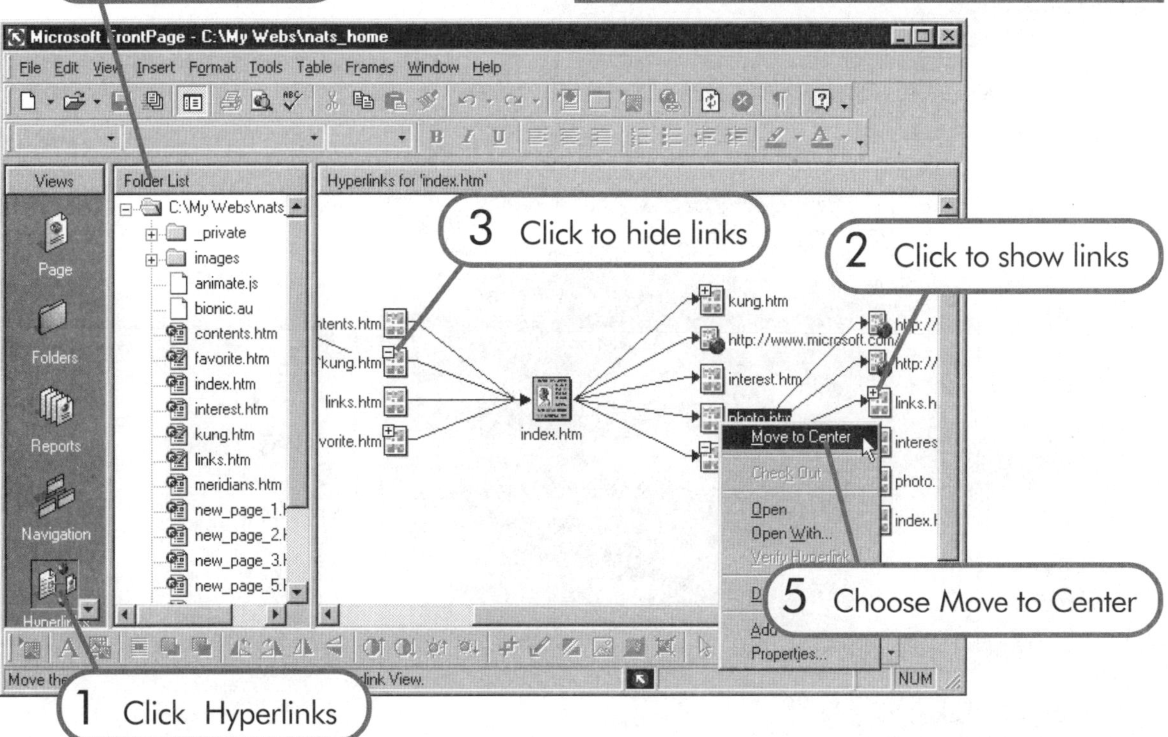
4 Click Folder List
3 Click to hide links
2 Click to show links
5 Choose Move to Center
1 Click Hyperlinks
Microsoft FrontPage - C:\My Webs\nats_home
Folder List
Hyperlinks for 'index.htm'
index.htm
Move to Center

# Page view

## Basic steps

The **Page view** is where you will spend most of your time; here you work on the pages themselves. Several pages can be open at once, and you can move between them as you work.

You can open pages in the web you are working on, or from elsewhere on your computer, or from webs you may have on the Internet.

When browsing choose:

- **History** for recently-used files
- **My Documents**, **Desktop** and **Favorites** for files in common places on your computer
- **Web Folders** for files you've already published to the Internet with FrontPage 2000

❑ For a new page:

1 Click on the Page button.

2 Double-click on a file in the Folder List.

*Or*

3 Choose Open… from the File menu.

4 Browse for a file.

5 Click Open.

❑ For a new page

6 Choose New, then Page… from the File menu.

7 Select a template.

8 Click OK.

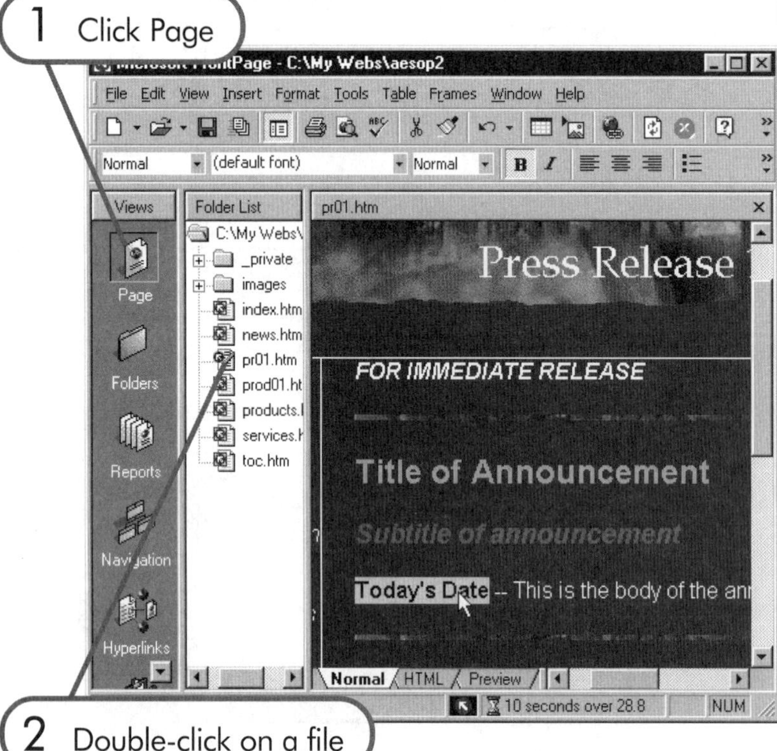
1 Click Page
FrontPage - C:\My Webs\aesop2
File Edit View Insert Format Tools Table Frames Window Help
Normal (default font) Normal
Views
Page
Folders
Reports
Navigation
Hyperlinks
Folder List
C:\My Webs\
_private
images
index.htm
news.htm
pr01.htm
prod01.ht
products.l
services.l
toc.htm
pr01.htm
Press Release
FOR IMMEDIATE RELEASE
Title of Announcement
Subtitle of announcement
Today's Date -- This is the body of the an
Normal HTML Preview
10 seconds over 28.8
NUM
2 Double-click on a file

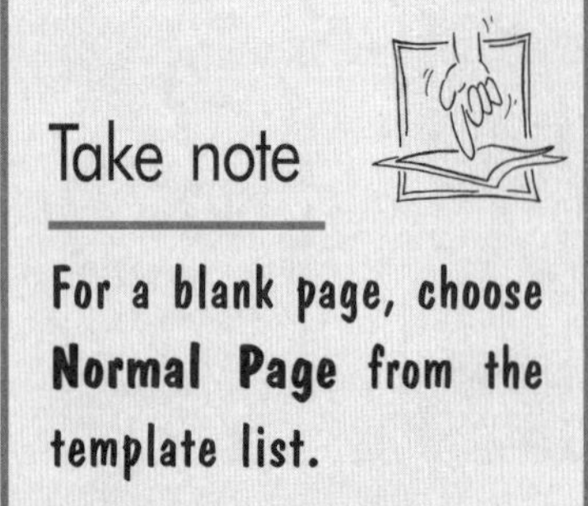

### Take note

**For a blank page, choose Normal Page from the template list.**

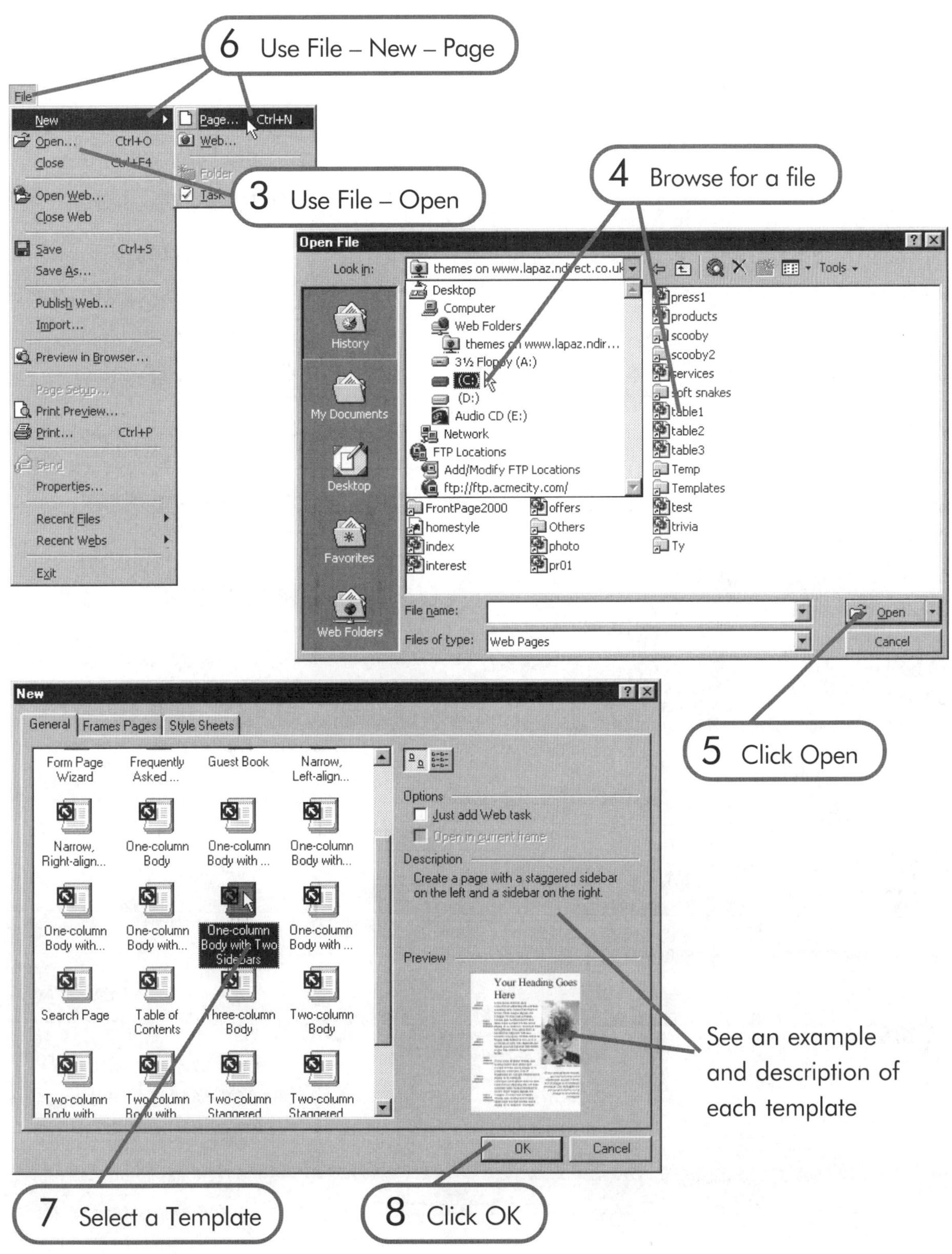

6 Use File – New – Page
3 Use File – Open
4 Browse for a file
5 Click Open
7 Select a Template
8 Click OK
See an example and description of each template

# To save pages

First rule of working with computers – save regularly! This ensures that you don't accidentally delete work or lose it in a program crash. When you save a page which contains images brought in from outside your web, you will be prompted to save any new images to it – this ensures that nothing gets missed out when you publish your web to the Internet.

## Basic steps

1 Choose Save As… from the File menu.
2 Enter a File name.
3 Click Change…
4 Enter a Page title and click OK.
5 Click Save.
6 If prompted to Save Embedded Files, click OK.

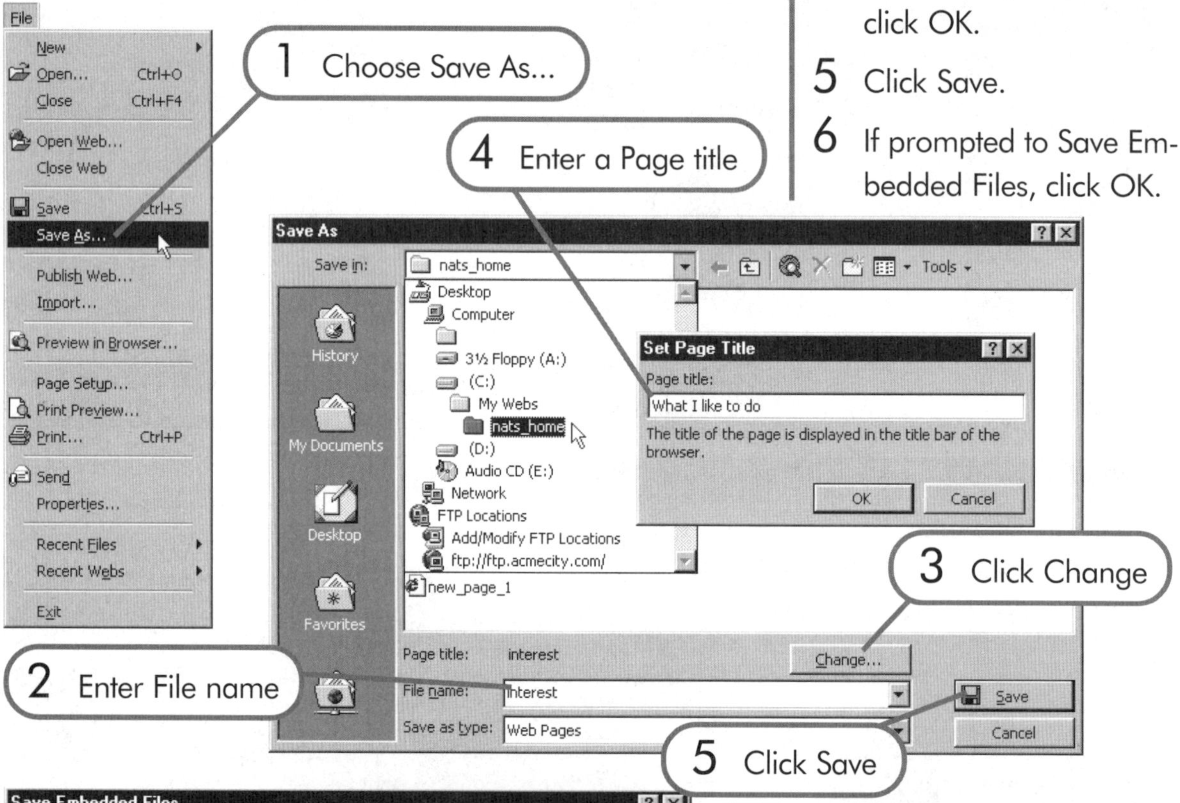

1 Choose Save As…

4 Enter a Page title

3 Click Change

2 Enter File name

5 Click Save

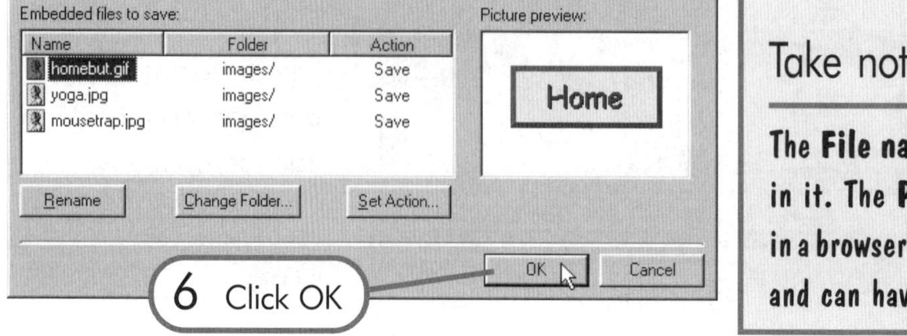

Save Embedded Files
Embedded files to save:
Name
Folder
Action
homebut.gif
images/
Save
yoga.jpg
images/
Save
mousetrap.jpg
images/
Save
Picture preview:
Home
Rename
Change Folder...
Set Action...
OK
Cancel


6 Click OK

### Take note

**The File name cannot have spaces in it. The Page title is displayed in a browser's title bar when viewed, and can have any characters in it.**

## Basic steps

# Page properties

1. Right-click anywhere on the page, and choose Page Properties…
2. Click on the Background tab.
3. Click the down arrow ▾ next to a colour setting to open the palette.
4. Select a colour.
5. Click More Colors... for a wider choice.
6. Repeat for the other settings and click OK.

From the **Page properties…** dialog box, you can set a colour scheme for your page, choose a background image, set margins, or link a sound file to it (see page 58).

## Setting colours

- **Background** – the default ‘paper’ colour.
- Normal **Text** – selected text can be recoloured later.
- **Hyperlink** – the initial colour for links.
- **Visited Hyperlink** – the colour of a link which you have already followed.
- **Active Hyperlink** – selects the colour that the link turns as you click on it.

Default colours are already set if you leave any of these settings on Automatic.

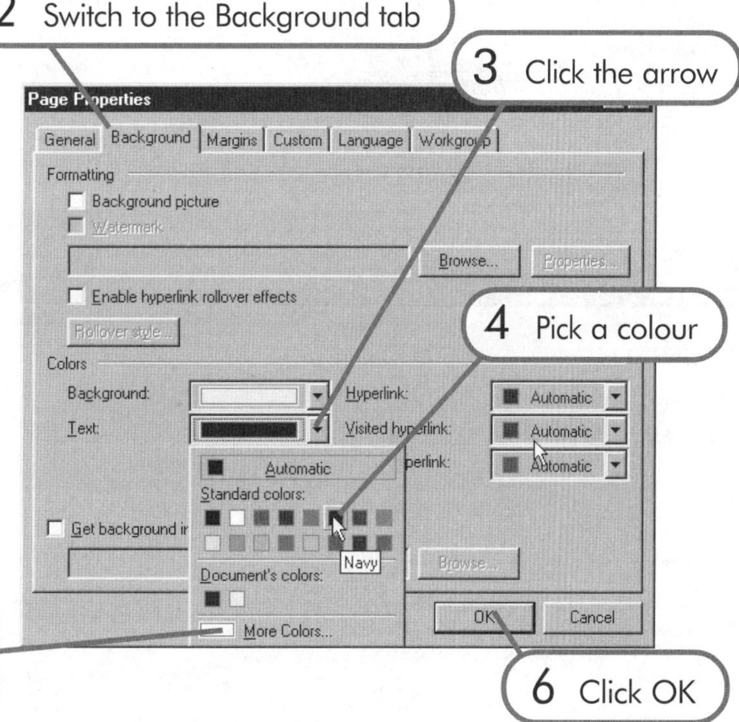
1 Right-click and choose Page Properties
Cut
Copy
Paste
Paste Special
Theme...
Shared Borders...
Page Properties...
Paragraph...
Font... Alt+Enter
2 Switch to the Background tab
3 Click the arrow
4 Pick a colour
5 Choose from More Colors...
6 Click OK
Page Properties
General
Background
Margins
Custom
Language
Workgroup
Formatting
Background picture
Watermark
Browse...
Properties...
Enable hyperlink rollover effects
Rollover style...
Colors
Background:
Text:
Hyperlink:
Visited hyperlink:
Automatic
Standard colors:
Navy
Document's colors:
More Colors...
Get background i
OK
Cancel

## Background images and watermarks

A background image can be screen-sized, or small and repeated to give a wallpaper effect. Small ones are often better as they download faster, and don't get in the way of the page's text. The Clip Art Gallery has a few good examples.

Watermarks only run on Microsoft Explorer at present. When you view the page, the background stays still and the rest of the page moves over it as you scroll up and down.

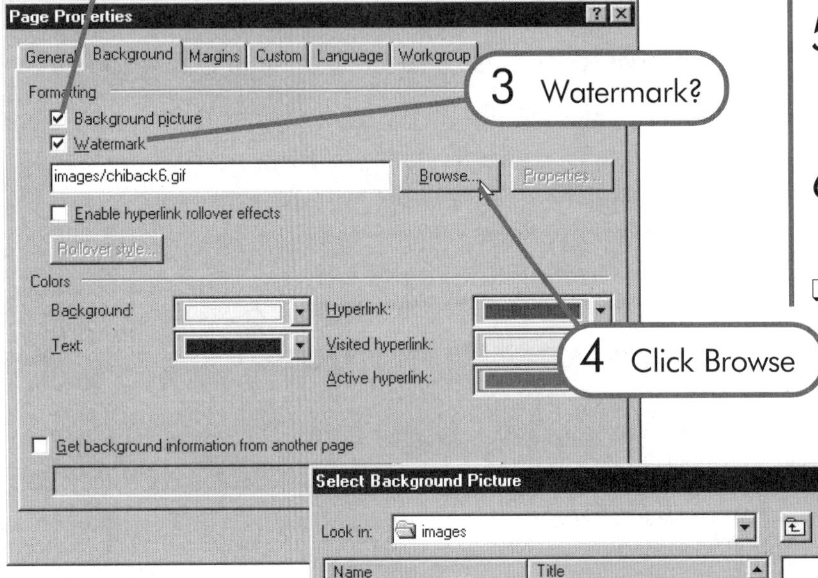
2 Choose Background picture
Page Properties
General
Background
Margins
Custom
Language
Workgroup
Formatting
Background picture
Watermark
3 Watermark?
images/chiback6.gif
Browse...
Properties...
Enable hyperlink rollover effects
Rollover style...
Colors
Background:
Text:
Hyperlink:
Visited hyperlink:
Active hyperlink:
4 Click Browse
Get background information from another page

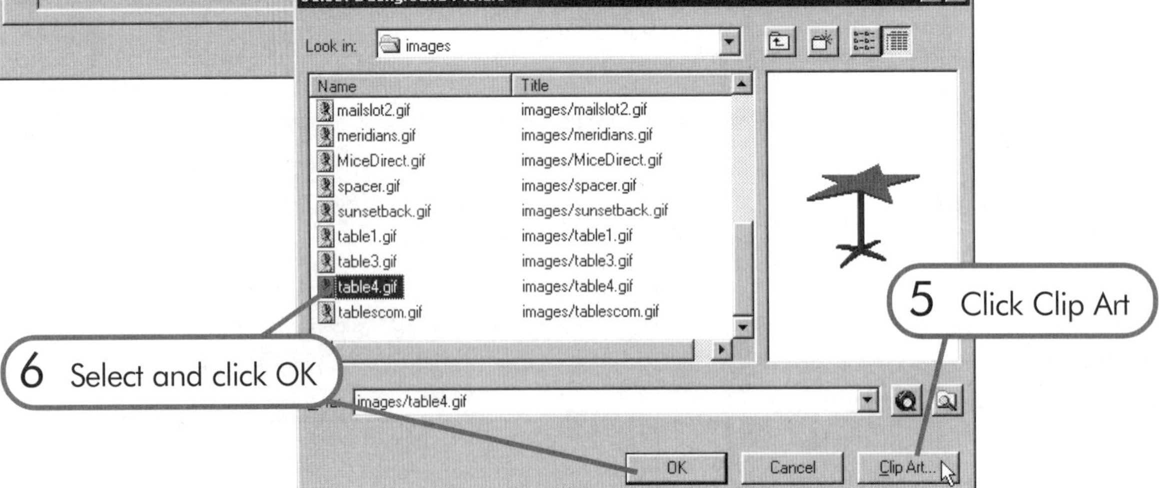
Select Background Picture
Look in:
images
Name
Title
mailslot2.gif
images/mailslot2.gif
meridians.gif
images/meridians.gif
MiceDirect.gif
images/MiceDirect.gif
spacer.gif
images/spacer.gif
sunsetback.gif
images/sunsetback.gif
table1.gif
images/table1.gif
table3.gif
images/table3.gif
table4.gif
images/table4.gif
tablescom.gif
images/tablescom.gif
6 Select and click OK
images/table4.gif
5 Click Clip Art
OK
Cancel
Clip Art...

## Basic steps

1 Open the Page Properties dialog box.

2 On the Background tab, first choose Background picture.

3 If you want the image to be a Watermark, check this box.

4 Click Browse...

5 Click the Clip Art button to search the Gallery.

6 Select a background image and click OK.

- To use your own image click [icon] to search your hard drive – see page 26 for finding images.

Basic steps

# Previewing pages

1 Choose Preview in browser... from the File menu.

2 Select a browser.

3 Choose a Window Size.

4 Check the Automatically save page box to save the page before opening it in the browser.

5 Click Preview.

FrontPage shows pages pretty much as they will appear in a browser window, but as browsers vary a little, you may want to check the appearance of your pages in a normal browser.

## Window size

If your pages are going to viewed on the World Wide Web, remember that not everyone has the same type of monitor. Pages that work well on your 1024 x 768 screen may look terrible when viewed on a 640 x 480! If you have any doubts about the layout, preview it in each of the screen sizes.

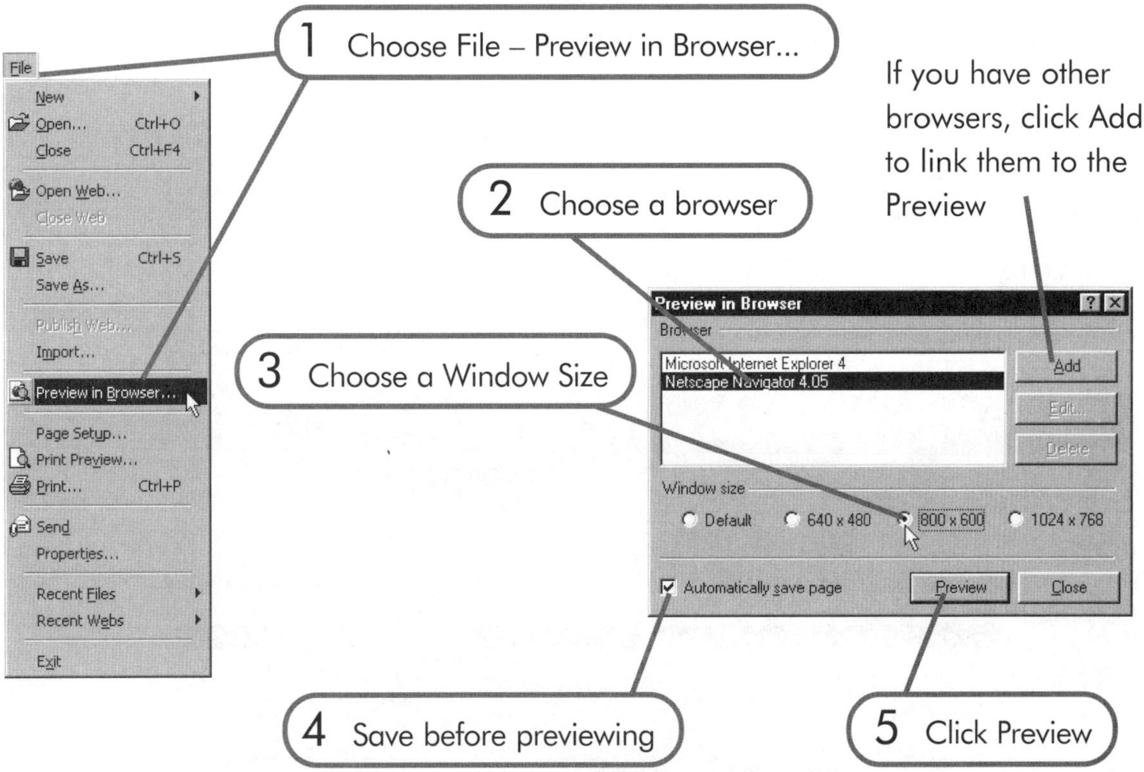

1 Choose File – Preview in Browser...

If you have other browsers, click Add to link them to the Preview

2 Choose a browser

3 Choose a Window Size

4 Save before previewing

5 Click Preview

# Tasks view

## Basic steps

Unless you sit down and construct an entire web in one sitting, the **Tasks** view can be very useful. It shows a list of tasks which need to be carried out on your web, along with information about them. In **Tasks** view, you can:

- add and remove reminders to do certain tasks;
- assign the task to a certain person if there are several people working on the web;
- set a priority rating for each task;
- make a note of any details in the **Description** field.

Completed tasks can either be hidden or displayed as a project record by selecting **Show History** on the **Edit – Task** menu.

Some wizards automatically write a few tasks on the **Task view** when they create your web template. These are associated with the page which needs editing so that you can go straight to it by clicking on **Start Task**.

❑ To add a task

1 Click the Tasks button.

2 Right-click anywhere in the window and select New Task...

3 Type a brief reminder of the job in the Task Name field.

4 Click on a radio button to assign the task a priority.

5 Assign the task to someone.

6 Enter a Description.

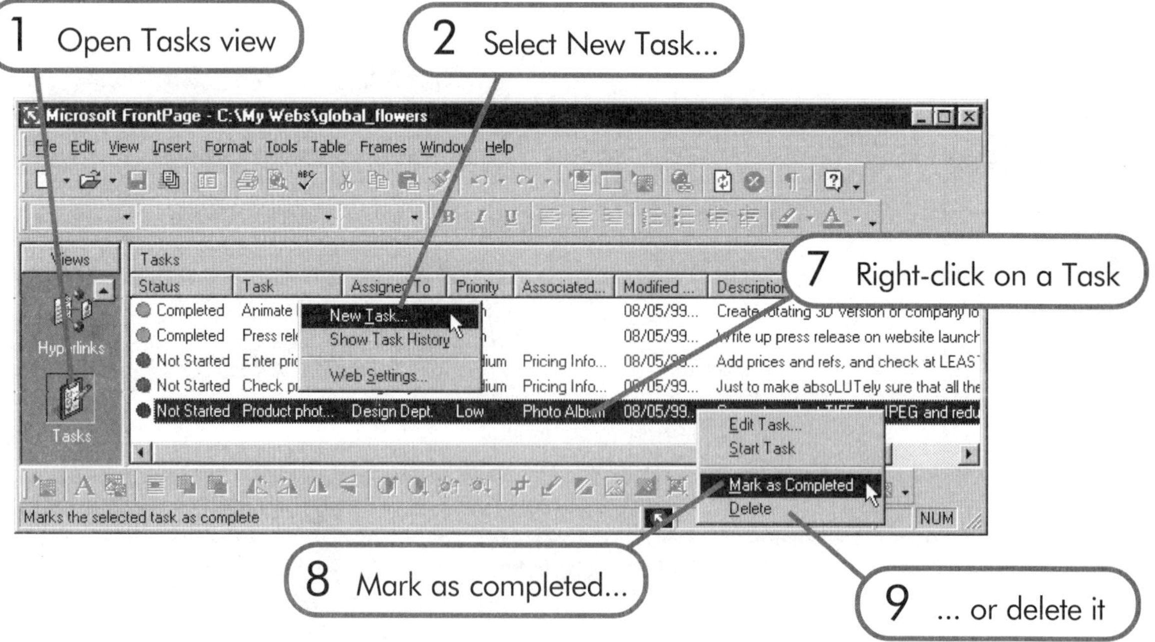

1 Open Tasks view
2 Select New Task...
7 Right-click on a Task
8 Mark as completed...
9 ... or delete it
Microsoft FrontPage - C:\My Webs\global_flowers
File Edit View Insert Format Tools Table Frames Window Help
Views
Hyperlinks
Tasks
Status
Task
Assigned To
Priority
Associated...
Modified ...
Description
Completed
Not Started
New Task...
Show Task History
Web Settings...
Product phot...
Design Dept.
Low
Pricing Info...
08/05/99...
Write up press release on website launch
Add prices and refs, and check at LEAST
Just to make absoLUTely sure that all the
Edit Task...
Start Task
Mark as Completed
Delete
Marks the selected task as complete
NUM

❑ To remove a task

7 Select a task and right-click on it.

8 Click Mark as completed.

Or

9 Delete this task if you do not need a record of it.

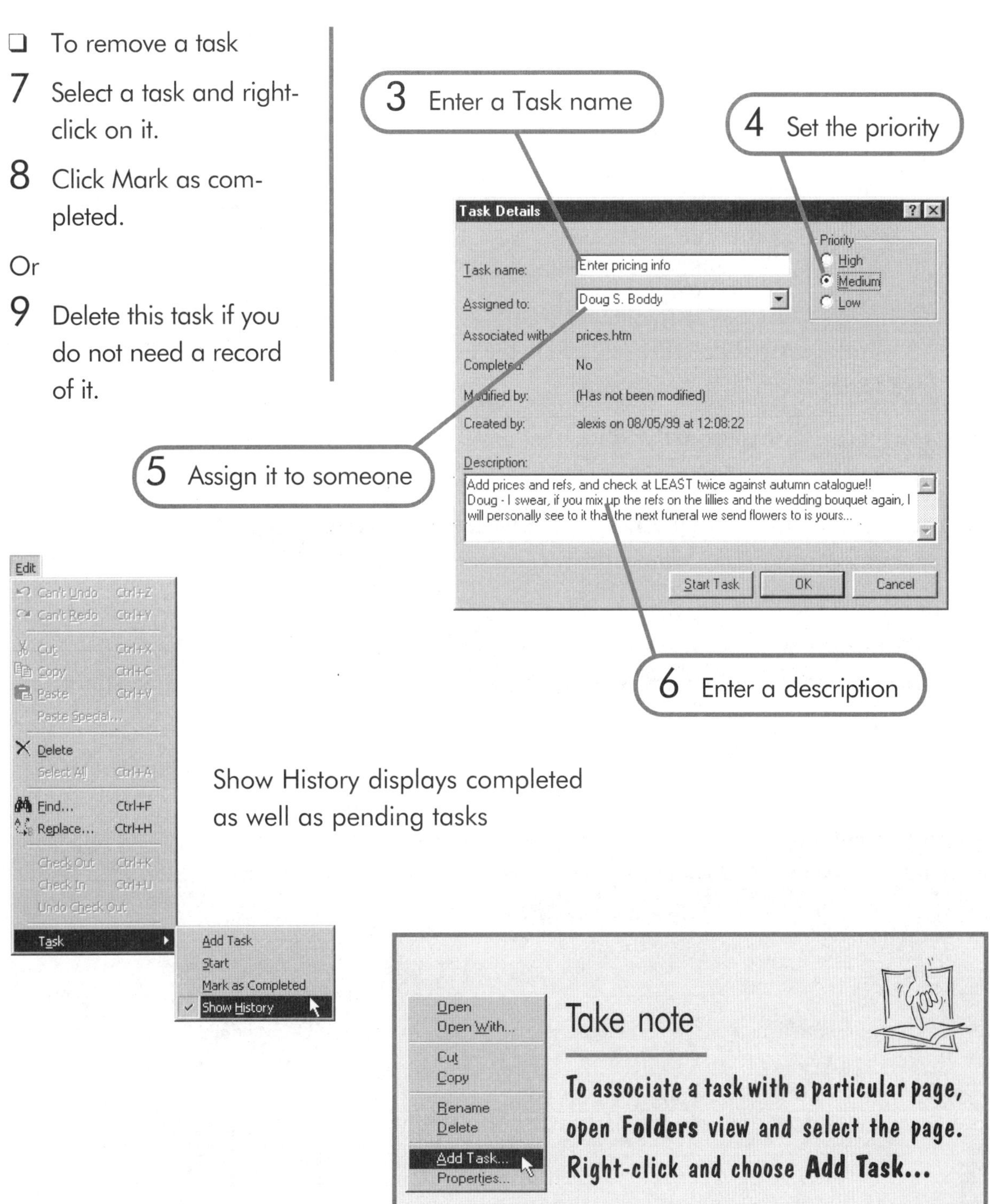

3 Enter a Task name
4 Set the priority
Task Details
Task name:
Enter pricing info
Assigned to:
Doug S. Boddy
Associated with:
prices.htm
Completed:
No
Modified by:
(Has not been modified)
Created by:
alexis on 08/05/99 at 12:08:22
Priority
High
Medium
Low
Description:
Add prices and refs, and check at LEAST twice against autumn catalogue!! Doug - I swear, if you mix up the refs on the lillies and the wedding bouquet again, I will personally see to it that the next funeral we send flowers to is yours...
Start Task
OK
Cancel
5 Assign it to someone
6 Enter a description
Edit
Can't Undo Ctrl+Z
Can't Redo Ctrl+Y
Cut Ctrl+X
Copy Ctrl+C
Paste Ctrl+V
Paste Special...
Delete
Select All Ctrl+A
Find... Ctrl+F
Replace... Ctrl+H
Check Out Ctrl+K
Check In Ctrl+U
Undo Check Out
Task
Add Task
Start
Mark as Completed
Show History
Open
Open With...
Cut
Copy
Rename
Delete
Add Task...
Properties...


Show History displays completed as well as pending tasks

## Take note

**To associate a task with a particular page, open Folders view and select the page. Right-click and choose Add Task...**

# Reports view

The **Reports View** displays statistics which give you an overview of the state of your web, and it is particularly useful if you find you have a lot of pages. It shows:

- the number of **files** and their total size;
- the number of **Picture** files (excluding video files);
- the number of **Slow pages** – large files which may take a long time to download;
- lists of **Recently added files** (created in the last 30 days) and **Older files**;
- the number of **hyperlinks** and whether any of them are **Broken** or **Unverified** (see pages 87);
- how many of your **hyperlinks** are **internal**, between pages of your web, and **external**, to files outside your web (see pages 80–83);
- whether you have any **errors** in automated **components** such as a Table of Contents (see Chapter 8);
- any **Uncompleted tasks**;
- any **Unused themes** which can be deleted (see page 39).

The **Site Summary** is the main **Reports** page – each section of the report can be double-clicked to show more details.

## Basic steps

1 Click on the Reports button.

2 Double-click on a section to see more details.

❑ To return to the Site Summary

3 Choose Reports – Site Summary from the View menu.

## Take note

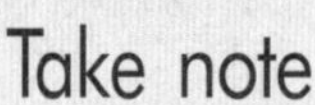

**The Reports view is also used for checking hyperlinks – see page 88.**

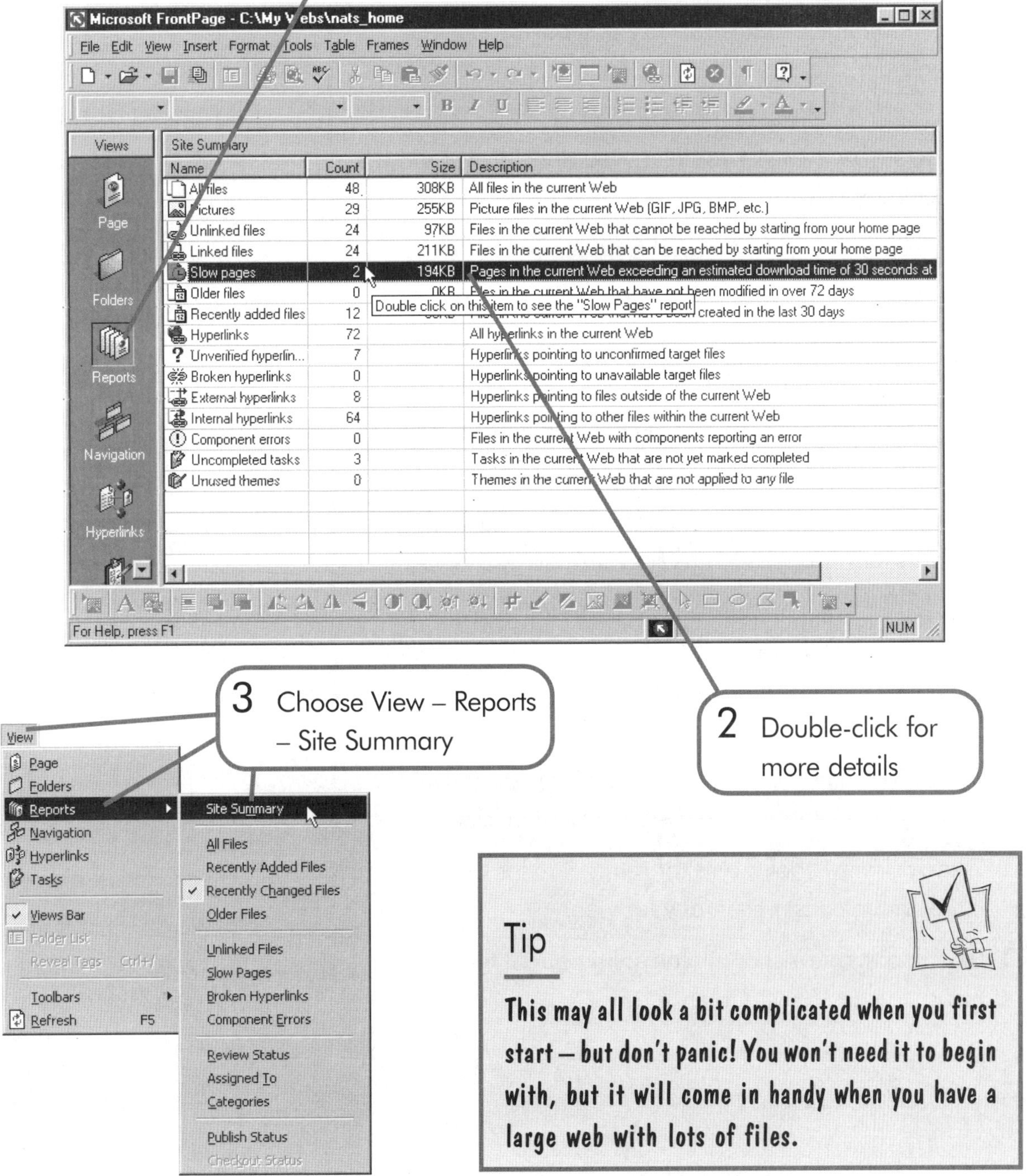
1 Click Reports
Microsoft FrontPage - C:\My Webs\nats_home
File Edit View Insert Format Tools Table Frames Window Help
Views
Page
Folders
Reports
Navigation
Hyperlinks
Site Summary
Name Count Size Description
All files 48 308KB All files in the current Web
Pictures 29 255KB Picture files in the current Web (GIF, JPG, BMP, etc.)
Unlinked files 24 97KB Files in the current Web that cannot be reached by starting from your home page
Linked files 24 211KB Files in the current Web that can be reached by starting from your home page
Slow pages 2 194KB Pages in the current Web exceeding an estimated download time of 30 seconds at
Older files 0 0KB Files in the current Web that have not been modified in over 72 days
Double click on this item to see the "Slow Pages" report
Recently added files 12 created in the last 30 days
Hyperlinks 72 All hyperlinks in the current Web
Unverified hyperlin... 7 Hyperlinks pointing to unconfirmed target files
Broken hyperlinks 0 Hyperlinks pointing to unavailable target files
External hyperlinks 8 Hyperlinks pointing to files outside of the current Web
Internal hyperlinks 64 Hyperlinks pointing to other files within the current Web
Component errors 0 Files in the current Web with components reporting an error
Uncompleted tasks 3 Tasks in the current Web that are not yet marked completed
Unused themes 0 Themes in the current Web that are not applied to any file
For Help, press F1
NUM
3 Choose View – Reports – Site Summary
2 Double-click for more details
View
Page
Folders
Reports
Navigation
Hyperlinks
Tasks
Views Bar
Folder List
Reveal Tags Ctrl+/
Toolbars
Refresh F5
Site Summary
All Files
Recently Added Files
Recently Changed Files
Older Files
Unlinked Files
Slow Pages
Broken Hyperlinks
Component Errors
Review Status
Assigned To
Categories
Publish Status
Checkout Status

## Tip

**This may all look a bit complicated when you first start – but don't panic! You won't need it to begin with, but it will come in handy when you have a large web with lots of files.**

# Summary

- ❑ A web is a set of HTML pages organised into a navigable system using hypertext links.
- ❑ The FrontPage window has a Views Bar on the left-hand side. The views are used for dealing with different aspects of building and managing your web.
- ❑ Folders view is where you can view and change the file structure of a web.
- ❑ Hyperlinks view shows how the pages of your web are linked.
- ❑ Save your work regularly to avoid losing it if you make a mistake or the program crashes.
- ❑ Page view is where the actual construction and editing of web pages takes place.
- ❑ Use the Page Properties dialog box to set basic characteristics for a page, such as background and default text colours.
- ❑ You can use a Background picture instead of a plain coloured background if you wish.
- ❑ Check the appearance of your page by previewing it in a browser, trying different Window Size settings if you have a layout that may not work well at all sizes.
- ❑ The Task view shows a set of reminders for keeping track of the construction of your web.
- ❑ The Reports view shows information about the state of your work.

# 2 Text and graphics

# Text

## Basic steps

Handling text in FrontPage is very similar to Microsoft Word in many basic respects. The Toolbar buttons and keystrokes for common commands are the same – opening and saving files, printing, checking spelling, undo and redo, cut, copy and paste, highlighted text and graphics, **bold**, *italic*, underlined text, etc.

Some things are different, though – for instance, when you press **[Enter]**, a blank line is inserted before the next paragraph. If you want to keep lines closer together, hold down **[Shift]** and press **[Enter]**.

- ❑ Headings

1 Position the cursor anywhere in a line.

2 Click on the down arrow next to the Style menu field.

3 Select a heading size.

- ❑ Font size

4 Highlight the text.

5 Select a Font size from the menu.

2 Open the list

1 Click into the line

Microsoft FrontPage
File Edit View Insert Format Tools Table Frames Window Help
Normal
(default font)
Normal
Formatted
Address
Heading 1
Heading 2
Heading 3
Heading 4
huge.htm
A heading style applies to a whole section of text...
... then when you press [Enter] a blank line is left beneath the heading, and the text reverts to ordinary size and style.
Folders
Normal HTML Preview
0 seconds over 28.8
NUM

3 Select a style

Use [Shift] and [Enter] if you want to break a heading into more than one line

5 Set the size

4 Highlight the text

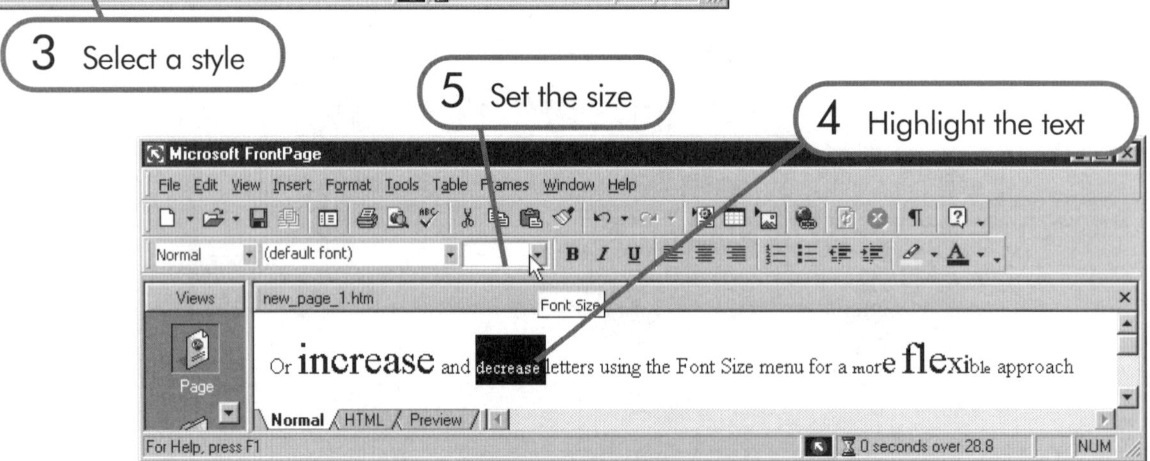
Microsoft FrontPage
File Edit View Insert Format Tools Table Frames Window Help
Normal
(default font)
Font Size
Views
new_page_1.htm
Page
Or increase and decrease letters using the Font Size menu for a more flexible approach
Normal HTML Preview
For Help, press F1
0 seconds over 28.8
NUM

## Headings and font size

**Tip**

**To select text, point to the start, hold down the left mouse button and drag to the end.**

FrontPage has seven font sizes – one for **normal** text, four larger sizes and two smaller.

The six **Headings** styles are a quick way of setting the size of a line of text; they are all set in **bold type**, and with a blank line below the text.

- **Font sizes** go from 7 (largest) down to 1.
- **Headings** go from 1 (largest) down to 6!

Heading 1 is the second largest font size, (but set in bold), and Heading 6 is the smallest.

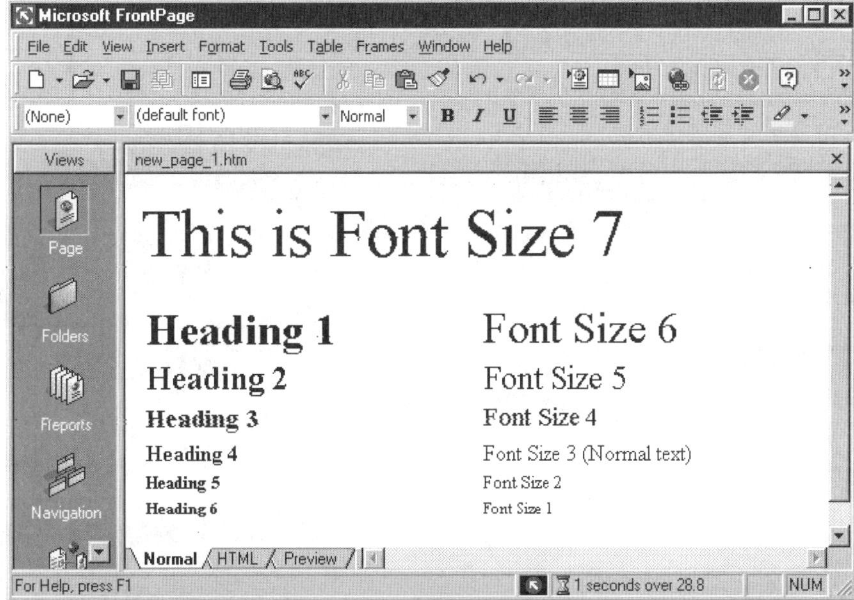
Microsoft FrontPage
File Edit View Insert Format Tools Table Frames Window Help
(None)
(default font)
Normal
Views
Page
Folders
Reports
Navigation
new_page_1.htm
This is Font Size 7
Heading 1
Heading 2
Heading 3
Heading 4
Heading 5
Heading 6
Font Size 6
Font Size 5
Font Size 4
Font Size 3 (Normal text)
Font Size 2
Font Size 1
Normal
HTML
Preview
For Help, press F1
1 seconds over 28.8
NUM

**Tip**

**If you find that changing the Heading size in the Style menu is having no effect on the text you want to change, there may be other, conflicting formats set on the text. Try clearing it down with Remove Formatting on the Format menu.**

# Fonts

## Basic steps

The standard font used in HTML is Times New Roman, but you can use other from the drop-down menu. Note that some fonts, such as Small fonts or System, cannot be set in different sizes, and that if your visitors do not have the font on their system, they will see the text in the standard font.

## Font colour

Any section of text – a paragraph, word or letter – can be shown in a different colour from whatever you set as the default.

1 Select the text.

2 Click the down arrow next to the Fonts field.

3 Choose a font from the list.

4 Click on the arrow next to the Font colour button.

5 Click on More Colors...

6 Pick a colour from the palette and click OK.

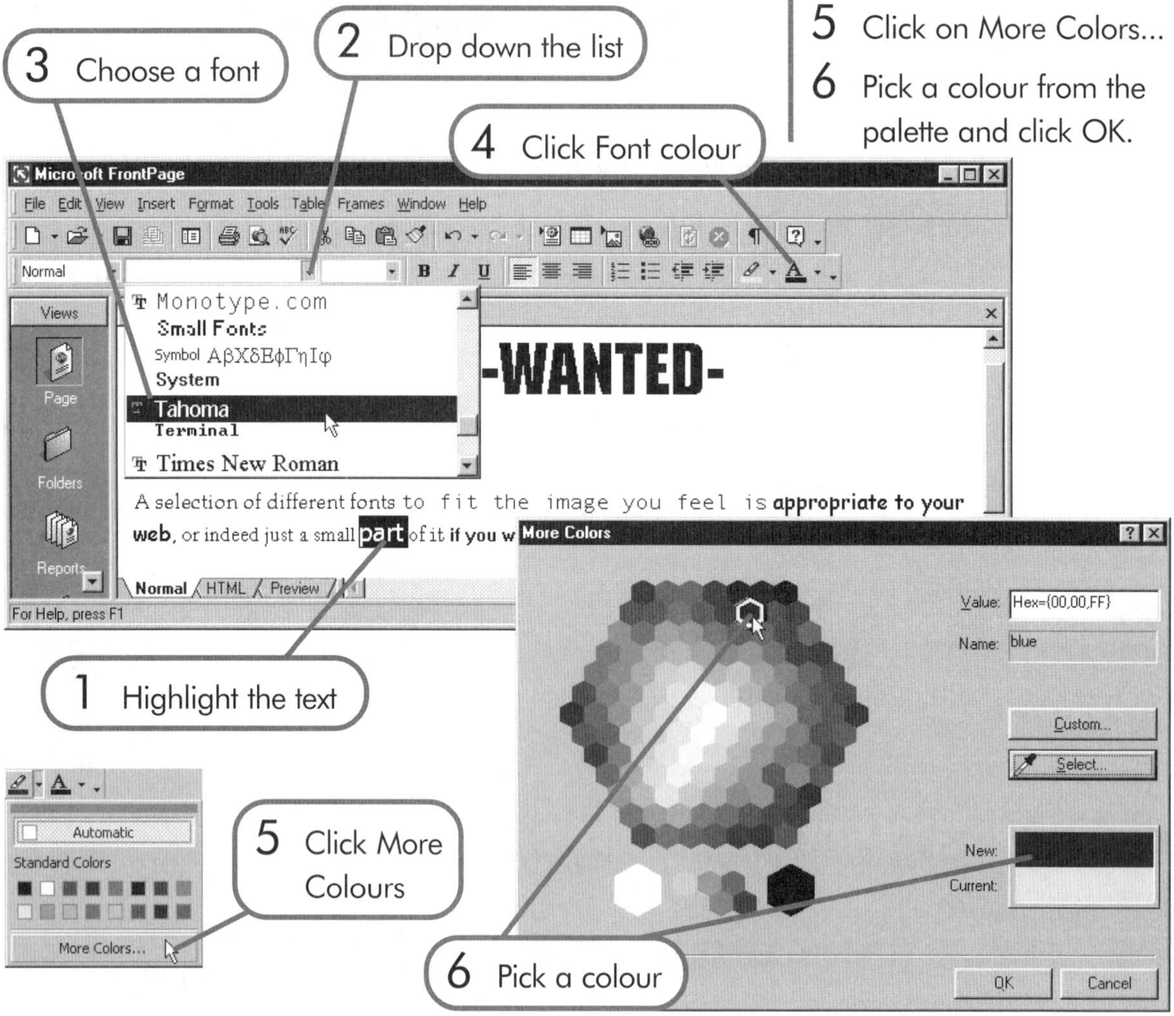

3 Choose a font

2 Drop down the list

4 Click Font colour

1 Highlight the text

5 Click More Colours

6 Pick a colour

## Basic steps

1 Select the text.
2 Select Font… from the Format menu.
3 Check the box next to an option to apply the effect.
4 Set other aspects of the format as needed.
5 Click OK.

## Special font styles

If you highlight a section of text and choose **Font…** from the **Format** menu, a dialog box appears which gives you various effects such as **Strikethrough** (rules a line through the text), **Blink** (flashing text), **Superscript**, **Subscript**, etc.

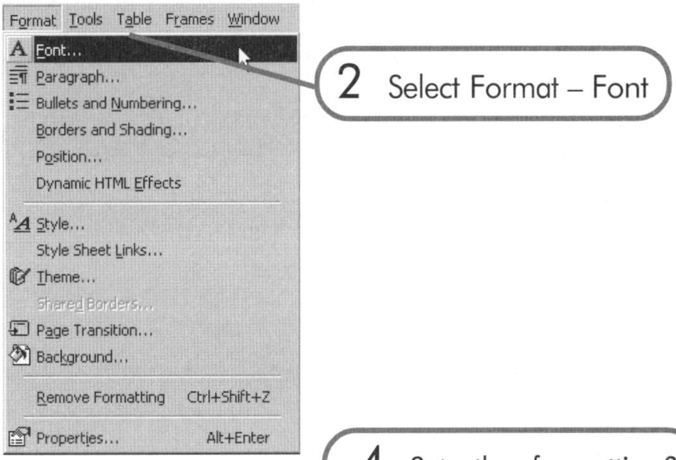

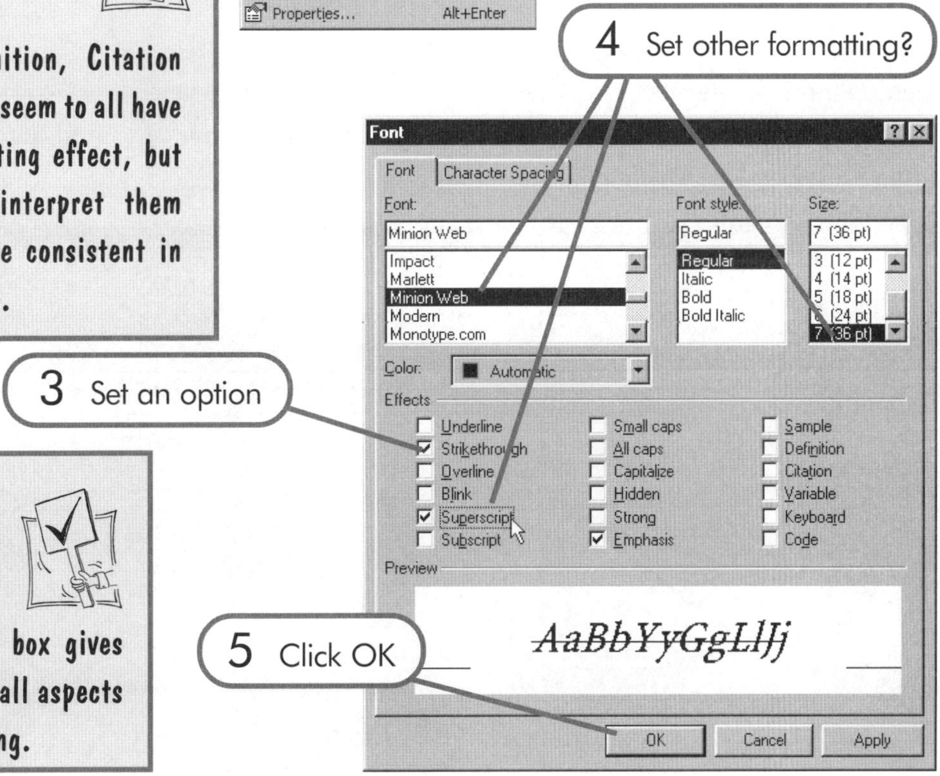

2 Select Format – Font

4 Set other formatting?

3 Set an option

5 Click OK

### Take note

**Emphasis, Definition, Citation and Variable may seem to all have the same formatting effect, but some browsers interpret them differently, so be consistent in your use of them.**

### Tip

**The Font dialog box gives you control over all aspects of text formatting.**

# Alignment and lists

## Aligning text

Place the cursor anywhere in a paragraph and click an **alignment** button to justify the text left, centre or right.

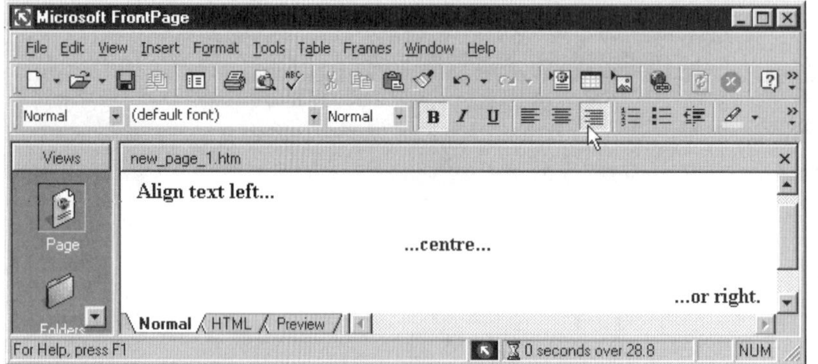
Microsoft FrontPage
Align text left...
...centre...
...or right.

## Lists

Lists can present information quickly and clearly on screen – wading through huge passages of text on screen is quite hard on the eyes. The bullets and numbers can be selected from a range of styles in the **List Properties...** dialog box.

## Basic steps

1 Click the Bulleted or the Numbered List button.

2 Type the first item and hit [Enter]. A bullet appears ready for the next item. After the last, there will be an unwanted one – press [←] to get rid of it.

- Changing the style

3 Right-click on the list and choose List Properties...

4 Select a different style from the Plain Bullets or Numbers panels.

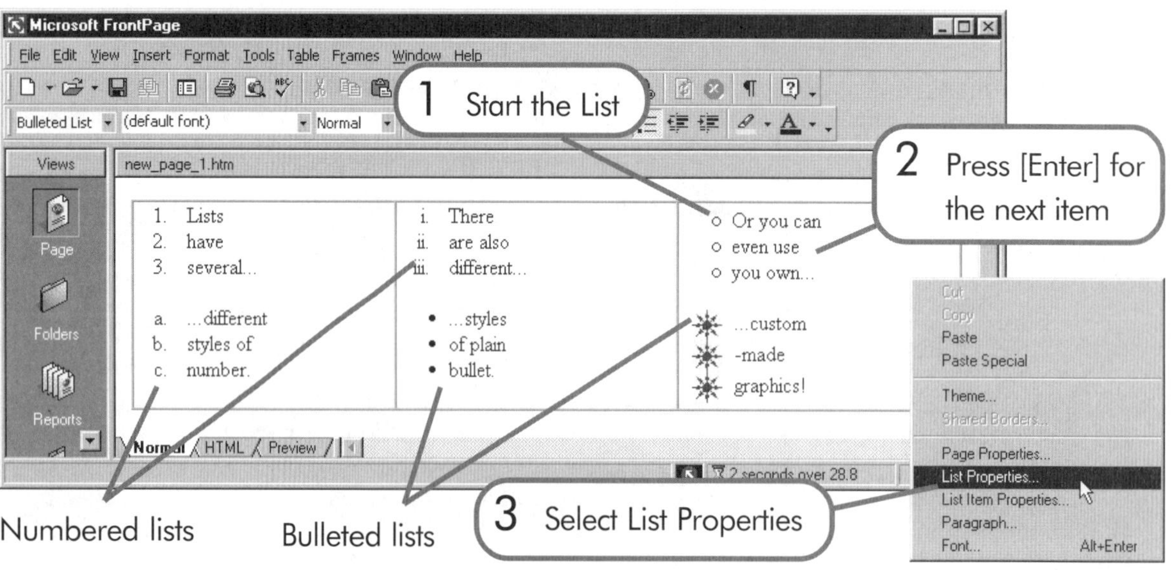
Microsoft FrontPage
1 Start the List
2 Press [Enter] for the next item
1. Lists
2. have
3. several...
a. ...different
b. styles of
c. number.
i. There
ii. are also
iii. different...
...styles
of plain
bullet.
Or you can
even use
you own...
...custom
-made
graphics!
Cut
Copy
Paste
Paste Special
Theme...
Shared Borders...
Page Properties...
List Properties...
List Item Properties...
Paragraph...
Font... Alt+Enter
Numbered lists
Bulleted lists
3 Select List Properties

*Or*

5 Go to the Picture Bullets panel and Browse... for Clip Art or a custom-made graphic.

**Tip**

**There are lots of places on the Internet where you can find free graphics to use as bullets. Try: http://www.alt-web.com**

- ❑ Definition lists

6 From the Style menu, choose Defined Term.

7 Type the term and press [Enter].

8 Type its definition and press [Enter].

9 After the last definition, choose Normal from the Style menu.

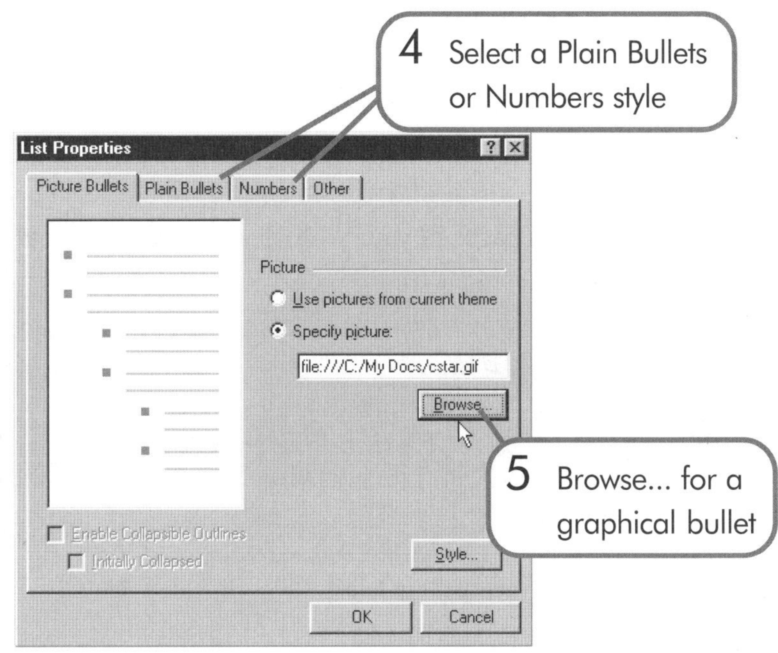

4 Select a Plain Bullets or Numbers style
List Properties
Picture Bullets
Plain Bullets
Numbers
Other
Picture
Use pictures from current theme
Specify picture:
file:///C:/My Docs/cstar.gif
Browse...
5 Browse... for a graphical bullet
Enable Collapsible Outlines
Initially Collapsed
Style...
OK
Cancel


## Definition list

This is a two-level list, normally used for a list of terms, each of which has its own definition indented below it. FrontPage arranges the list in pairs of **Defined Terms** and **Definitions**.

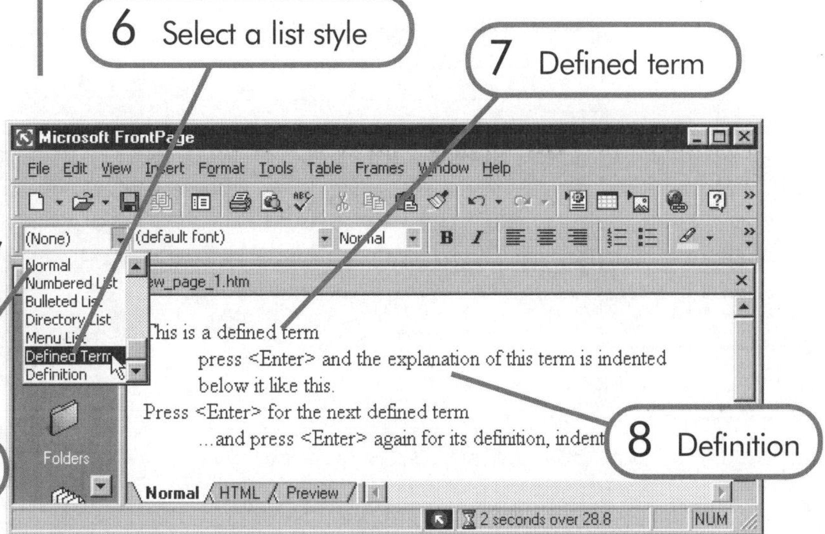

6 Select a list style
7 Defined term
Microsoft FrontPage
File Edit View Insert Format Tools Table Frames Window Help
(None)
(default font)
Normal
Numbered List
Bulleted List
Directory List
Menu List
Defined Term
Definition
This is a defined term
press <Enter> and the explanation of this term is indented below it like this.
Press <Enter> for the next defined term
...and press <Enter> again for its definition, indent
8 Definition
9 Back to Normal
Folders
Normal
HTML
Preview
2 seconds over 28.8
NUM

# Placing images

## Basic steps

You will no doubt want some pictures on your pages to make them more attractive – though you should be careful about the amount of time large images take to download. Images can be imported from other pages in your web, from a folder on your hard drive, or even from a World Wide Web location.

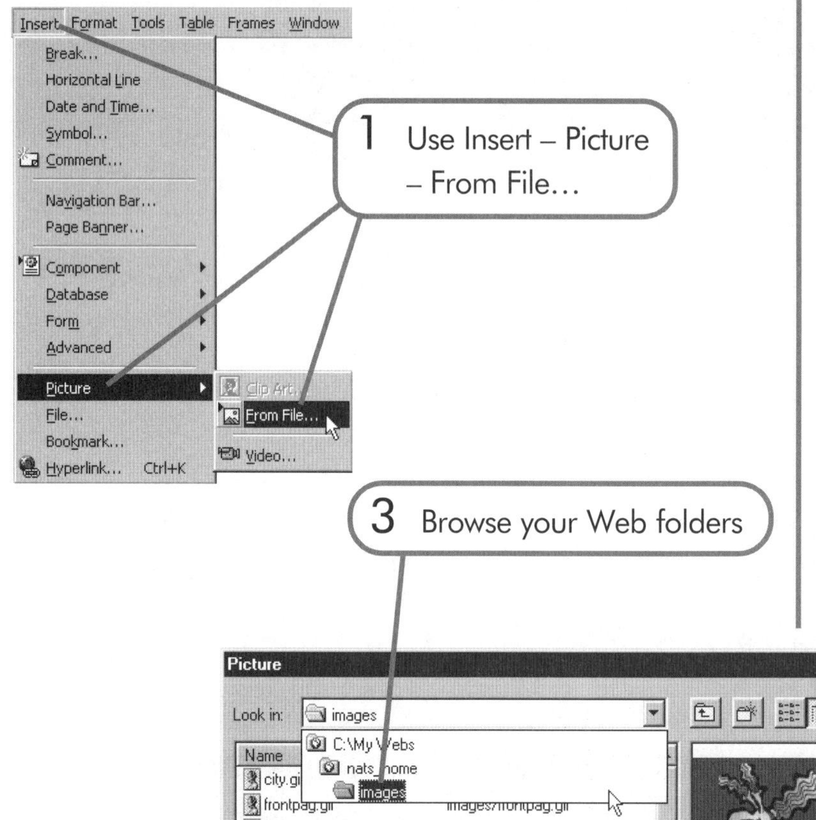

Insert Format Tools Table Frames Window
Break...
Horizontal Line
Date and Time...
Symbol...
Comment...
Navigation Bar...
Page Banner...
Component
Database
Form
Advanced
Picture
File...
Bookmark...
Hyperlink... Ctrl+K
Clip Art...
From File...
Video...
1 Use Insert – Picture – From File...
3 Browse your Web folders
Picture
Look in: images
C:\My Webs
nats_home
images
Name
city.gif
frontpag.gif
homebut.gif images/homebut.gif
kadmium1.gif images/kadmium1.gif
kadmium3.gif images/kadmium3.gif
kadthmb1.gif images/kadthmb1.gif
label.gif
larrow.gif
4 Open the file
9 Paste the URL
URL: http://www.alt-web.com/bullets.html
OK
Cancel
Clip Art...
Parameters...
Scan...


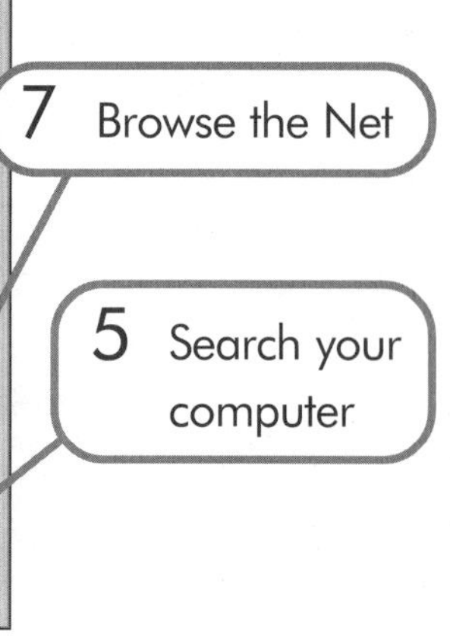

7 Browse the Net
5 Search your computer


1 From the Insert menu, choose Picture, then From file...

*Or*

2 Click on the Insert Image button.

- ❑ Images from a FrontPage web

3 Browse through the folders.

4 Select a file and click OK.

- ❑ From your hard drive

5 Click on the File button or choose from the Clip Art Gallery.

6 Select a file and click OK.

- From the Internet

7 Click on the Internet button and browse the Internet for an image.

8 Right-click on the image and choose Copy image location.

9 In the URL field, press [Ctrl]+[v] to paste the image URL in.

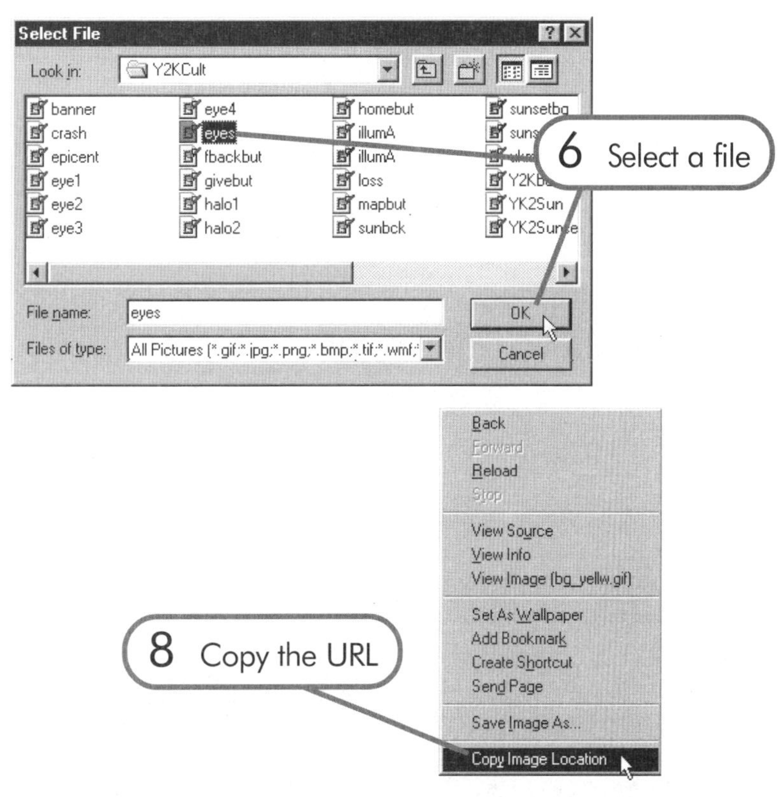
Select File
Look in: Y2KCult
banner
crash
epicent
eye1
eye2
eye3
eye4
eyes
fbackbut
givebut
halo1
halo2
homebut
illumA
illumA
loss
mapbut
sunbck
sunsetbg
YK2Sun
6 Select a file
File name: eyes
Files of type: All Pictures (*.gif;*.jpg;*.png;*.bmp;*.tif;*.wmf;
OK
Cancel
Back
Forward
Reload
Stop
View Source
View Info
View Image (bg_yellw.gif)
Set As Wallpaper
Add Bookmark
Create Shortcut
Send Page
Save Image As...
Copy Image Location
8 Copy the URL

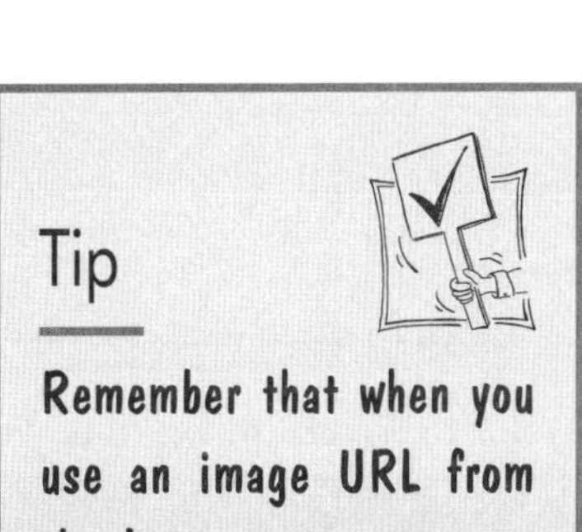

## Tip

**Remember that when you use an image URL from the Internet, you are using the image from someone else's server - so if they update or remove it, it will change on your page too. This can be very useful in some cases; e.g. a regularly-updated graph of your share prices.**

## Copy and Paste images

If you have been editing an image in a graphics package, you can use the **Copy** command to save it to the Clipboard, and then **Paste** it into FrontPage.

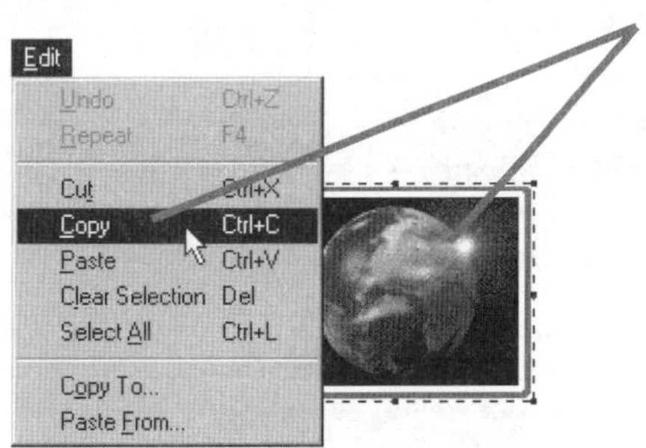
Edit
Undo Ctrl+Z
Repeat F4
Cut Ctrl+X
Copy Ctrl+C
Paste Ctrl+V
Clear Selection Del
Select All Ctrl+L
Copy To...
Paste From...
Select the image and click Copy – in any Windows application

# Drag and drop images

A neat feature of FrontPage allows you to hunt for a file using the Windows Explorer or Find File tool and then drag it onto the page you are working on.

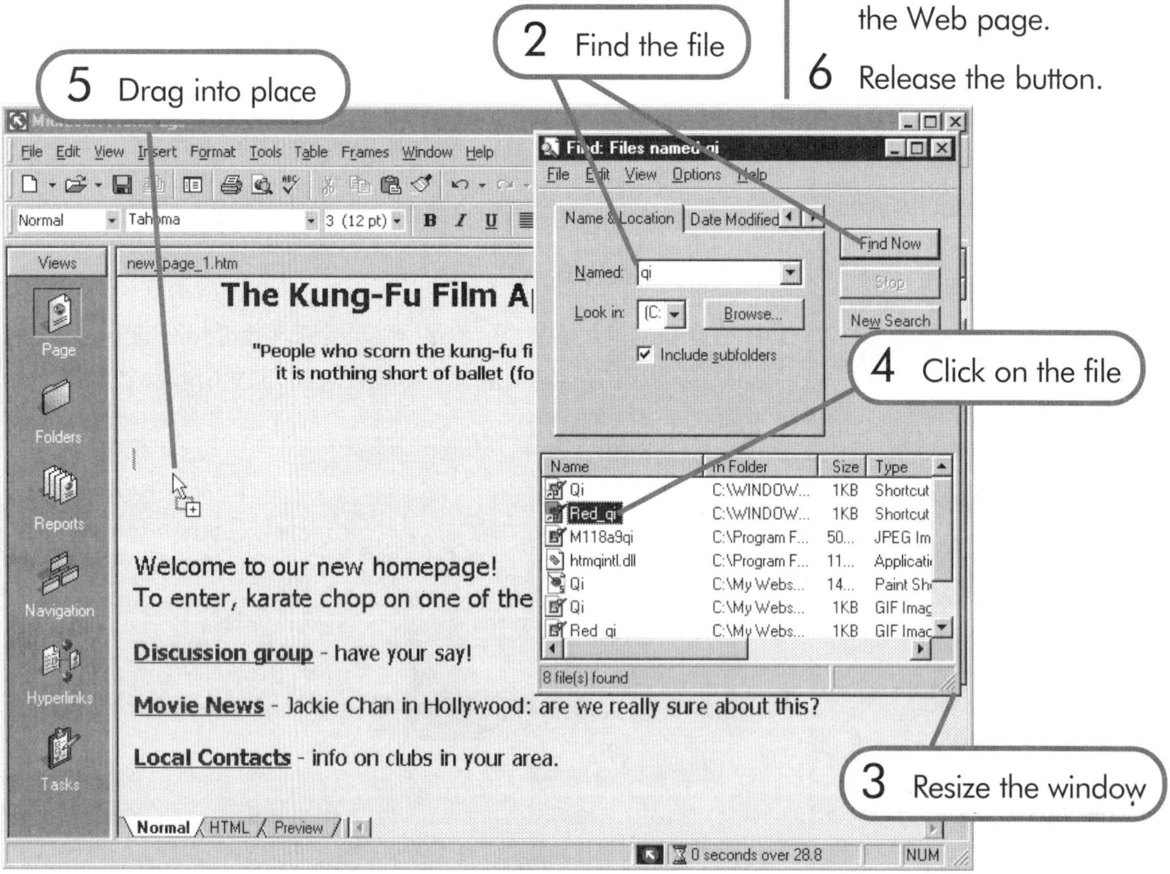

## Basic steps

1 Run Find – Files from the Start menu.
2 Find the file you want.
3 Resize the window so that you can see where to put the image.
4 Click on the file name and hold the mouse button down.
5 Drag the cursor where you want the image on the Web page.
6 Release the button.

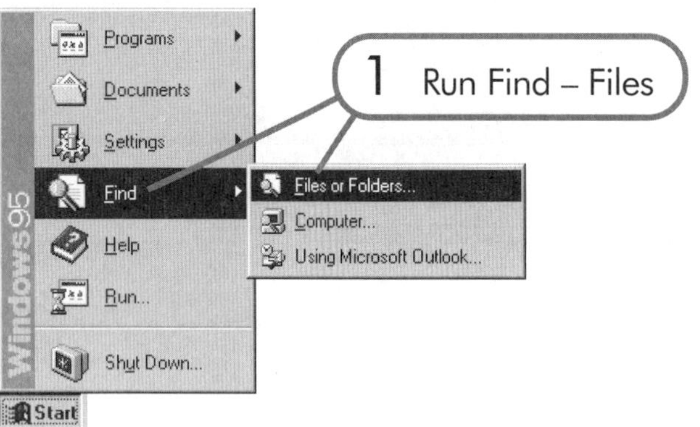
1 Run Find – Files
Programs
Documents
Settings
Find
Help
Run...
Shut Down...
Files or Folders...
Computer...
Using Microsoft Outlook...
Windows95
Start

2 Find the file

5 Drag into place

4 Click on the file

3 Resize the window

# Picture properties

1 Right-click an image to open its contexxt menu and select Picture properties…

2 Click on the Appearance tab.

3 Turn on Specify Size.

4 Set the Width and Height by entering values and choosing in Pixels or in Percent.

5 If you want a border, set its Thickness.

An image has properties you can set or change. Some of these alter the appearance of the image itself – its **Size** and **Border**, while others determine its relation to the accompanying text – the **Alignment**, **Horizontal** and **Vertical Spacing**.

- **Size** can be set in pixels (giving precise control), or as a percentage of the window (ensuring that larger images don't run off the edge of a viewer's screen). **Keep aspect ratio** couples the width and height, to avoid distortion.
- **Border Thickness** is set in pixels. A value of 4 will give you a reasonably thick line.

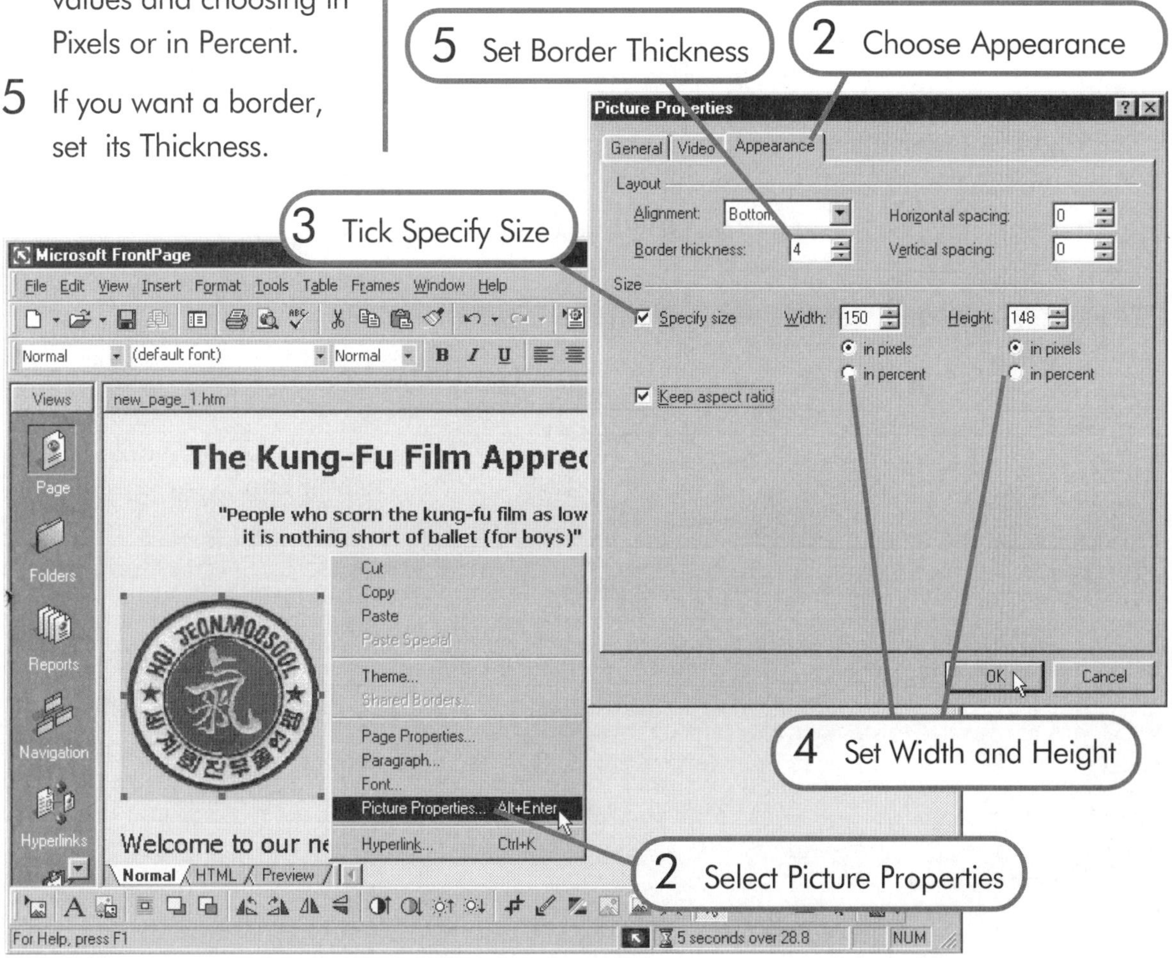

5 Set Border Thickness

2 Choose Appearance

3 Tick Specify Size

4 Set Width and Height

2 Select Picture Properties

# Image alignment

- **Horizontal** and **Vertical Spacing** is also set in pixels, and refers to the distance between the edge of the picture and any surrounding text.

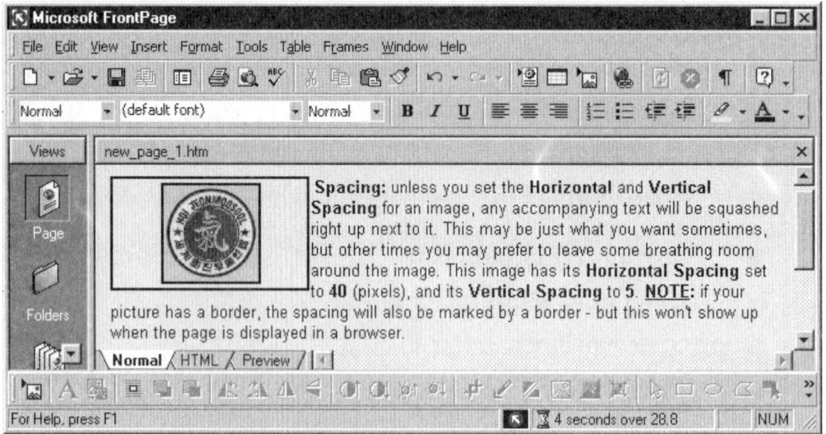
Microsoft FrontPage
File Edit View Insert Format Tools Table Frames Window Help
Normal
(default font)
Normal
Views
Page
Folders
new_page_1.htm
Spacing: unless you set the Horizontal and Vertical Spacing for an image, any accompanying text will be squashed right up next to it. This may be just what you want sometimes, but other times you may prefer to leave some breathing room around the image. This image has its Horizontal Spacing set to 40 (pixels), and its Vertical Spacing to 5. NOTE: if your picture has a border, the spacing will also be marked by a border - but this won't show up when the page is displayed in a browser.
Normal HTML Preview
For Help, press F1
4 seconds over 28.8
NUM

The Vertical distance is also affected by the spacing between the lines of text

- **Alignment** determines how text is arranged around the image. The most useful options are **Top, Middle** and **Bottom** for captions, and **Left** and **Right** when the image is embedded in text.

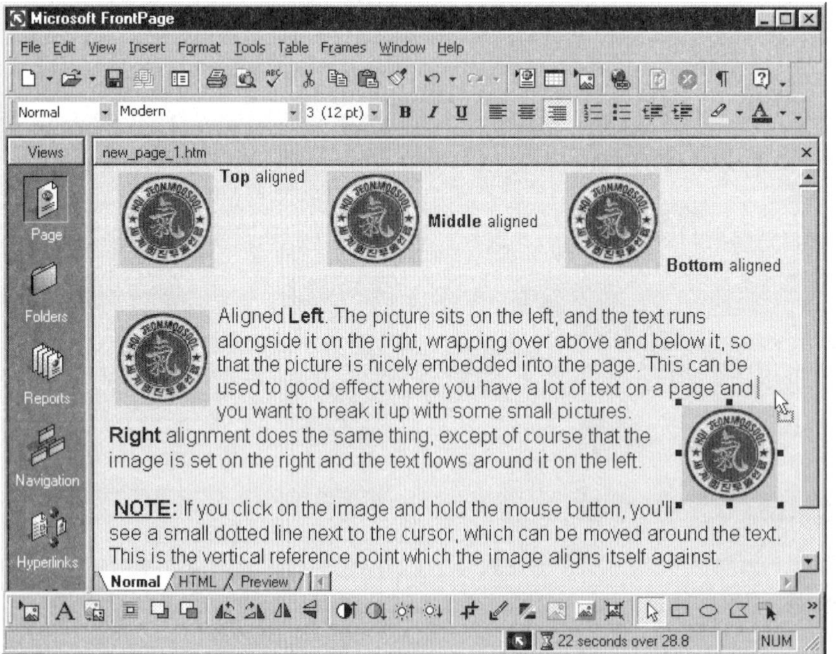
Microsoft FrontPage
File Edit View Insert Format Tools Table Frames Window Help
Normal
Modern
3 (12 pt)
Views
Page
Folders
Reports
Navigation
Hyperlinks
new_page_1.htm
Top aligned
Middle aligned
Bottom aligned
Aligned Left. The picture sits on the left, and the text runs alongside it on the right, wrapping over above and below it, so that the picture is nicely embedded into the page. This can be used to good effect where you have a lot of text on a page and you want to break it up with some small pictures.
Right alignment does the same thing, except of course that the image is set on the right and the text flows around it on the left.
NOTE: If you click on the image and hold the mouse button, you'll see a small dotted line next to the cursor, which can be moved around the text. This is the vertical reference point which the image aligns itself against.
Normal HTML Preview
22 seconds over 28.8
NUM

Use Top, Middle or Bottom with a single line of text

Use Left or Right when the image is beside a block of text

## Basic steps

# Alternative representations

1 Click on the General tab.

2 At the Text field, enter a title or descriptive message.

3 Click Browse by the Low-Res field to find a thumbnail image, if you created one.

4 Click OK.

As some people turn off the **View Images** option on their browser so that pages download faster, it is good practice to have a text label which appears in place of your images. Also, a small Low resolution version of a large image gives people an idea of what they are waiting for, rather than making them sit around twiddling their thumbs for ages.

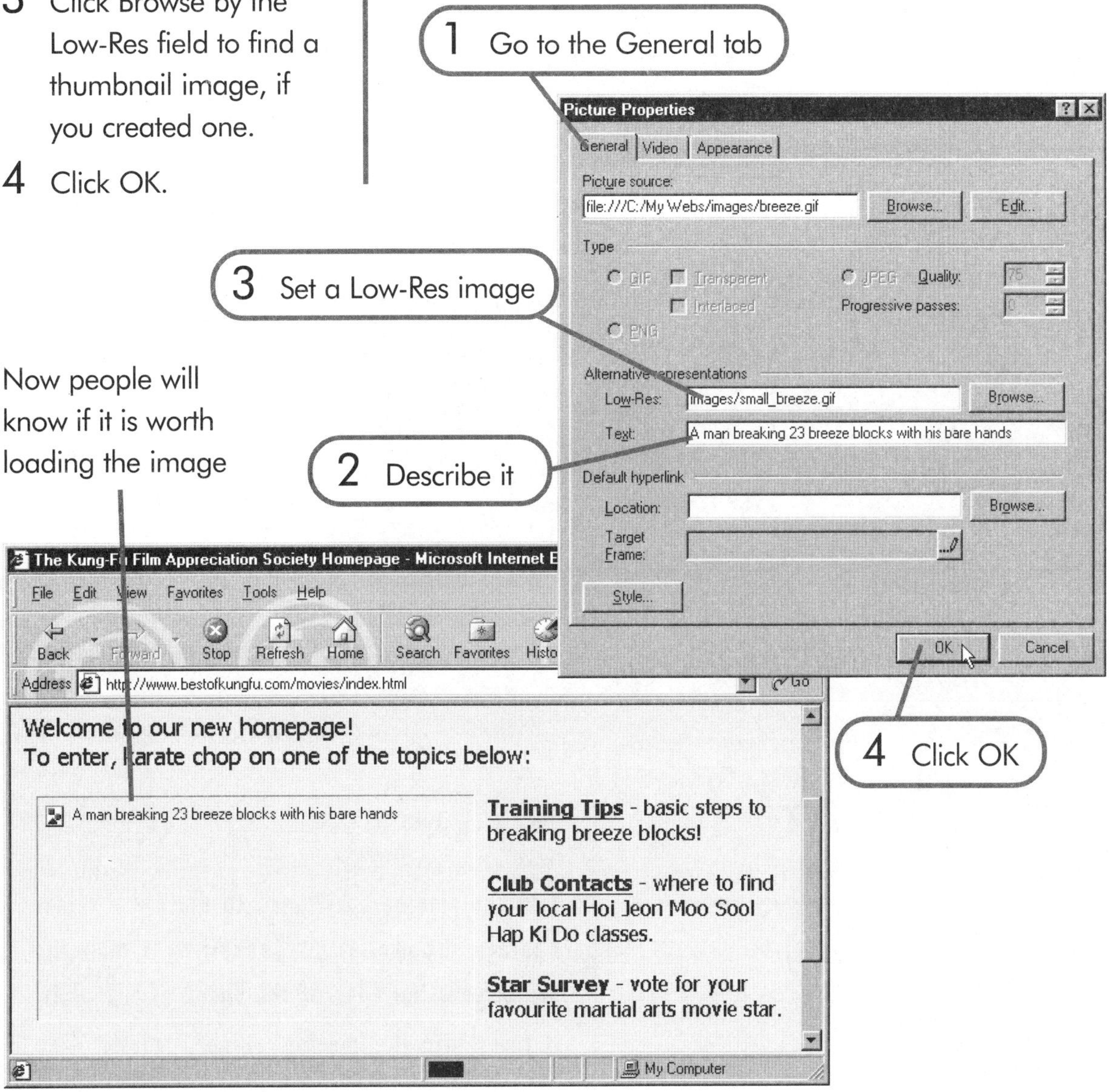

1 Go to the General tab

Picture Properties

General | Video | Appearance

Picture source: file:///C:/My Webs/images/breeze.gif Browse... Edit...

Type

GIF Transparent Interlaced JPEG Quality: 75 Progressive passes: 0 PNG

3 Set a Low-Res image

Alternative representations

Low-Res: images/small_breeze.gif Browse...

Text: A man breaking 23 breeze blocks with his bare hands

2 Describe it

Default hyperlink

Location: Browse...

Target Frame:

Style...

OK Cancel

4 Click OK

Now people will know if it is worth loading the image

The Kung-Fu Film Appreciation Society Homepage - Microsoft Internet E

File Edit View Favorites Tools Help

Back Forward Stop Refresh Home Search Favorites Histo

Address http://www.bestofkungfu.com/movies/index.html Go

Welcome to our new homepage!
To enter, karate chop on one of the topics below:

A man breaking 23 breeze blocks with his bare hands

**Training Tips** - basic steps to breaking breeze blocks!

**Club Contacts** - where to find your local Hoi Jeon Moo Sool Hap Ki Do classes.

**Star Survey** - vote for your favourite martial arts movie star.

My Computer

# Positioning

There is a drag-and-drop feature of FrontPage called **absolute positioning**, which allows you to position images anywhere on the page – including on top of, or behind text and other images. However, be warned that this only works when the page is viewed with Internet Explorer – other browsers may not support the feature, in which case the image will be dropped in wherever the image was *originally* placed (before you dragged-and-dropped it).

1 Select the image

5 Bring Forward

4 Send Backward

2 Position Absolutely

## Basic steps

1. Left-click on an image.
2. Click on the Position Absolutely button .
3. Click on the image and drag it to wherever you want it.
4. Click on the Send Backward button to put the image behind other text and images.
5. Click on the Bring Forward button to float it on top of them.
6. Click on the Position Absolutely button again to return to normal image mode.

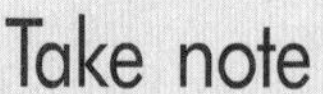

### Take note

**Text can also be positioned absolutely – select a paragraph and click . To position it, move the cursor over the edge of the chunk of text until it turns into the 'moving' cursor, usually .**

## Basic steps

1 Left-click on an image.
2 Click the Picture toolbar buttons to rotate, flip or adjust.
❑ Cropping an image:
3 Click the Crop button.
4 Click and drag to define an area.
5 Click the Crop button again.
❑ After editing:
6 Save the page.
7 Click Rename to save as a new file.
8 Click OK.

### Take note

**Sometimes when you use the Crop function, the cropped area may be adjusted to the same size and shape as the original image. To fix this, go into Picture Properties and uncheck the Specify size box.**

# Image manipulation

With FrontPage you can do more than just plonk an image onto the page – the **Picture** toolbar along the bottom of the screen has several useful image-editing features:

**Rotate Left / Right** – rotate the image 90° left or right.

**Flip Vertical / Horizontal** – Flip the picture over to give a mirror image.

**Increase / Decrease Contrast** – as your TV controls!

**Increase / Decrease Brightness** – again, as on TV!

**Crop** –Trim the unwanted edges off your picture.

Once you've changed an image with these tools, you'll need to save it, because the changes are made to the image itself. Remember to save it as a new image if you want to keep the original for use elsewhere.

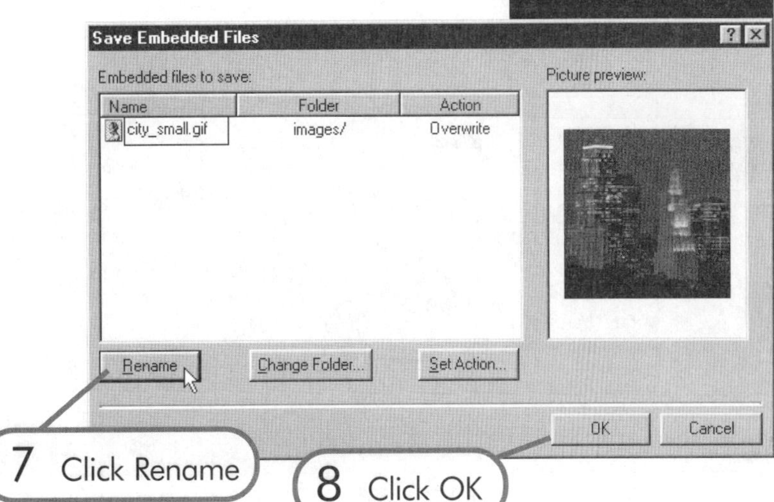
4 Click and drag to Define an Area
Save Embedded Files
Embedded files to save:
Picture preview:
Name
Folder
Action
city_small.gif
images/
Overwrite
Rename
Change Folder...
Set Action...
OK
Cancel
7 Click Rename
8 Click OK

## Text

If you want to overlay text such as a caption onto the picture, use the **Text** button. This opens a resizeable text box on the picture which you can type the text in. The text can be formatted as for normal text. Note that this only works with GIFs – FrontPage will prompt you to save JPG images as GIFs.

### More image tools

**Black and White** – convert from colour to greyscale.

**Wash Out** – bleach the colour out of an image to use it in the background.

**Bevel** – give a 'button' effect with a bevelled edge.

**Resample** – when you resize an image in FrontPage, the original picture file remains unchanged. This tool is useful if you shrink an image, because it reduces the file size, making your page load faster.

## Basic steps

1 Click the Text button.
2 Type into the box.
3 Click outside the box to finish typing.
4 Click inside and drag the box into position.
5 Format the text as normal.

### Tip

**Use the handles to change the text box size and shape.**

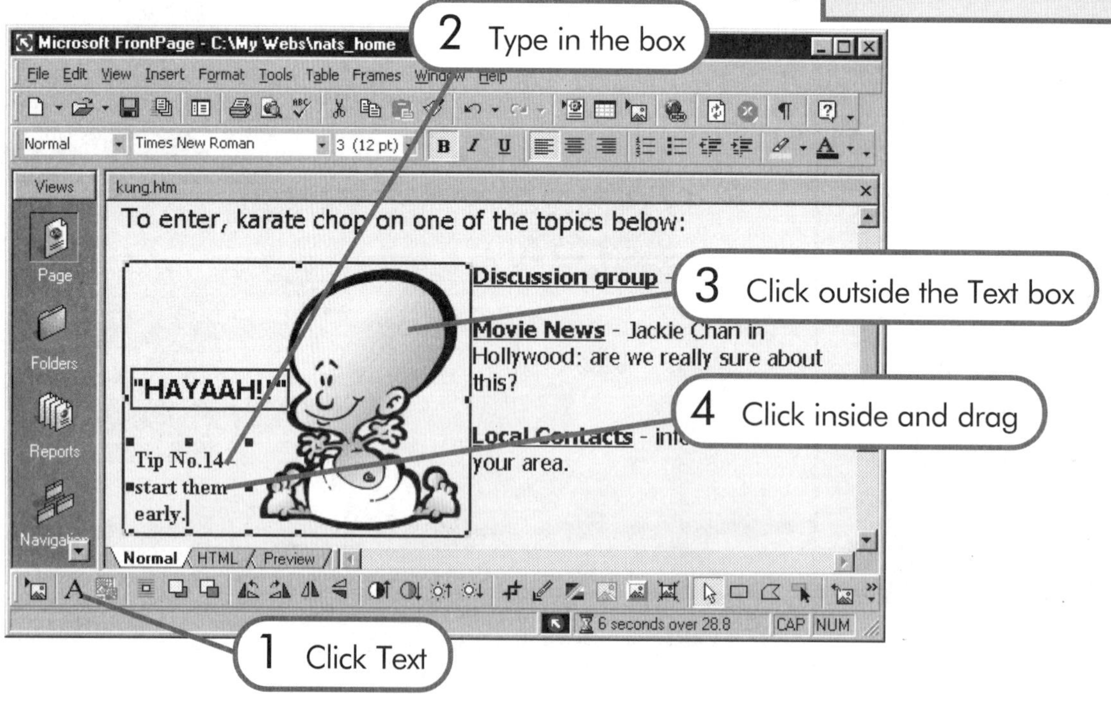
Microsoft FrontPage - C:\My Webs\nats_home
2 Type in the box
File Edit View Insert Format Tools Table Frames Window Help
Normal
Times New Roman
3 (12 pt)
Views
kung.htm
To enter, karate chop on one of the topics below:
Page
Folders
Reports
Navigation
Discussion group
3 Click outside the Text box
Movie News - Jackie Chan in Hollywood: are we really sure about this?
"HAYAAH!!"
4 Click inside and drag
Local Contacts
your area.
Tip No.14 - start them early.
Normal HTML Preview
6 seconds over 28.8
CAP NUM
1 Click Text

## Basic steps

1 Select the image.

2 Click the Make transparent button.

3 Click anywhere on the background colour to make it transparent.

## Transparent colours

The background colour of an image can be set to be transparent, allowing the page behind to show through. This breaks up the monotony of having all the pictures enclosed in rectangular boxes, and is especially useful for stylised text.

1 Select the image

3 Click on the colour

2 Click Make Transparent

The image is stamped across the background instead of being enclosed in a large coloured box

# Style sheets

These are special documents which are never actually seen by your visitors; they hold new definitions for text, background, and other styles. For example, the Heading 1 style normally displays text in Times New Roman, black, bold and 24 points in size. A style sheet might redefine it to be Arial, red, italic and 21 points. HTML pages can be linked to style sheets to apply their settings, which saves you respecifying them on every page and ensures a consistent look for your web. There are ready-made style sheets, or you can customise one to your liking.

## Basic steps

1 Choose New – Page... from the File menu.

2 Click on the Style Sheets tab and choose a template.

3 Choose Style... from the Format menu or from the Style toolbar.

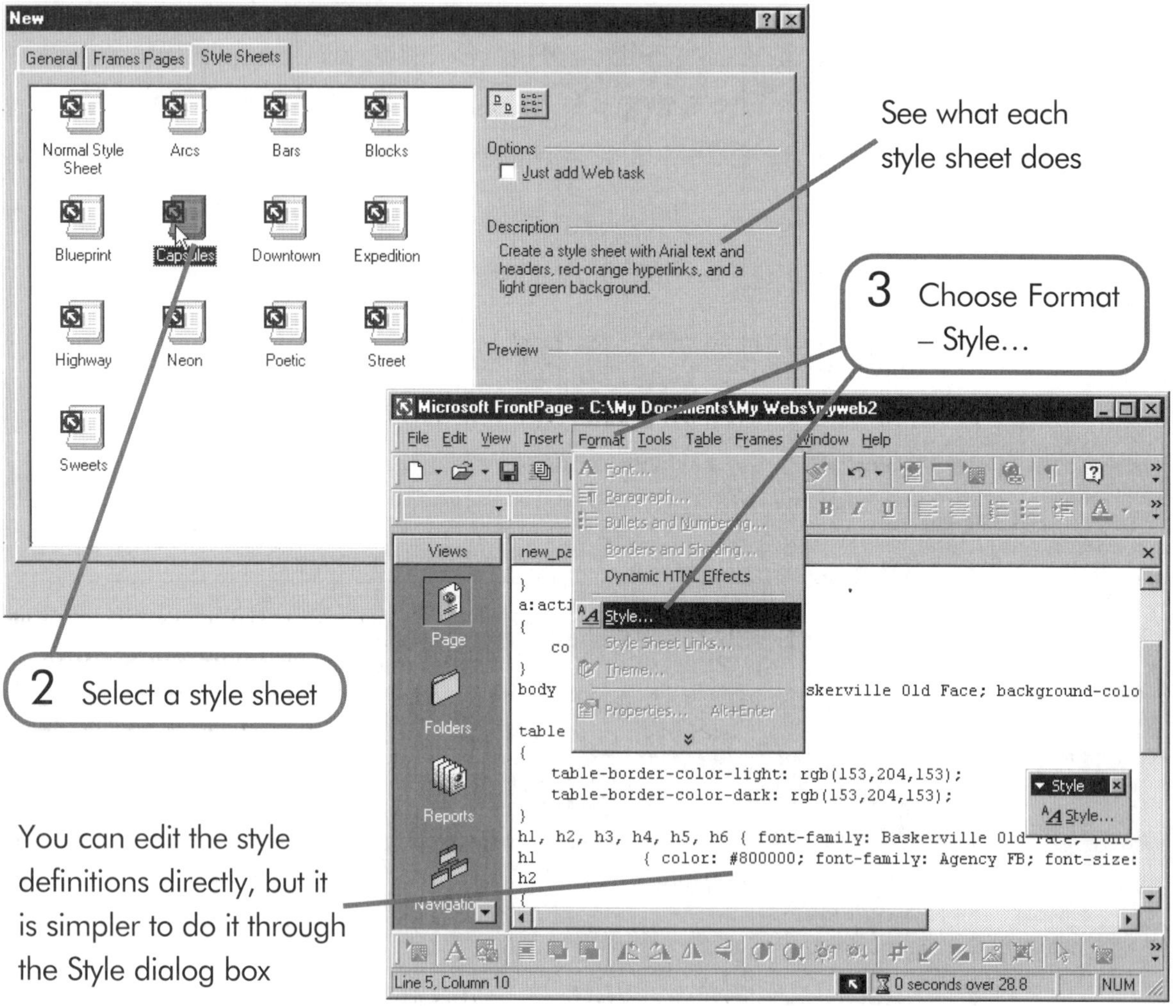

See what each style sheet does

3 Choose Format – Style...

2 Select a style sheet

You can edit the style definitions directly, but it is simpler to do it through the Style dialog box

4 Select a Style, e.g. h1 (Heading 1), body text, etc.

5 Click Modify…

6 Click on the Format button and choose what to modify.

7 Edit the style as you would normally.

8 Click OK.

9 Save the page – it will be given a .css (Cascading Style Sheet) extension.

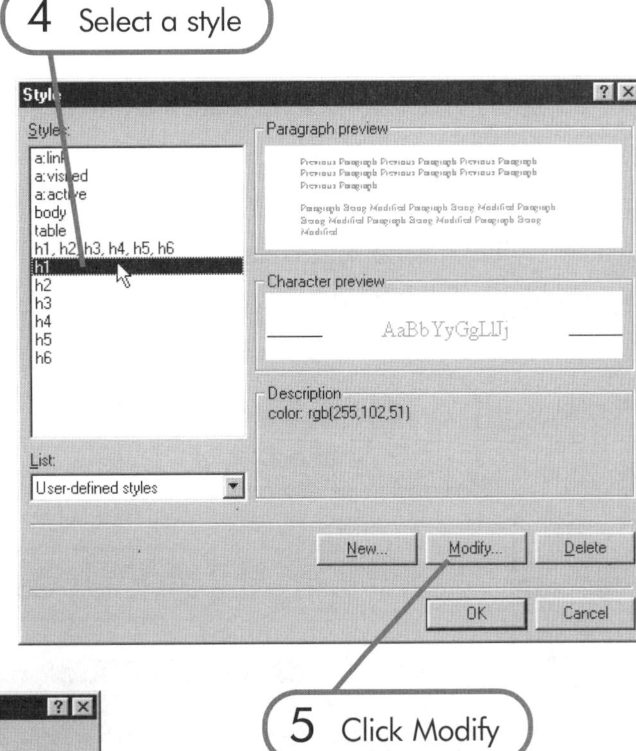

4 Select a style
Style
Styles:
a:link
a:visited
a:active
body
table
h1, h2, h3, h4, h5, h6
h1
h2
h3
h4
h5
h6
Paragraph preview
Character preview
AaBbYyGgLlJj
Description
color: rgb(255,102,51)
List:
User-defined styles
New...
Modify...
Delete
OK
Cancel
5 Click Modify


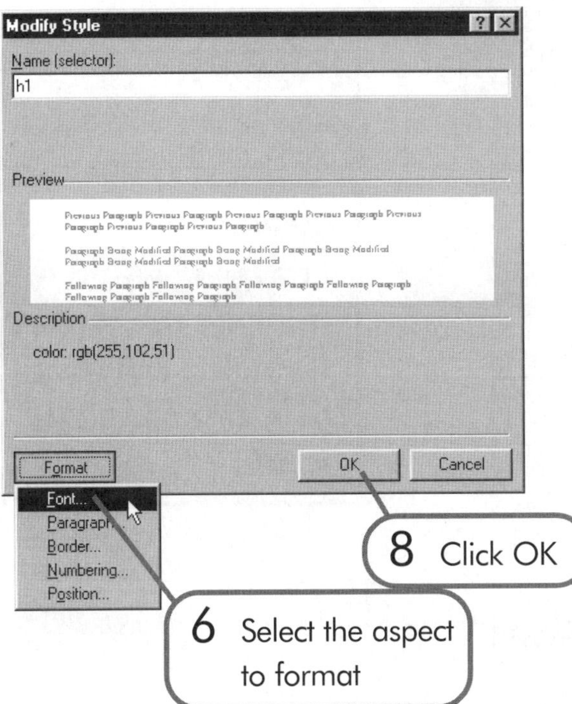

Modify Style
Name (selector):
h1
Preview
Description
color: rgb(255,102,51)
Format
OK
Cancel
Font...
Paragraph...
Border...
Numbering...
Position...
8 Click OK
6 Select the aspect to format


## Take note

**If you want to use a ready-made style sheet – without modifications – you must still save the new sheet. If you do not, it won't be available in your web.**

**They are called 'cascading' style sheets because you can have more than one, each used by distinct subsections of your web – useful if you have a large web.**

## Applying the styles

You now need to switch turn to the pages that you want to apply the style sheet to.

- If you are going to apply the style sheet to a single page, do it from that page in Page view and you can see the effects immediately.
- If you are styling several pages the same, you can do it in one operation in Folders view.

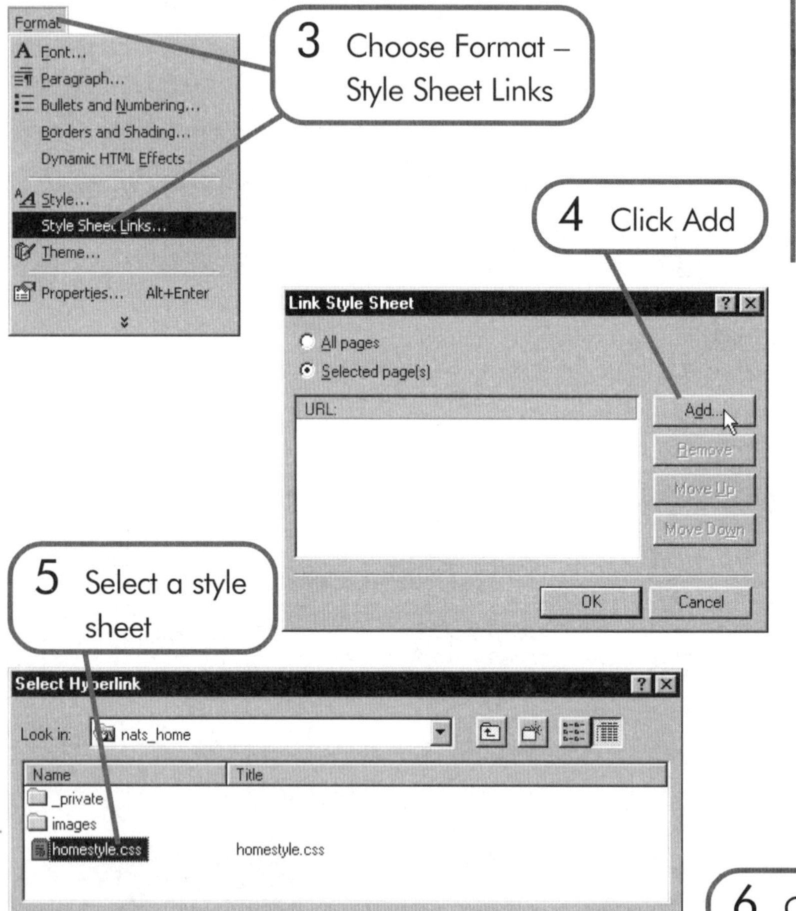

Format
Font...
Paragraph...
Bullets and Numbering...
Borders and Shading...
Dynamic HTML Effects
Style...
Style Sheet Links...
Theme...
Properties... Alt+Enter
3 Choose Format – Style Sheet Links
4 Click Add
Link Style Sheet
All pages
Selected page(s)
URL:
Add...
Remove
Move Up
Move Down
OK
Cancel
5 Select a style sheet
Select Hyperlink
Look in: nats_home
Name
Title
_private
images
homestyle.css
homestyle.css
URL: homestyle.css
OK
Cancel
6 Click OK


## Basic steps

1. Open the (single) page to be styled.

Or

2. Click on the Folders button and select the file(s).
3. Choose Style Sheet Links from the Format menu.
4. Click Add...
5. Select the style sheet you have just saved.
6. Click OK.

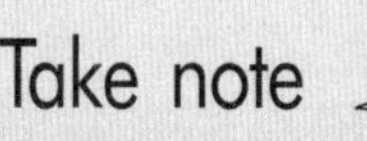

Take note

**Browers older than Netscape or Explorer 4 cannot use style sheets. Pages will be displayed on these in the default style formats.**

# Themes

1. Open the Format menu and choose Theme…
2. Select a theme.
3. Apply it to All pages or Selected page(s).
4. Set the display options: Choose Vivid colours for variations. Active graphics look nicer but the 'hover' effect may not work on older browsers. Turn off Background picture for a plain colour.
5. Turn off Apply using CSS.
6. Click OK.

Themes are suites of graphics and font settings which you can apply to a page or to your whole web to give it a polished look. Some themes come with FrontPage – you can use these 'off-the-rack' or customise them if you prefer.

Themes can applied using style sheets rather than changing the HTML code of each bit of text, but there's little advantage, and CSS you get plain horizontal rules instead of the graphic ones.

You can apply a theme to all pages from Page or Folders view. If you only want to apply it to selected pages, switch to Folders view and highlight the pages, then open the **Themes** dialog box and select **Apply Theme to Selected page(s)**.

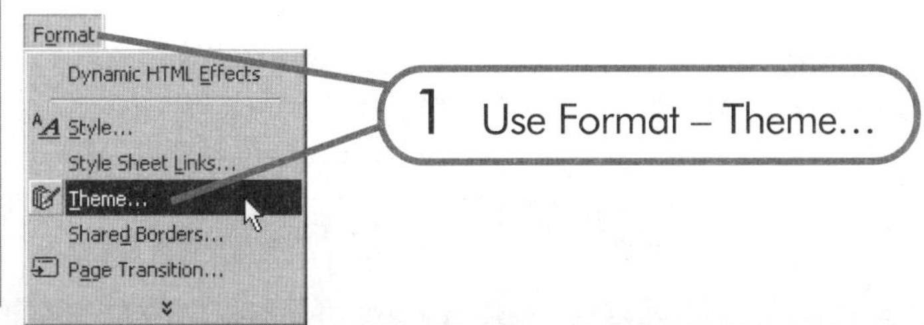
Format
Dynamic HTML Effects
Style...
Style Sheet Links...
Theme...
Shared Borders...
Page Transition...
1 Use Format – Theme…

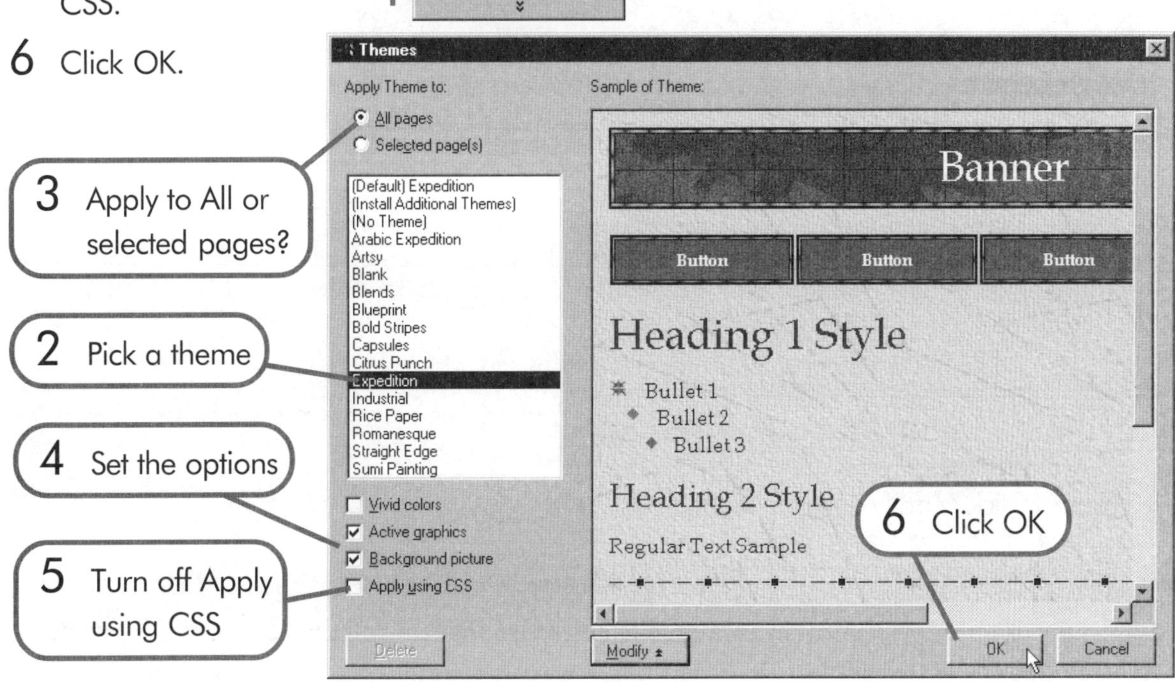
Themes
Apply Theme to:
All pages
Selected page(s)
Sample of Theme:
(Default) Expedition
(Install Additional Themes)
(No Theme)
Arabic Expedition
Artsy
Blank
Blends
Blueprint
Bold Stripes
Capsules
Citrus Punch
Expedition
Industrial
Rice Paper
Romanesque
Straight Edge
Sumi Painting
Banner
Button
Button
Button
Heading 1 Style
Bullet 1
Bullet 2
Bullet 3
Heading 2 Style
Regular Text Sample
Vivid colors
Active graphics
Background picture
Apply using CSS
Delete
Modify
OK
Cancel
3 Apply to All or selected pages?
2 Pick a theme
4 Set the options
5 Turn off Apply using CSS
6 Click OK

# Customising themes

## Basic steps

All aspects of a theme can be modified from the **Themes** dialog box – colours, font styles and sizes, background and button graphics.

If you you modify a theme, you will be prompted to save it at the end – give it a new name if you also want to retain the original theme.

## Colours

You can change the background colour (if you're not using an image) and the colour of different kinds of text – normal body text, headings, hyperlinks, navigation button text, etc.

1 Choose Theme… from the Format menu.

2 Select a theme.

3 Click Modify…

4 Click Colors… .

5 Choose a Color Scheme from the list.

*Or*

6 Click the Custom tab.

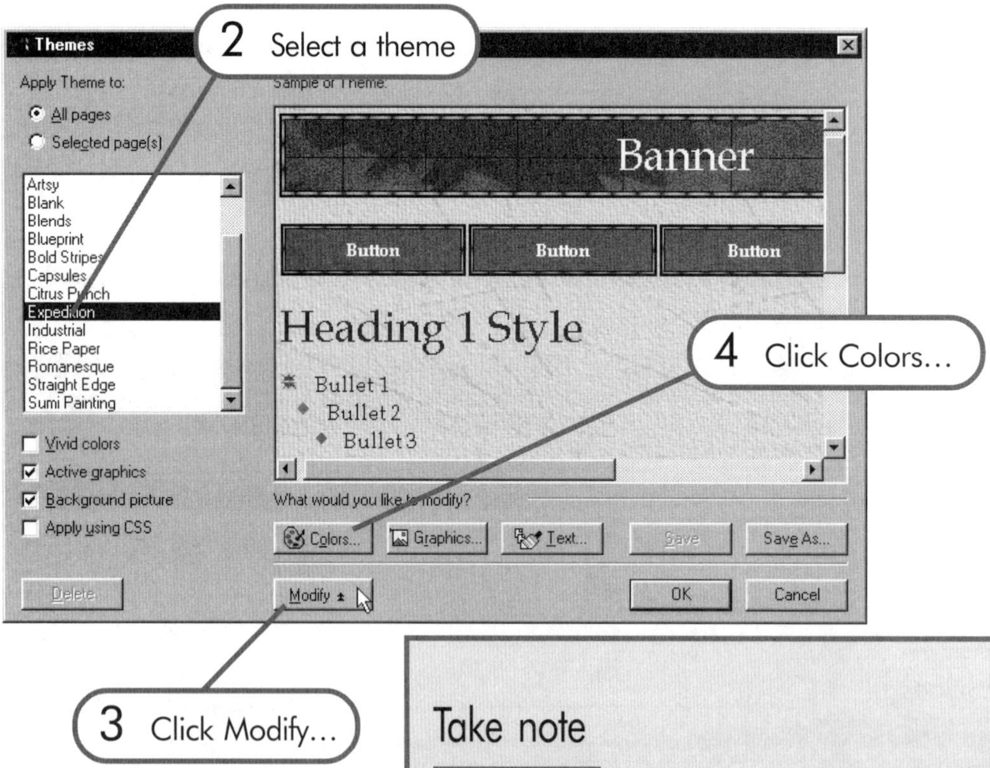

2 Select a theme

4 Click Colors…

3 Click Modify…

### Take note

**FrontPage themes are not the same as desktop themes, which are used to customise the look of your PC screen and sounds.**

7 Select an element from the menu.

8 Choose a colour.

9 Click OK.

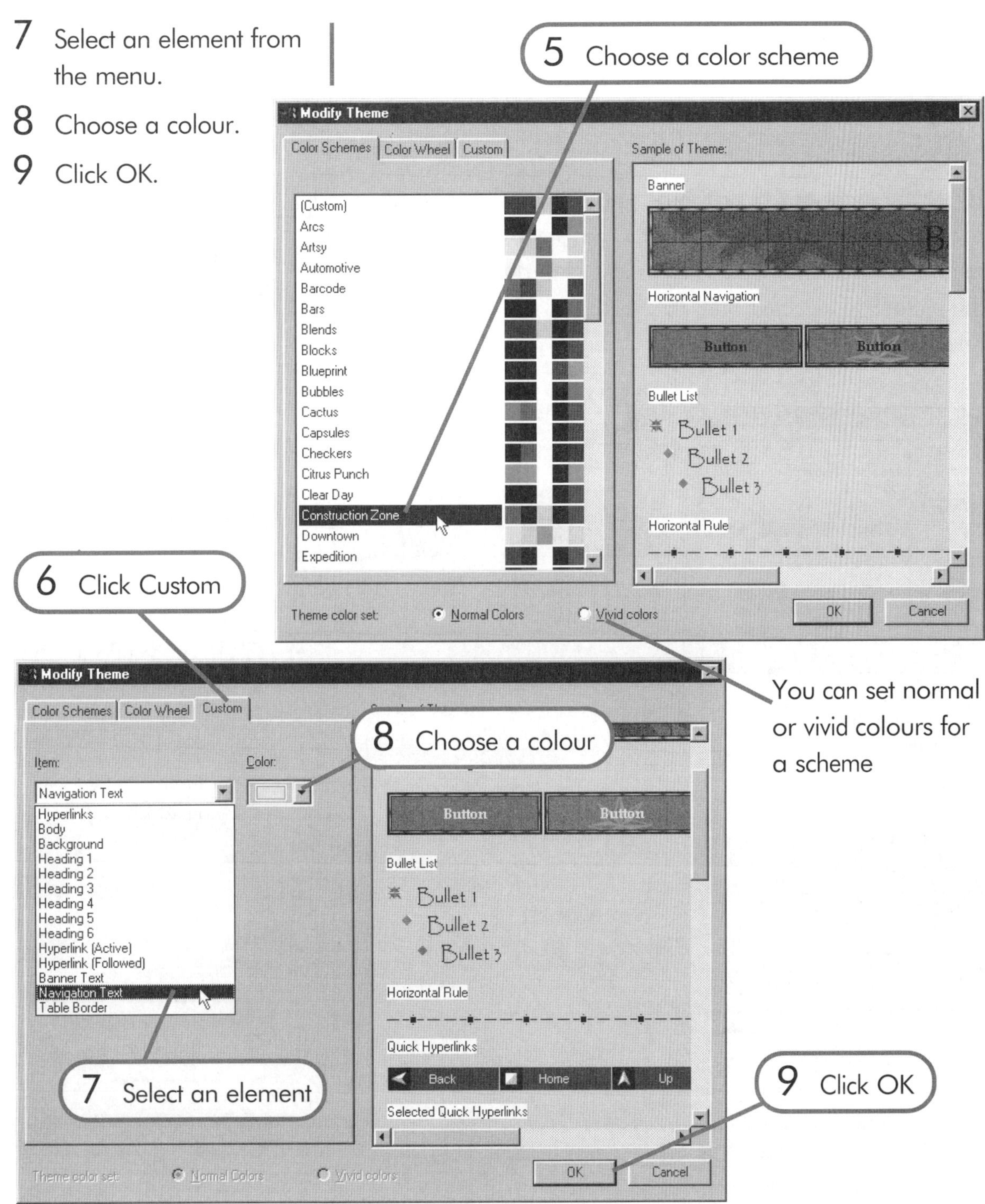
5 Choose a color scheme
Modify Theme
Color Schemes
Color Wheel
Custom
Sample of Theme:
(Custom)
Arcs
Artsy
Automotive
Barcode
Bars
Blends
Blocks
Blueprint
Bubbles
Cactus
Capsules
Checkers
Citrus Punch
Clear Day
Construction Zone
Downtown
Expedition
Banner
Horizontal Navigation
Button
Bullet List
Bullet 1
Bullet 2
Bullet 3
Horizontal Rule
Theme color set:
Normal Colors
Vivid colors
OK
Cancel
6 Click Custom
You can set normal or vivid colours for a scheme
Item:
Color:
Navigation Text
Hyperlinks
Body
Background
Heading 1
Heading 2
Heading 3
Heading 4
Heading 5
Heading 6
Hyperlink (Active)
Hyperlink (Followed)
Banner Text
Navigation Text
Table Border
8 Choose a colour
Quick Hyperlinks
Back
Home
Up
Selected Quick Hyperlinks
7 Select an element
9 Click OK

## Graphics

If you fancy yourself as a bit of an artist, you can design your own – or you can find libraries of ready-made graphics on the Internet. Remember that your buttons will have text on them, and you want it to be legible, so beware of over-jazzy designs.

If you are using **Active graphics**, you will need to choose two images for each button: one normal one, and one for when the mouse is hovering over it. There is also a third option for when the picture is 'selected', but this feature doesn't work in this release of the program! (v. 4.02)

## Basic steps

1. Click the Graphics... button [Graphics...]
2. Select a graphical element.
3. Browse for an image – with Active graphics, choose the other images for the button.

❑ To style the button text

4. Click on the Font tab.
5. Choose a Font.
6. Set the Style, Size, etc.
7. Click OK.

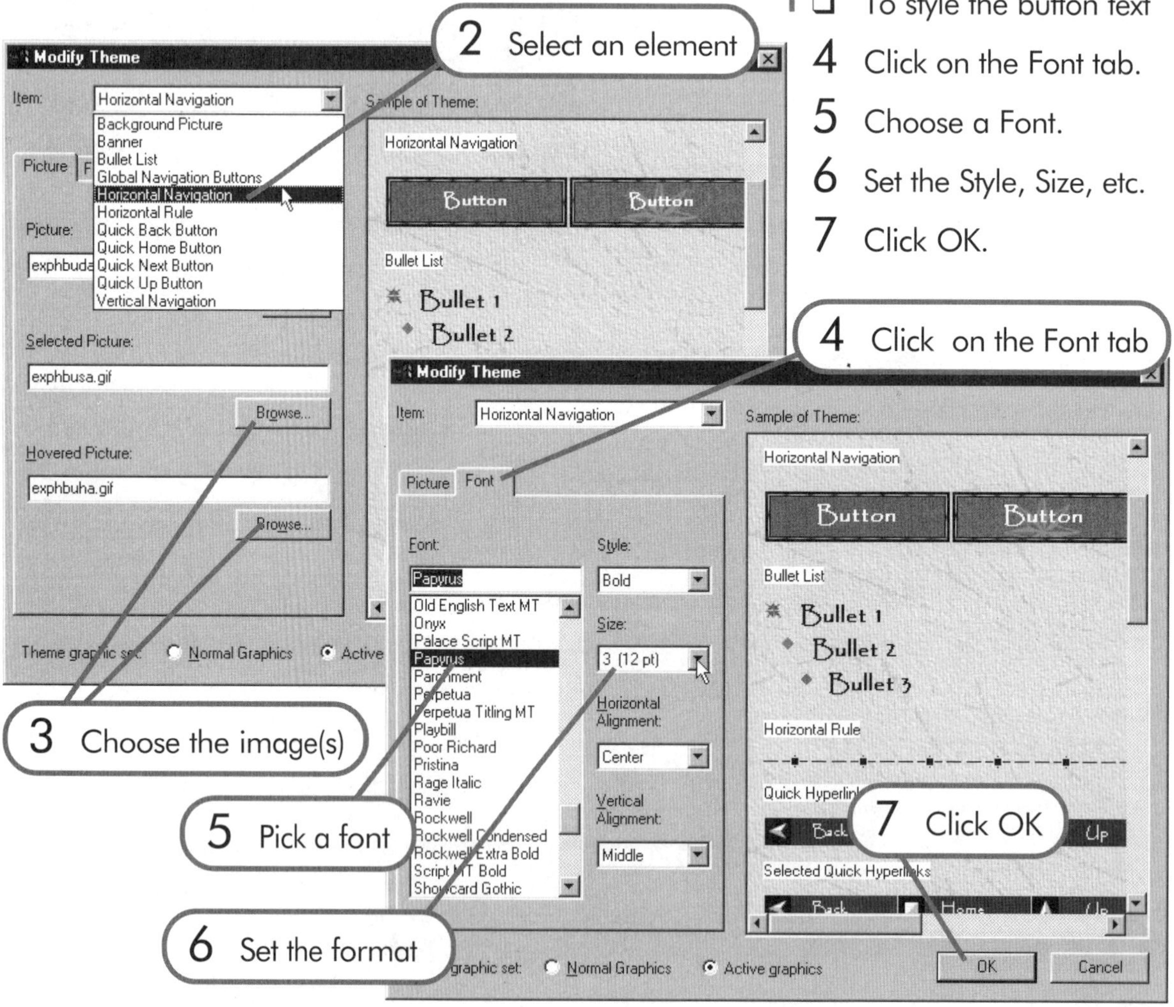

2 Select an element

3 Choose the image(s)

4 Click on the Font tab

5 Pick a font

6 Set the format

7 Click OK

## Basic steps

1. Click the Text... button [Text...].
2. Select what to change from the menu.
3. Choose a Font.
4. Click OK.

## Text

The Themes dialog box lets you change the font style and size of all text, including the text which appears on the navigation buttons and banners.

Note that the wording of the text on the buttons is taken from the settings in **Navigation view** (see page 126). To change this, you have to close the Themes dialog box and switch to Navigation view. Right-click on a file and choose **Rename** – then type what you want to appear on the navigation button and banner for that page (this does not affect the page Title).

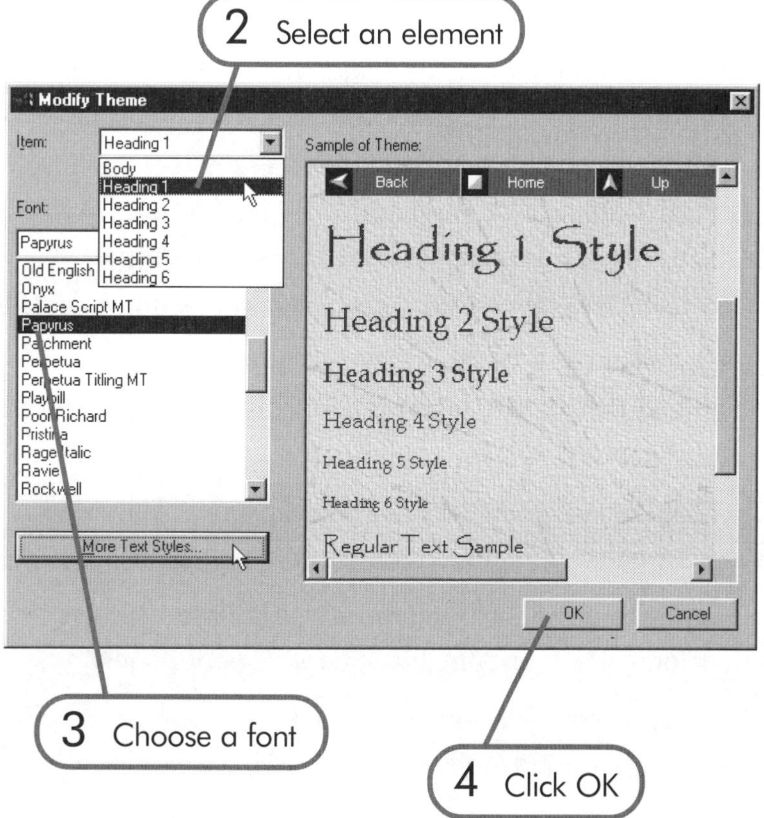
2 Select an element
Modify Theme
Item:
Heading 1
Body
Heading 1
Heading 2
Heading 3
Heading 4
Heading 5
Heading 6
Font:
Papyrus
Old English
Onyx
Palace Script MT
Papyrus
More Text Styles...
Sample of Theme:
Back
Home
Up
Heading 1 Style
Heading 2 Style
Heading 3 Style
Heading 4 Style
Heading 5 Style
Heading 6 Style
Regular Text Sample
OK
Cancel
3 Choose a font
4 Click OK

### Take note

**If you want to change the size and style of text as well as the font, click More text styles... and format the text as described in the section on style sheets on page 37.**

# Summary

- ❑ Set the size of text using the Font buttons, or Style drop-down menus.
- ❑ Change text colour by highlighting it and clicking the Font Color button to bring up a colour palette.
- ❑ Use Lists to make information more visually accessible.
- ❑ You can insert an image from elsewhere on a FrontPage Web, from your computer, or from the Internet.
- ❑ You can also drag an image from Windows Explorer or the Find File window and drop it into the page, or copy one from an image editor and paste it in.
- ❑ Change an image's size, alignment and relation to surrounding text, or give it a border from the Picture properties... dialog box.
- ❑ Give an image Alternative text or a thumbnail image to be displayed so that visitors don't have to wait around for pictures which they might not want to see.
- ❑ Use the Picture Toolbar for more effects - to float an image behind text, rotate or flip it, adjust the brightness and contrast, etc.
- ❑ Give an image a transparent background if you don't want it in a boring rectangular box.
- ❑ Style sheets will help to ensure that your text styles and colours are consistent throughout a set of pages.
- ❑ A theme can give your web a polished look. You can modify the ready-made themes to your own design.

# 3 Active content

# Animated GIFs

These are images which move – in fact, they are several images stored in one file and displayed in sucession. They are inserted on a page in exactly the same way as an ordinary static image.

There are lots of places on the Internet which offer animated graphics to use free of charge (usually only for home use, though), and plenty which do not charge very much!

If you prefer, you can try your hand at making your own – there are a number of very reasonable shareware packages for animating GIFs. Try a download site such as **www.tucows.com** and search for GIF animation.

Tip

**When constructing your web pages, try to strike a balance between impressive looking graphics, movie clips and other attention-grabbers, and the boredom involved in waiting for large files to download.**

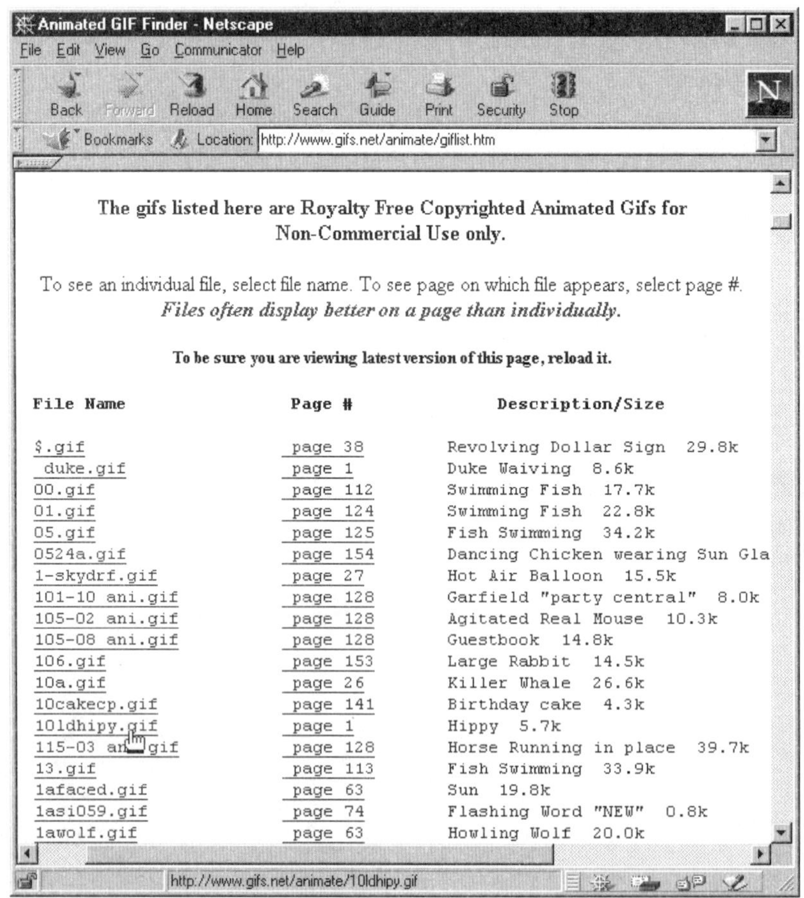

Animated GIF Finder - Netscape
File Edit View Go Communicator Help
Back Forward Reload Home Search Guide Print Security Stop
Bookmarks Location: http://www.gifs.net/animate/giflist.htm
The gifs listed here are Royalty Free Copyrighted Animated Gifs for Non-Commercial Use only.
To see an individual file, select file name. To see page on which file appears, select page #.
Files often display better on a page than individually.
To be sure you are viewing latest version of this page, reload it.
File Name Page # Description/Size
$.gif page 38 Revolving Dollar Sign 29.8k
duke.gif page 1 Duke Waiving 8.6k
00.gif page 112 Swimming Fish 17.7k
01.gif page 124 Swimming Fish 22.8k
05.gif page 125 Fish Swimming 34.2k
0524a.gif page 154 Dancing Chicken wearing Sun Gla
1-skydrf.gif page 27 Hot Air Balloon 15.5k
101-10 ani.gif page 128 Garfield "party central" 8.0k
105-02 ani.gif page 128 Agitated Real Mouse 10.3k
105-08 ani.gif page 128 Guestbook 14.8k
106.gif page 153 Large Rabbit 14.5k
10a.gif page 26 Killer Whale 26.6k
10cakecp.gif page 141 Birthday cake 4.3k
10ldhipy.gif page 1 Hippy 5.7k
115-03 ani.gif page 128 Horse Running in place 39.7k
13.gif page 113 Fish Swimming 33.9k
1afaced.gif page 63 Sun 19.8k
1asi059.gif page 74 Flashing Word "NEW" 0.8k
1awolf.gif page 63 Howling Wolf 20.0k
http://www.gifs.net/animate/10ldhipy.gif


At the time of writing, there was an excellent GIF animation source page at: http://www.gifs.net/animate/animate.htm
Check it out – it should still be there.

Basic steps

# AVI and MOV video clips

1 From the Insert menu, choose Picture, then Video...

2 Choose from a video already in one of your FrontPage Webs.

*Or*

3 Click on the Select File button.

4 Find a video file on your computer.

*Or*

5 Browse the Internet for a file and copy the URL – but remember that if you link to someone else's page, the clip may change when they update.

6 Click OK.

The way video clips are displayed varies from browser to browser. FrontPage is designed for use with **AVI** and **MOV** files, and is very fussy about them – it will not display files of other formats in the list of FrontPage files.

If you use **AVI** or **MOV** files and your visitors use MS Explorer, video clips will be played wherever you put them on the page, and you can also customise the way they are displayed.

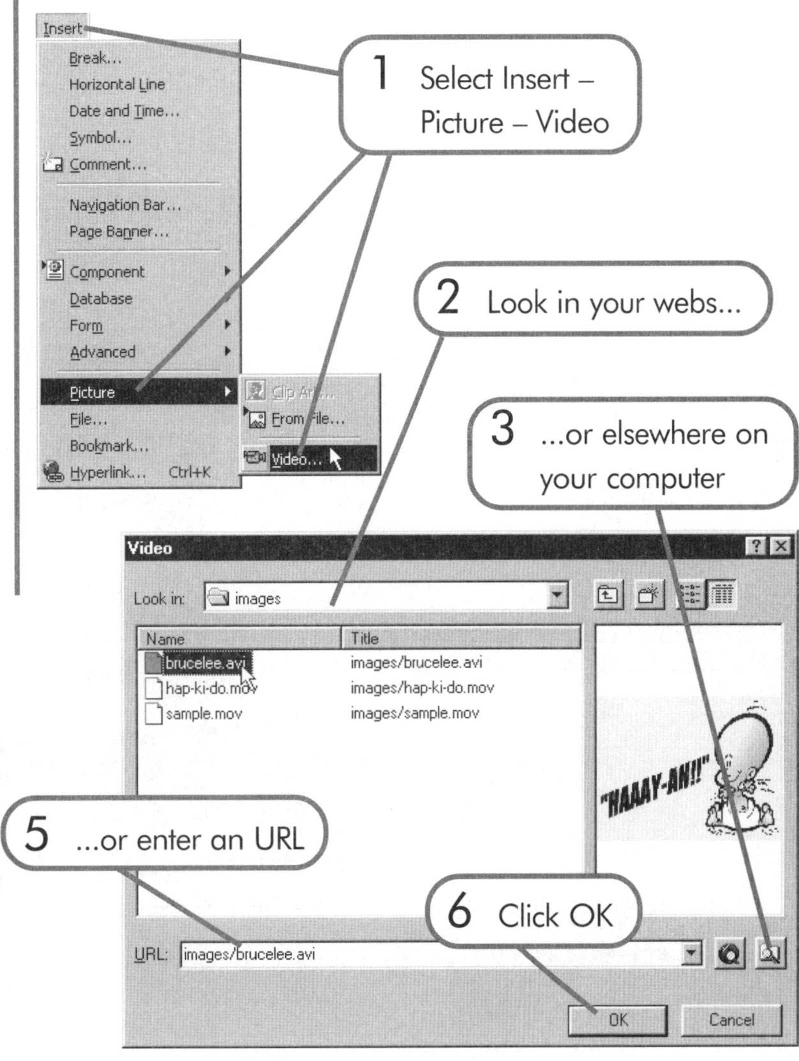

1 Select Insert – Picture – Video
2 Look in your webs...
3 ...or elsewhere on your computer
5 ...or enter an URL
6 Click OK
Insert
Break...
Horizontal Line
Date and Time...
Symbol...
Comment...
Navigation Bar...
Page Banner...
Component
Database
Form
Advanced
Picture
File...
Bookmark...
Hyperlink... Ctrl+K
Clip Art...
From File...
Video...
Video
Look in: images
Name
Title
brucelee.avi
hap-ki-do.mov
sample.mov
images/brucelee.avi
images/hap-ki-do.mov
images/sample.mov
"HAAAY-AH!!"
URL: images/brucelee.avi
OK
Cancel


## Take note

**AVI stands for Audio-Visual Interleaved and is the format used by Window's Media Player.**

## AVI and MOV display options

There are a few options that you can set to control how the .AVI or .MOV clip is displayed.

- **Show controls in browser** – if this is checked, it allows visitors to stop and start the clip, though in fact, this feature is often not supported.
- **Loop** – specifies the number of times to repeat the clip.
- **Forever** – sets the clip into a continuous loop.
- **Loop Delay** – the delay between repeat showings.
- **Start On File Open** – starts the animation as soon as the clip is loaded.
- **Start On MouseOver** – loads the clip and waits for the cursor to move over the first frame before starting to play.

## Basic steps

1 Right-click on the video image and choose Picture Properties...
2 Click on the Video tab.
3 Set the options as required.
4 Click OK.

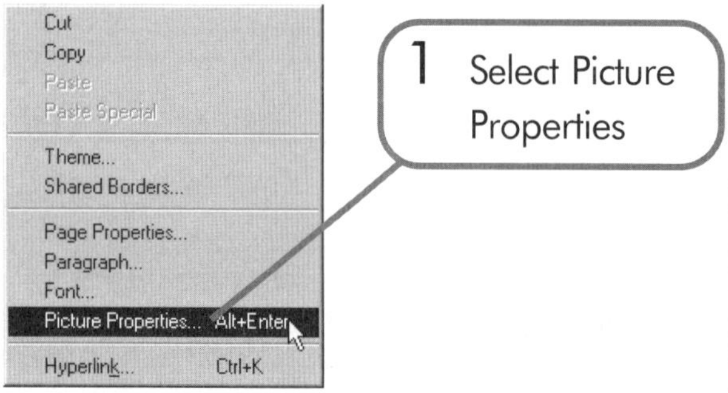

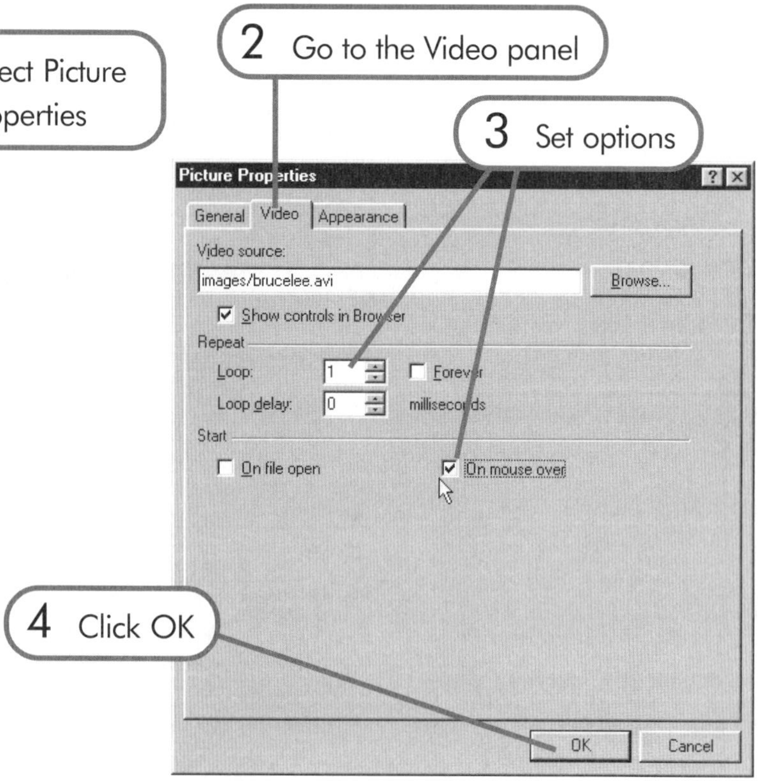

Cut
Copy
Paste
Paste Special
Theme...
Shared Borders...
Page Properties...
Paragraph...
Font...
Picture Properties... Alt+Enter
Hyperlink... Ctrl+K
1 Select Picture Properties
2 Go to the Video panel
3 Set options
Picture Properties
General
Video
Appearance
Video source:
images/brucelee.avi
Browse...
Show controls in Browser
Repeat
Loop:
1
Forever
Loop delay:
0
milliseconds
Start
On file open
On mouse over
4 Click OK
OK
Cancel


### Tip

**Use the resizing handles around the edges of a video clip to change the size at which it is played.**

## Basic steps

1. Choose Import… from the File menu.
2. Click Add File… and browse for a file.
3. Click OK.
4. Select text or an image to serve as a link.
5. Click the Create Hyperlink button.
6. Browse your folders for the file.
7. Click OK.

# Other video formats

Unfortunately for FrontPage users, many clips available are in other formats such as .mpeg, and many people prefer to use a Netscape browser! The best solution is to create a link to the video file instead of embedding it into a page. This does mean that you lose the extra display options, but your visitors will appreciate being given the choice of whether to download a large video file or not. (See Chapter 5 for more on creating hyperlinks.)

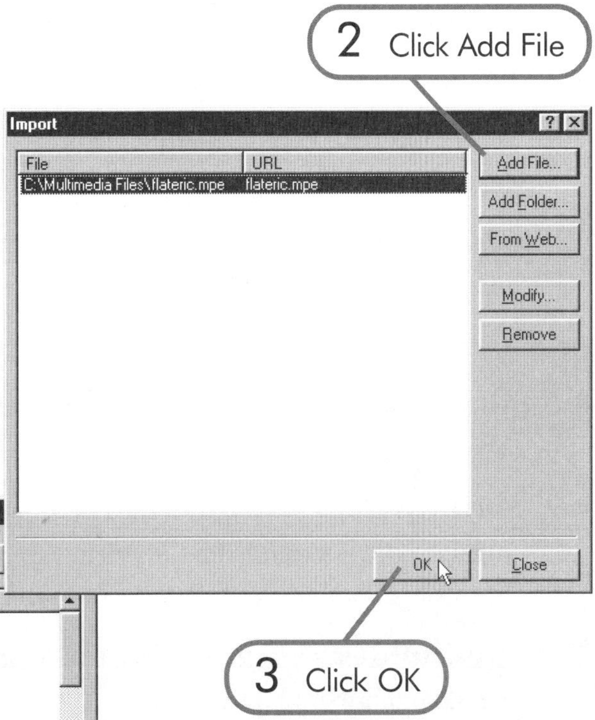

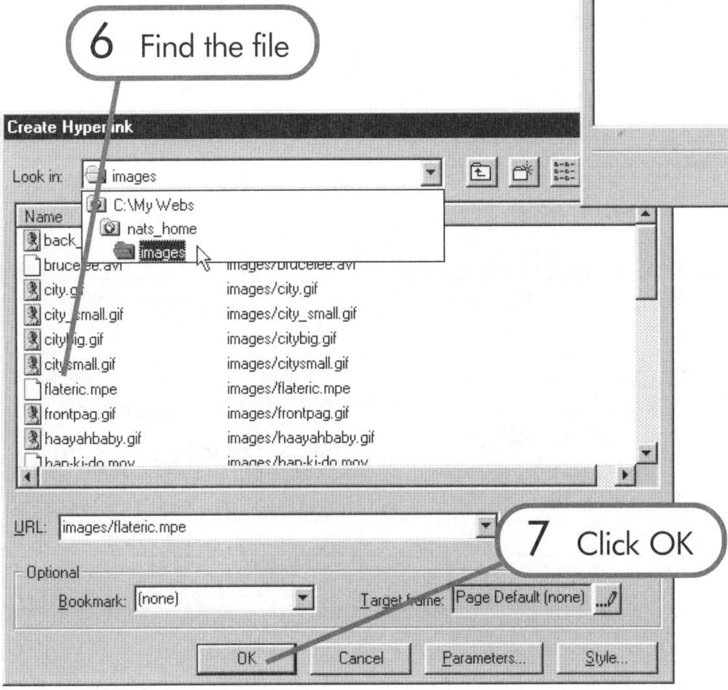

2 Click Add File

3 Click OK

6 Find the file

7 Click OK

### Take note

**Import brings a file into the Web folder, but does not insert it into the page.**

# Marquees

A Marquee is a FrontPage component which will make text scroll or bounce from left to right across the screen. There are several properties which you can edit:

- **Direction** determines whether the text scrolls to the Left or Right.
- **Movement Speed** sets the *Delay* in milliseconds between each step of the animation and the motion – *Amount* it moves each step, measured in pixels.
- **Behavior** – sets how the marquee moves.

  *Scroll* runs text onto the marquee box at one side and off the other;

  *Slide* makes text slide onto the marquee and stay still when it reaches the other side

  *Alternate* makes text slide back and forth.
- **Align with text** sets the vertical alignment of any text surrounding the marquee.
- **Specify Width** and **Height** – by default, these are determined by the size of the text in the marquee, but you can set values if you wish.
- **Repeat** makes the action repeat *Continuously* or for a specified number of *Times*.
- **Background color** – change the background colour.
- **Automatic** – gives the Marquee a transparent background.

## Basic steps

1. From the Insert menu, choose Component, then Marquee...
2. Type a message.
3. Set the Direction and Speed of motion.
4. Select a Behavior style.
5. Set text alignment.
6. Specify the Width and/ or Height.
7. Decide how many times the action is repeated.
8. Set a Background color.
9. Click OK.

### Tip

**A marquee's text can be formatted as normal – just highlight it and use the toolbar to set the font, size and colour.**

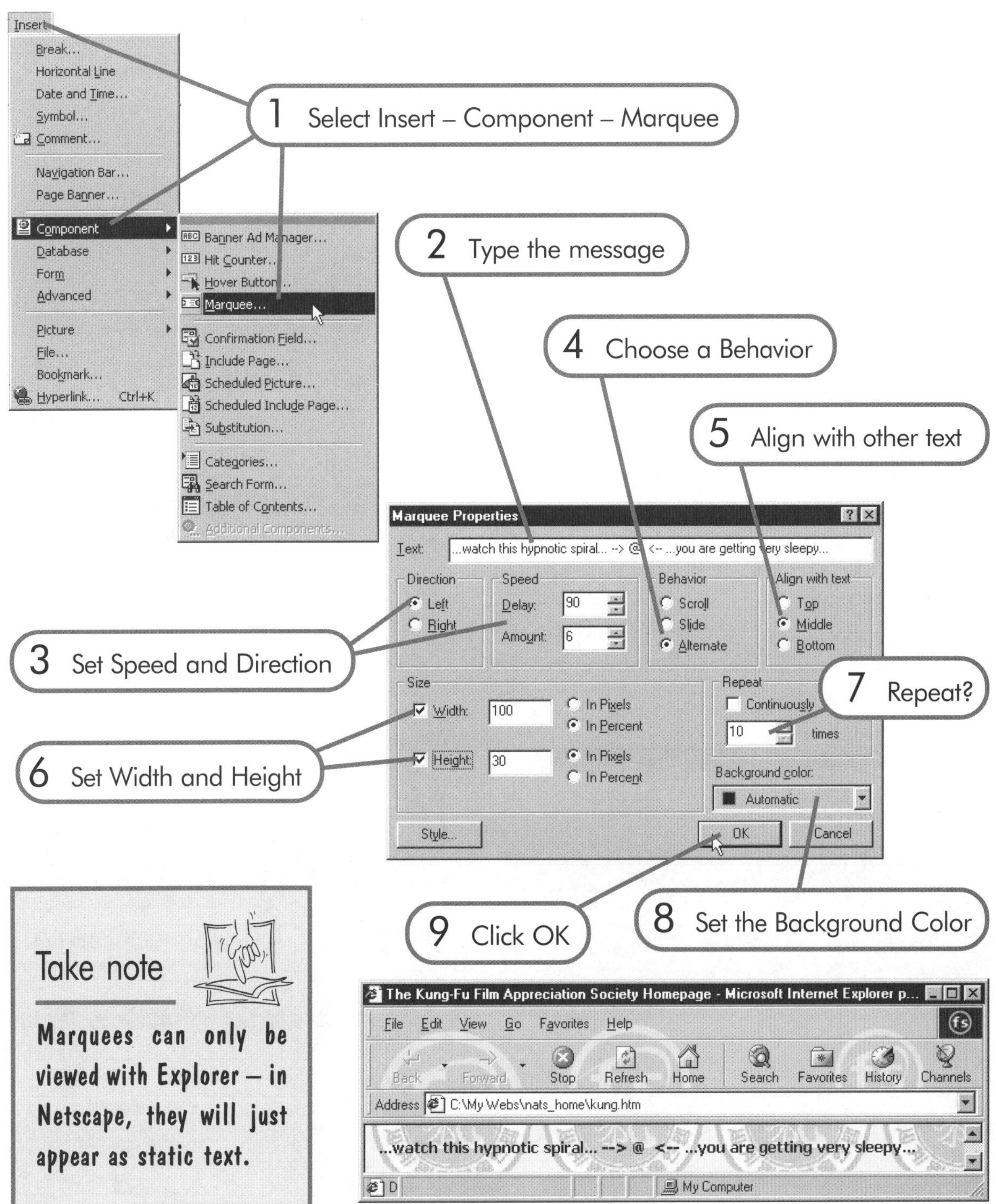
Insert
Break...
Horizontal Line
Date and Time...
Symbol...
Comment...
Navigation Bar...
Page Banner...
Component
Database
Form
Advanced
Picture
File...
Bookmark...
Hyperlink... Ctrl+K
Banner Ad Manager...
Hit Counter...
Hover Button...
Marquee...
Confirmation Field...
Include Page...
Scheduled Picture...
Scheduled Include Page...
Substitution...
Categories...
Search Form...
Table of Contents...
Additional Components...
1 Select Insert – Component – Marquee
2 Type the message
3 Set Speed and Direction
4 Choose a Behavior
5 Align with other text
6 Set Width and Height
7 Repeat?
8 Set the Background Color
9 Click OK
Marquee Properties
Text: ...watch this hypnotic spiral... --> @ <-- ...you are getting very sleepy...
Direction
Left
Right
Speed
Delay: 90
Amount: 6
Behavior
Scroll
Slide
Alternate
Align with text
Top
Middle
Bottom
Size
Width: 100
In Pixels
In Percent
Height: 30
In Pixels
In Percent
Repeat
Continuously
10 times
Background color:
Automatic
Style...
OK
Cancel
The Kung-Fu Film Appreciation Society Homepage - Microsoft Internet Explorer p...
File Edit View Go Favorites Help
Back Forward Stop Refresh Home Search Favorites History Channels
Address C:\My Webs\nats_home\kung.htm
...watch this hypnotic spiral... --> @ <-- ...you are getting very sleepy...
My Computer

## Take note

**Marquees can only be viewed with Explorer – in Netscape, they will just appear as static text.**

# Hover buttons

FrontPage uses Java to create interactive buttons called *hover buttons*. When a visitor's mouse cursor 'hovers' over the button, one of several kinds of visual effect can be applied to it.

- **Color fill** – changes the **Button color** to the **Effect color**.
- **Color average** – changes to a colour mid-way between the **Button color** and **Effect color**.
- **Glow** – shines a 'spotlight' of the **Effect color** on the middle of the button.
- **Reverse glow** – shines the **Effect color** spotlight on the edges.
- **Light glow** – like **Glow**, but with white light.
- **Bevel out** – makes the button 'pop up' in 3D.
- **Bevel in** – makes the button 'sink in'.

## Basic steps

1 Open the Insert menu, choose Component, then Hover button…

2 Type in the text to go on the button.

3 Click Font…

4 Select the font, style, size, and colour of the text and click OK.

5 Browse… for the file to be hyperlinked.

6 Choose a Button color and Effect color.

7 Select an Effect.

8 Set the button's Width and Height (optional).

9 Click OK.

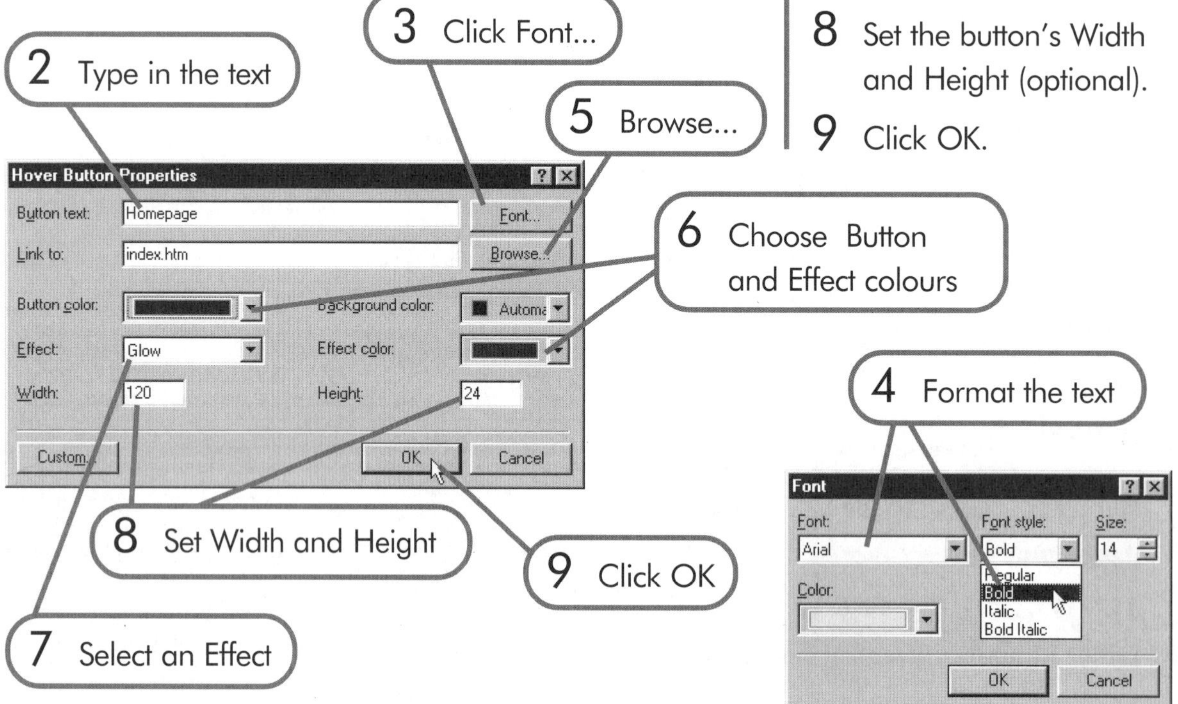

2 Type in the text
3 Click Font...
5 Browse...
Hover Button Properties
Button text:
Homepage
Font...
Link to:
index.htm
Browse...
Button color:
Background color:
Automa
Effect:
Glow
Effect color:
Width:
120
Height:
24
Custom...
OK
Cancel
6 Choose Button and Effect colours
4 Format the text
Font
Font:
Arial
Font style:
Bold
Size:
14
Regular
Bold
Italic
Bold Italic
Color:
OK
Cancel
8 Set Width and Height
9 Click OK
7 Select an Effect

## Basic steps

1 Click on the Custom… button.

2 Browse… for .au sound files to play *On click* and/or *On hover*.

3 Browse… for a Button image.

❑ If using a second image

4 Browse… for an image to display *On hover*.

5 Click OK.

## Custom hover buttons

Instead of having a plain text button, you can use an image as a hover button. The same effects as for text buttons can be applied, or you can choose a second image to replace the first as the hover effect. Sound files can also be set to play either when the mouse passes over the button, or when it is clicked (or have a different sound for each). Note that only sound files in Sun's .AU format can be used for this.

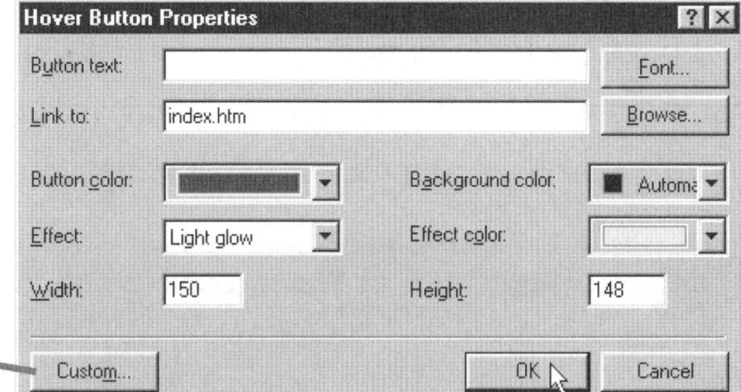
Hover Button Properties
Button text:
Font...
Link to:
index.htm
Browse...
Button color:
Background color:
Automa
Effect:
Light glow
Effect color:
Width:
150
Height:
148
Custom...
OK
Cancel
1 Click Custom...

### Take note

**If you have no text on your button because you are using an image, watch out! Whenever you open the Hover button properties dialog box, the default text 'Button text' will re-appear and must be deleted again.**

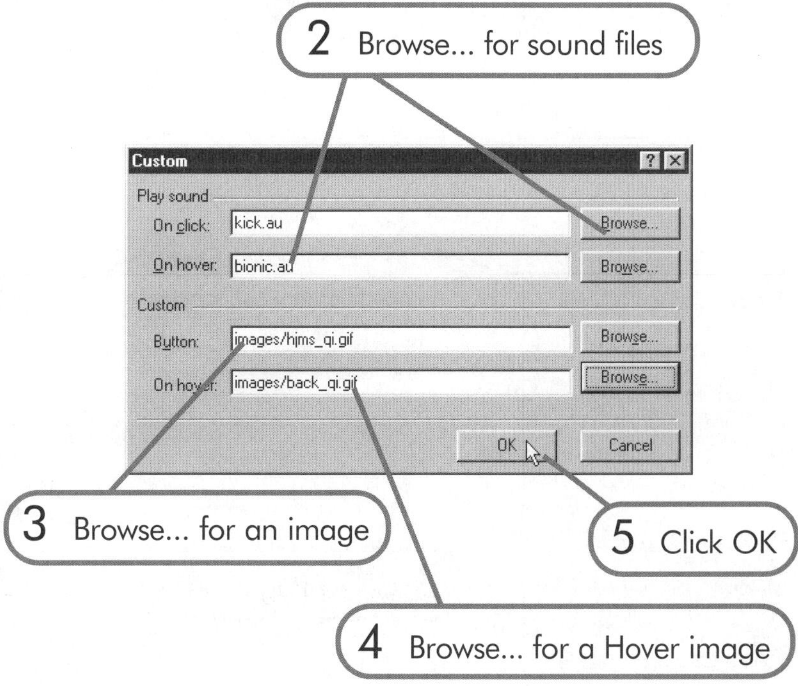
2 Browse... for sound files
Custom
Play sound
On click:
kick.au
Browse...
On hover:
bionic.au
Browse...
Custom
Button:
images/hjms_qi.gif
Browse...
On hover:
images/back_qi.gif
Browse...
OK
Cancel
3 Browse... for an image
5 Click OK
4 Browse... for a Hover image

# Dynamic HTML

Dynamic HTML (DHTML) is a new development which can animate text and graphics, and add interactive effects to pages. It performs some nifty tricks, but only when viewed in browsers which are geared up to it, so test-drive your pages carefully!

DHTML effects which are triggered by mouse movement or clicks all work in Explorer 4.0 and higher, but not (to date) in Navigator. The other effects change the way paragraphs or images are loaded into the page. The table shows which of these **On page load** effects work in each browser and which don't. 'Sort of', it means that the effect is supposed to work word by word, but in Navigator the whole paragraph moves as a chunk!

| DHTML effect | In Navigator | In Explorer? |
|---|---|---|
| Drop in by word | Sort of | Yes |
| Elastic | Yes | Yes |
| Fly in | Yes | Yes |
| Hop | Sort of | Yes |
| Spiral | Yes | Yes |
| Wave | Sort of | Yes |
| Wipe | No | No |

## Basic steps

1 Select text or image(s).

2 Open the Format menu and choose Dynamic HTML Effects.

3 Choose Page load from the first menu on the DHTML Effects toolbar.

4 Select an effect.

5 Choose the settings, if applicable.

6 A lightly shaded box will appear to show that the effect has been applied.

See opposite for more about these effects

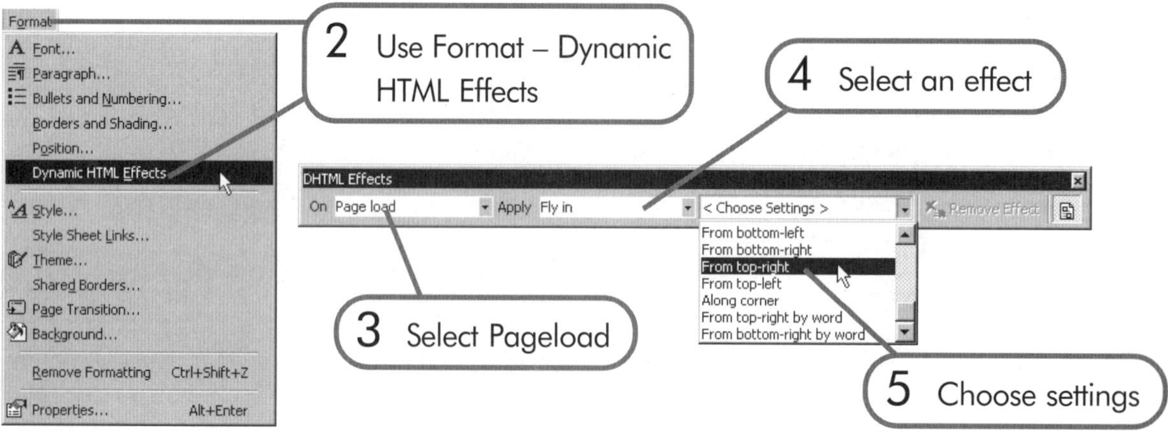
Format
Font...
Paragraph...
Bullets and Numbering...
Borders and Shading...
Position...
Dynamic HTML Effects
Style...
Style Sheet Links...
Theme...
Shared Borders...
Page Transition...
Background...
Remove Formatting Ctrl+Shift+Z
Properties... Alt+Enter
2 Use Format – Dynamic HTML Effects
4 Select an effect
DHTML Effects
On Page load
Apply Fly in
< Choose Settings >
Remove Effect
From bottom-left
From bottom-right
From top-right
From top-left
Along corner
From top-right by word
From bottom-right by word
3 Select Pageload
5 Choose settings

## On page load effects

### Take note

**People who use a non-compatible browser may not be able to see some of the text or images which have DHTML effects applied to them.**

These effects can be applied to images or whole paragraphs and headings. Just highlight the text you want to animate and choose an effect. Some of these have extra settings, for instance to determine which side of the screen the text flies in from.

- **Drop in by word** – each word of a sentence, or images from a set in one line, drops in from the top of the window in turn.
- **Fly in** – the text flies into position from the side .
- **Elastic** – as **Fly in**, but bounces when it reaches its target.
- **Hop** – text 'leapfrogs' into position word by word.
- **Wave** – like **Hop**, but alternate words bounce over or under each other.
- **Spiral** – text flies into position in a big loop.
- **Wipe** – text appears in a smooth sweep, as if a cover was being drawn off it.
- **Zoom** – text appears small and enlarges into its proper size, or appears large and is shrunk down to size.

If you apply a 'word by word' effect to a row of images each is animated in turn (IE4.0+ only)

Microsoft FrontPage - C:\My Webs\nats_home
File Edit View Insert Format Tools Table Frames Window Help
Heading 5
(default font)
Normal
Views
Page
Folders
Reports
DHTML Effects
On Page load
Apply Fly in
From top-right by word
Remove Effect
"HAAAY-AH!!"
"HAAAY-AH!!"
"HAAAY-AH!!"
"HAAAY-AH!!"
"Daaa-i-eeee! Watch out! Incoming kamikaze babies!"
Normal
HTML
Preview
35 seconds over 28.8
NUM

## Mouse-driven effects

DHTML can be used to affect text or images in response to a 'mouse event' – when the mouse passes over them (on **Mouse over**), or when they are clicked (on **Click** or **Double-click**).

The effects are **Fly out** (not available for **Mouse over**), which sends the text or image zipping off the screen, and **Formatting**, which allows you to add a border or background shading to the element. With text, you can also change the font size and style.

## Basic steps

1. Choose a mouse event.
2. Select Fly out and choose a direction.

Or

3. Select Formatting.
4. Select Choose Font… and set the format.
5. Select Choose Border…
6. Set the Border and Shading options and click OK.

1 Choose a mouse event

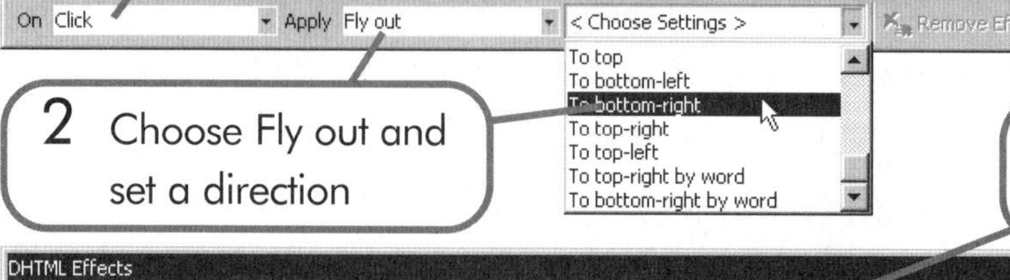
DHTML Effects
On Click
Apply Fly out
< Choose Settings >
Remove Effect
To top
To bottom-left
To bottom-right
To top-right
To top-left
To top-right by word
To bottom-right by word

2 Choose Fly out and set a direction

4 Select Choose Font... and set the format options

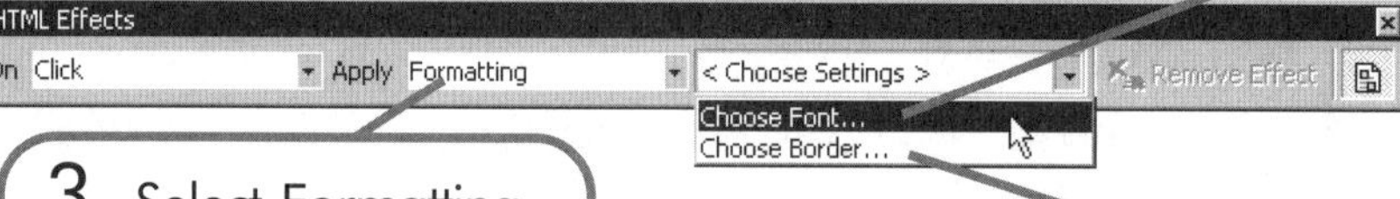
DHTML Effects
On Click
Apply Formatting
< Choose Settings >
Remove Effect
Choose Font...
Choose Border...

3 Select Formatting

5 Select Choose Border...

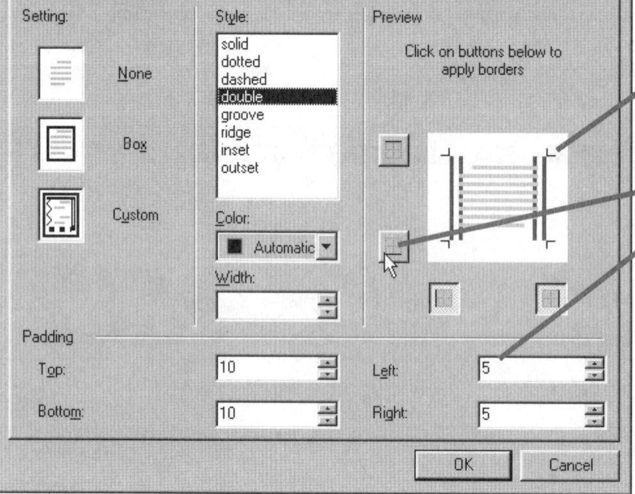
Borders and Shading
Borders
Shading
Setting:
None
Box
Custom
Style:
solid
dotted
dashed
double
groove
ridge
inset
outset
Color:
Automatic
Width:
Preview
Click on buttons below to apply borders
Padding
Top:
10
Bottom:
10
Left:
5
Right:
5
OK
Cancel

Experiment with the settings, using the Preview to guide you

6 Set the options

### Take note

**To get rid of an effect on an element, select it and click Remove Effect.**

## Basic steps

1 Select Page transition from the Format menu.
2 Select the event.
3 Choose an effect.
4 Specify how long the effect takes to complete.
5 Repeat for all events as needed.
6 Click OK.

## Page transitions

These change the way a page appears as it loads into the browser window, giving it a 'curtain' effect, for instance. If you have used a program like PowerPoint, you may be familiar with some of these effects. There are four events which trigger a page transition.

**Page enter/Page exit:** on loading or leaving the page, and

**Site enter/Site exit:** when a hyperlink goes into or out of the page from somewhere outside of your web site.

If a page has a Page enter transition, it will override the Page exit of the page it came from; also, Site enter and exit events override Page enter and exit transitions.

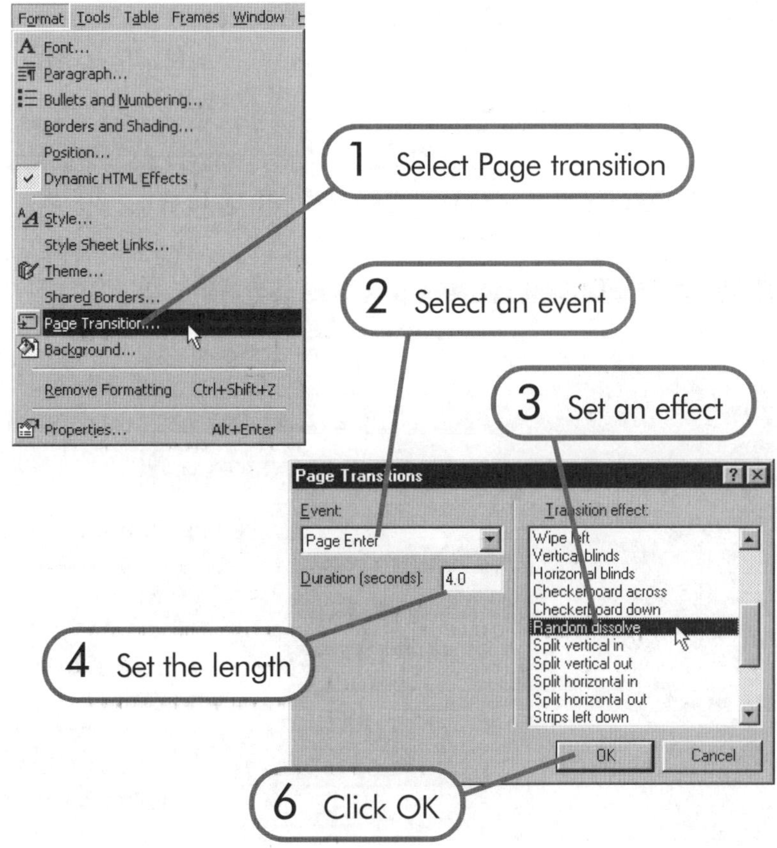
Format Tools Table Frames Window
Font...
Paragraph...
Bullets and Numbering...
Borders and Shading...
Position...
Dynamic HTML Effects
Style...
Style Sheet Links...
Theme...
Shared Borders...
Page Transition...
Background...
Remove Formatting Ctrl+Shift+Z
Properties... Alt+Enter
1 Select Page transition
2 Select an event
3 Set an effect
Page Transitions
Event:
Page Enter
Duration (seconds):
4.0
Transition effect:
Vertical blinds
Random dissolve
Split vertical in
Split vertical out
Split horizontal in
Split horizontal out
Strips left down
OK
Cancel
4 Set the length
6 Click OK

### Take note

**If you have more than one point of entry to your site, site enter and exit transitions must be set separately for each page – sounds tedious, but it means you can achieve different effects, depending on where a visitor first enters your site.**

# Background sounds

## Basic steps

If you have a sound file – a spoken message or some music – it can be attached to a page to play in the background when the page is opened. There are several kinds of sound file – the file extension identifies the format.

**AU** Sun's audio format – can be handled directly by Internet Explorer and by Netscape's LiveAudio plug-in. Most people should be able to hear these.

**AIFF** The Apple sound format.

**MID** MIDI sequence, played on Windows systems by MPlayer – normally linked to the browser.

**WAV** Wave format, played by Windows' sound software.

**RAM** (or **RM**) RealAudio 'play-as-you-download' format, needs the RealAudio software (available free from **www.real.com**).

1 Open the Page Properties... dialog box.

2 On the General tab, find Background Sound.

3 Browse... for a sound file.

4 Set the number of times to repeat playing the file.

or to repeat indefinitely

5 Check the Forever box.

6 Click OK.

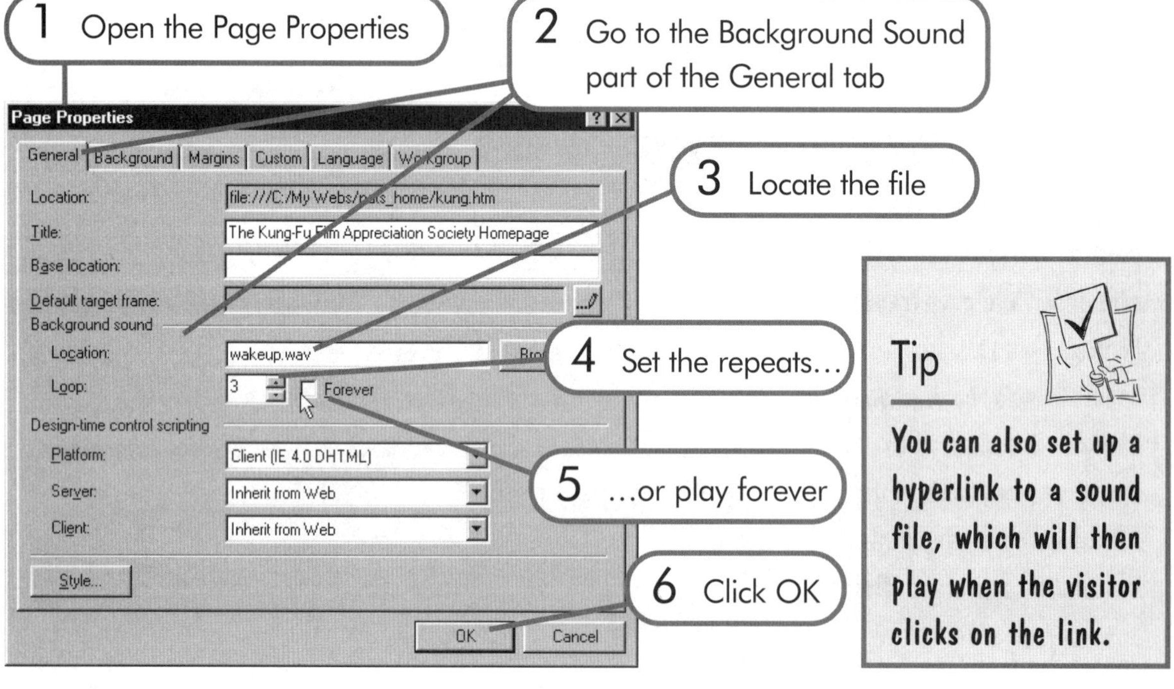
1 Open the Page Properties
2 Go to the Background Sound part of the General tab
3 Locate the file
4 Set the repeats...
5 ...or play forever
6 Click OK
Page Properties
General
Background
Margins
Custom
Language
Workgroup
Location:
file:///C:/My Webs/pats_home/kung.htm
Title:
The Kung-Fu Film Appreciation Society Homepage
Base location:
Default target frame:
Background sound
Location:
wakeup.wav
Loop:
3
Forever
Design-time control scripting
Platform:
Client (IE 4.0 DHTML)
Server:
Inherit from Web
Client:
Inherit from Web
Style...
OK
Cancel

## Tip

**You can also set up a hyperlink to a sound file, which will then play when the visitor clicks on the link.**

# Java, ActiveX and JavaScript

These are fairly complex computer language systems which you would need a bit of time to master. Fortunately for those of us who don't particularly want to become programmers, small chunks of program written by experts can be used by amateurs.

> **Tip**
>
> **Don't reject the idea of using these languages – the Links and Resources page (page 139) has the addresses of a couple of good sites where you can get simple advice and instruction on how to use them, as well as links to other sites showing them at work.**
>
> **If you want to learn these languages, why not try *Java Made Simple* and *JavaScript Made Simple*.**

## Java

Java applets are mini-programs which are loaded onto your hard drive and then run from your machine – they might run animations, or allow users to interact with the on-screen display, for example.

## ActiveX

ActiveX controls are simple modules of code which can be linked together to perform more complex tasks – even if they are stored in different sites around the Internet.

## JavaScript

This is considerably easier to learn than either of the others, but is more limited in what it can do. Small blocks of JavaScript code can be attached to the elements in your pages and forms, to make them more interactive. Unfortunately, only those visitors who use Netscape or Internet Explorer 4.0 will be able to get the real benefit, as earlier versions of Internet Explorer cannot handle JavaScript (a Netscape development)!

Most ready-made applets and controls are accompanied by text files explaining how they work. They may lok complicated, but if you read carefully and take a little time to experiment, you'll find that you can customise them to your needs.

# Summary

- Animated GIFs will liven up a page. There are many freely available on the Net, or you can get GIF animator software to create your own.
- Embed AVI and MOV video clips wherever you want in a page and set control options.
- Video clips in other file formats will need to have a hyperlink to the file set up.
- Make text scroll or slide to and fro like a banner with the Marquee feature.
- Use Hover buttons to spice up your links with some interactivity.
- Dynamic HTML will add special effects to your page – but visitors must have suitable browsers to see them.
- On page load effects animate the way text and graphics are loaded into a page.
- Mouse-driven effects add another interactive element to your page.
- Page transitions can make browsing through your site look very slick.
- Add a Background sound to your page, to play as the page is loaded.

## Tip

**Check out the Java, ActiveX and JavaScript sites in the Links and Resources (page 143) to see how to make your site truly interactive.**

# 4 Tables

# Creating a table

## Basic steps

FrontPage 2000 offers several flexible ways to create tables, including a tool which allows you to sketch a table out on-screen (see page68). We'll start by creating a table with roughly the right number of rows and columns for our purposes, as it can be adjusted later.

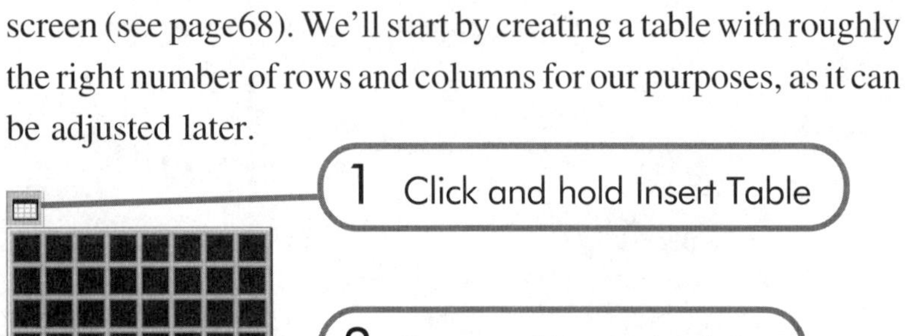
1 Click and hold Insert Table
2 Drag to the required size
8 by 8 Table

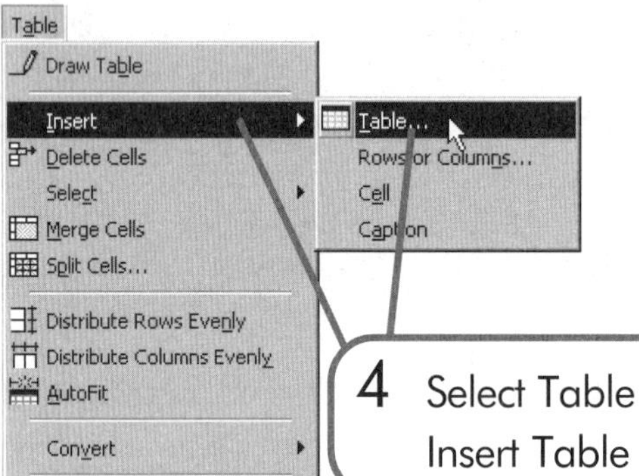
Table
Draw Table
Insert
Delete Cells
Select
Merge Cells
Split Cells...
Distribute Rows Evenly
Distribute Columns Evenly
AutoFit
Convert
Properties
Table...
Rows or Columns...
Cell
Caption
4 Select Table – Insert Table

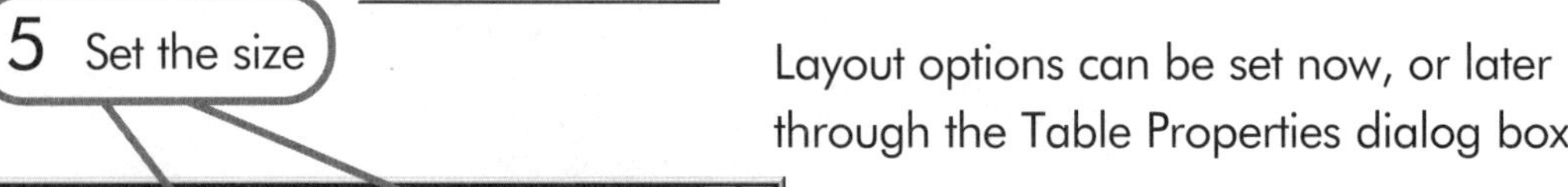
5 Set the size

Layout options can be set now, or later through the Table Properties dialog box

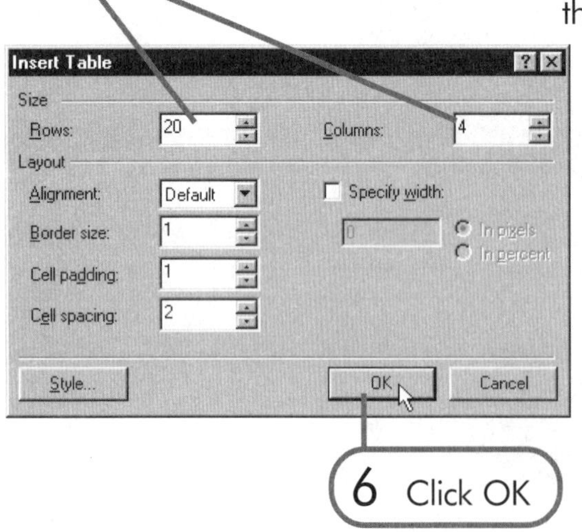
Insert Table
Size
Rows: 20
Columns: 4
Layout
Alignment: Default
Specify width:
Border size: 1
In pixels
In percent
Cell padding: 1
Cell spacing: 2
Style...
OK
Cancel
6 Click OK

1 On the Toolbar, click and hold the Insert Table button.

2 Drag the cursor down and to the right until you have the size you want.

3 Release the mouse button.

*Or*

4 Choose Insert – Table from the Table menu.

5 Set the number of rows and columns.

6 Click OK.

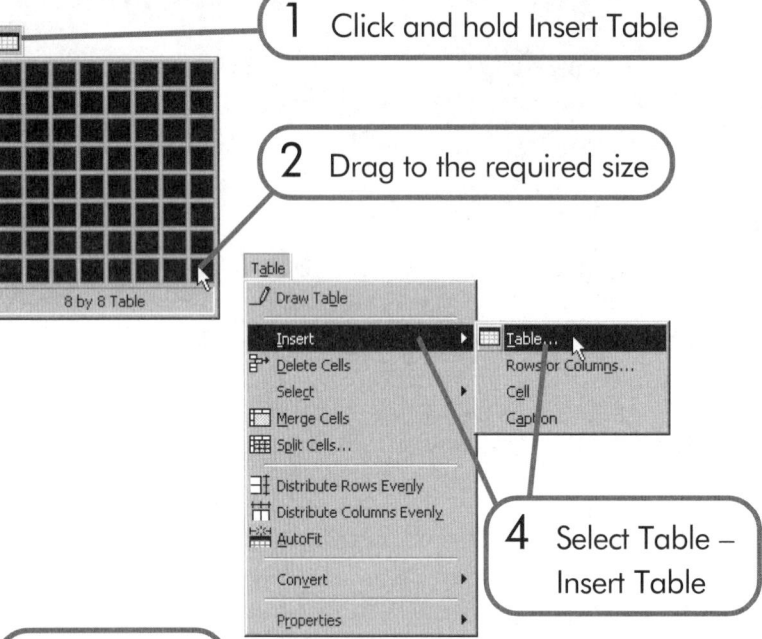

### Take note

**A new table has a maximum size of 25 rows by 25 columns. This can be increased later, but it is advisable to break large tables up where possible, as some browsers do not display anything until the whole table is loaded.**

## Basic steps

1. Highlight a cell or cells.
2. Right click and choose Cell Properties…
3. Edit the properties as required.
4. Click OK.

### Take note

**If you use the Draw Table toolbar to create a table, you will find that cell widths are set to very unlikely numbers. It's worth fixing this by highlighting all the cells in the table and turning off the Specify Width option in the Cell Properties dialog box.**

# Editing cells

To enter or edit text, just place the cursor in a cell and type as normal, using the arrow keys or **Tab** to move between cells.

You can format the text in cells exactly as you would format normal text. Cells also have additional features that can be changed through the **Cell Properties** dialog box:

- **Horizontal** and **Vertical Alignment** – determine how the contents of a cell are aligned within it.
- **Rows** and **Columns Spanned** – makes a cell span more than one row or column. You'll find it easier to use the **Merge Cells** function for this, though.
- **Header Cell** – identifies text as a row or column header (usually shown in browsers by bold type)
- **No Wrap** – tells browsers to make the cell wider rather than wrap text onto a new line within the cell.
- **Specify Width** and **Height** – set cell width and height in pixels or as a percentage of the table width.
- **Border** and **Background** – set border colours and background colour or image to distinguish the cell(s) from the rest of the table.

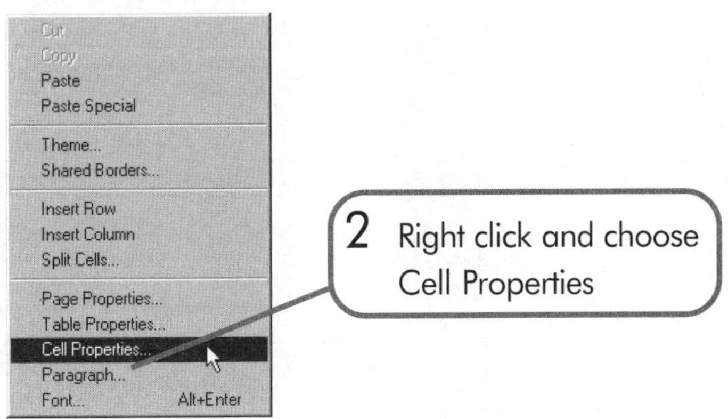
Cut
Copy
Paste
Paste Special
Theme...
Shared Borders...
Insert Row
Insert Column
Split Cells...
Page Properties...
Table Properties...
Cell Properties...
Paragraph...
Font...
Alt+Enter
2 Right click and choose Cell Properties

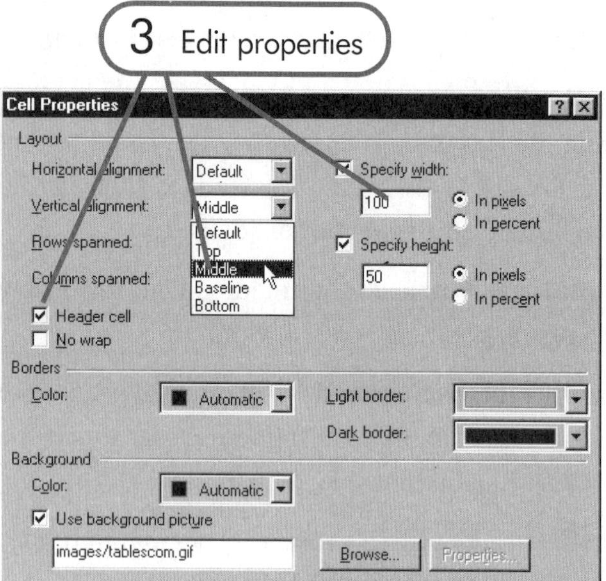
3 Edit properties
Cell Properties
Layout
Horizontal alignment:
Default
Vertical alignment:
Middle
Rows spanned:
Columns spanned:
Default
Top
Middle
Baseline
Bottom
Header cell
No wrap
Specify width:
100
In pixels
In percent
Specify height:
50
In pixels
In percent
Borders
Color:
Automatic
Light border:
Dark border:
Background
Color:
Automatic
Use background picture
images/tablescom.gif
Browse...
Properties...
Style...
OK
Cancel
Apply

4 Click OK

## Tip

**Test these settings in more than one browser if possible, as browsers are unreliable in the way they interpret them, especially the Cell Width and Height.**

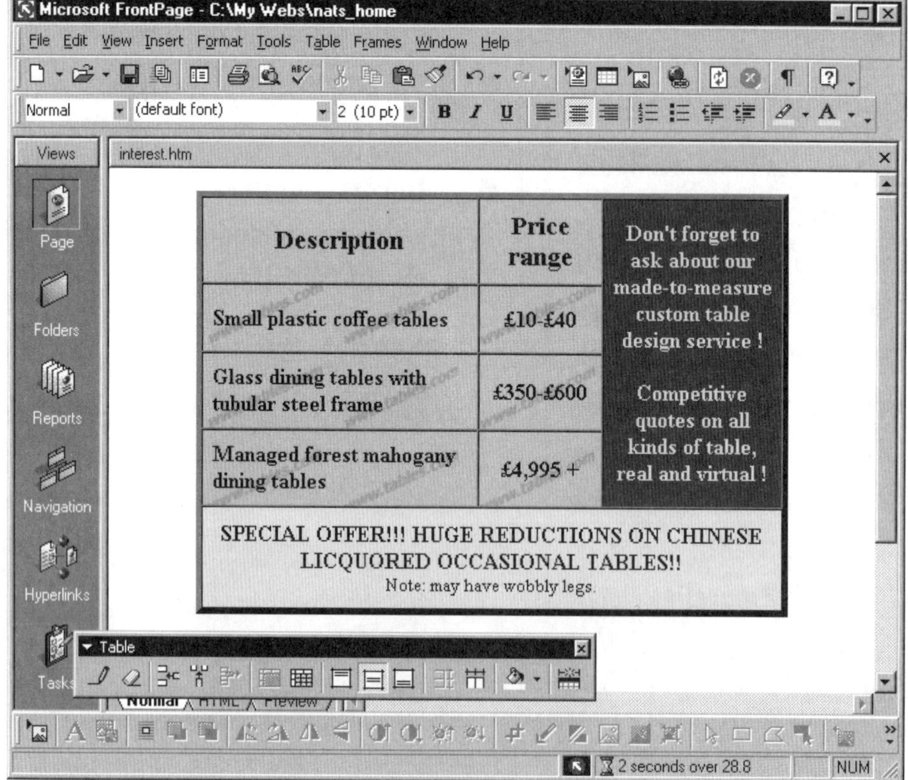
Microsoft FrontPage - C:\My Webs\nats_home
File Edit View Insert Format Tools Table Frames Window Help
Normal
(default font)
2 (10 pt)
Views
Page
Folders
Reports
Navigation
Hyperlinks
Tasks
interest.htm
Description
Price range
Don't forget to ask about our made-to-measure custom table design service !
Competitive quotes on all kinds of table, real and virtual !
Small plastic coffee tables
£10-£40
Glass dining tables with tubular steel frame
£350-£600
Managed forest mahogany dining tables
£4,995 +
SPECIAL OFFER!!! HUGE REDUCTIONS ON CHINESE LICQUORED OCCASIONAL TABLES!!
Note: may have wobbly legs.
Table
2 seconds over 28.8
NUM

## Basic steps

# Adjusting the size

- ❑ To insert lines

1 Place the cursor in the table where you want to insert a new row or column.

2 Choose Insert Rows or Columns… from the Table menu.

3 Select Rows or Columns.

4 Set the number to insert.

5 Choose where to put them in relation to where the cursor is.

- ❑ To delete lines

6 Move the cursor to the left or top edge of the table until it turns into a solid black arrow, then click to select the entire row or column.

7 Hold the mouse button and drag it to select more than one at a time.

8 Press [Backspace] or [Delete].

If you want to change the size of a table, rows and columns can be easily inserted or deleted.

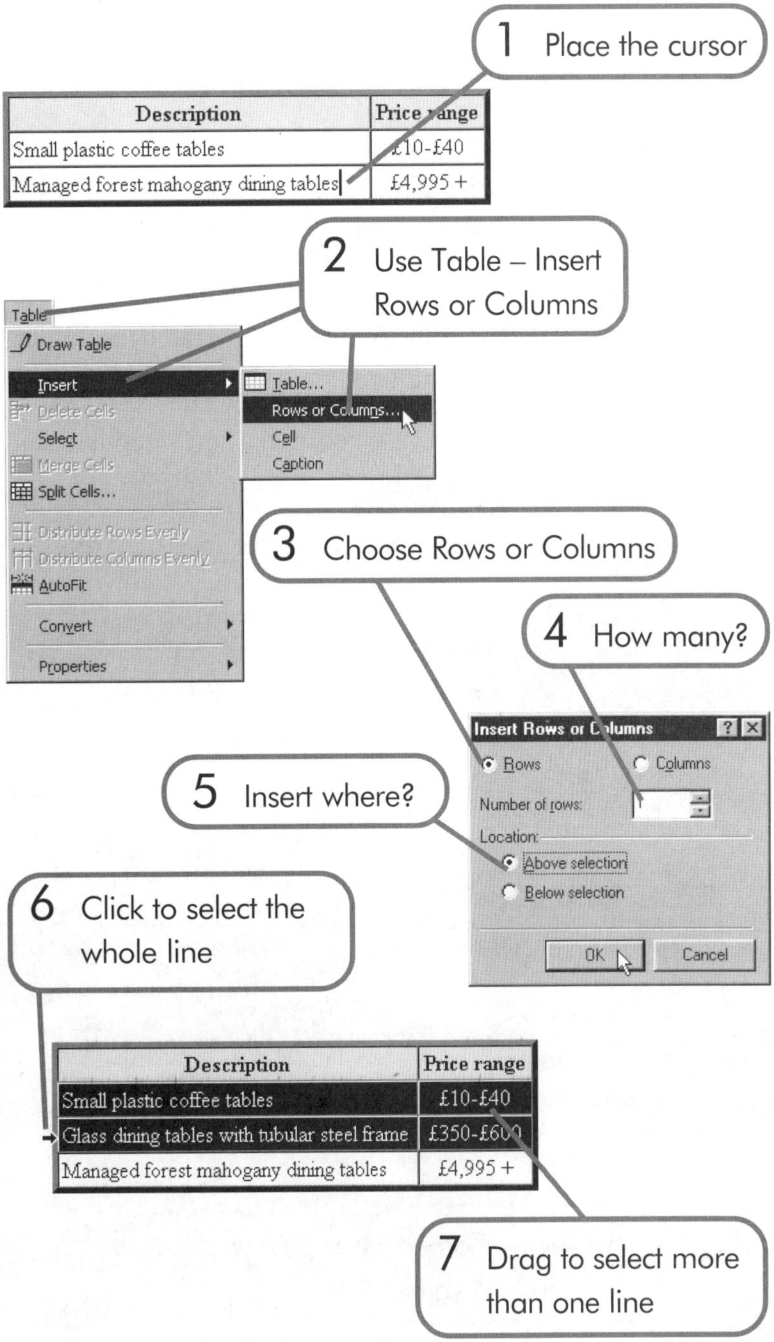

1 Place the cursor

| Description | Price range |
|---|---|
| Small plastic coffee tables | £10-£40 |
| Managed forest mahogany dining tables | £4,995 + |

2 Use Table – Insert Rows or Columns

Table
Draw Table
Insert
Delete Cells
Select
Merge Cells
Split Cells…
Distribute Rows Evenly
Distribute Columns Evenly
AutoFit
Convert
Properties

Table…
Rows or Columns…
Cell
Caption

3 Choose Rows or Columns

4 How many?

Insert Rows or Columns
Rows
Columns
Number of rows:
Location:
Above selection
Below selection
OK
Cancel

5 Insert where?

6 Click to select the whole line

| Description | Price range |
|---|---|
| Small plastic coffee tables | £10-£40 |
| Glass dining tables with tubular steel frame | £350-£600 |
| Managed forest mahogany dining tables | £4,995 + |

7 Drag to select more than one line

# Table properties

A table consists of cells, which can be coloured individually – but there are certain properties in the **Table Properties** dialog box which apply to all cells, or to the whole table:

- **Alignment** sets the position across the page.
- **Width** can be set in pixels or as a percentage of the browser window. If a width is not specified, the table size is determined by its contents.
- **Border** – the thickness in pixels of the table's outer border. A value of 0 will arrange data in a table format, but without a border or gridlines.
- **Cell padding** – the margin between a cell's contents and its inner edge, set in pixels.
- **Cell spacing** – the gap between cells, also in pixels.

## Basic steps

1. Right-click on the table and choose Table Properties...
2. Select an Alignment from the drop-down menu.
3. Set the Border, Cell Padding and Cell Spacing values.
4. Click Specify Width.
5. Enter a value, in Pixels or Percent.
6. Click OK.

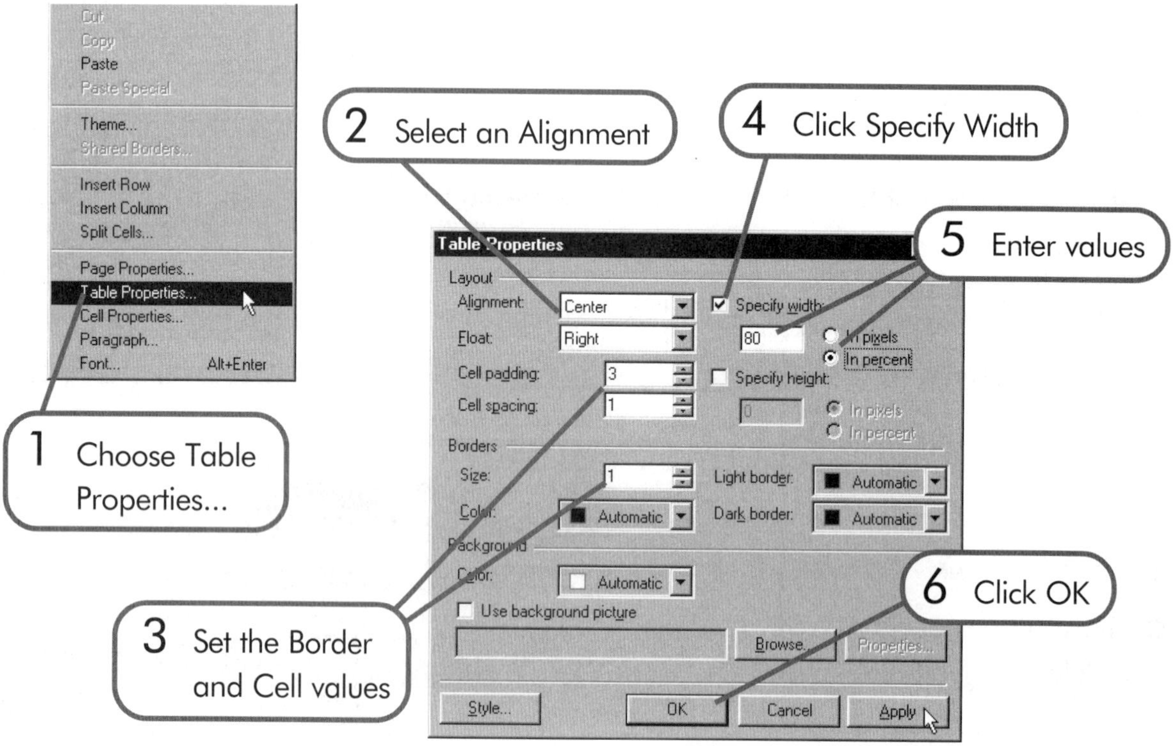

1 Choose Table Properties...

2 Select an Alignment

3 Set the Border and Cell values

4 Click Specify Width

5 Enter values

6 Click OK

## Basic st... and images

1 Op... ...oose the background colour of the cells, or set a erti... image to be tiled across the whole table.

2 Ch... border, set a colour for a plain flat **Border**, or give fla... ...ct with a **Light Colour** and a **Dark Colour** (you ...r width of a few pixels to notice this).

*Or*

3 Chc... for c...

4 Choo... Color.

*Or*

5 Click Use... Image an... the one you...

6 Click OK.

...he colour for ...t border...

3 ... or both colours for a 3-D border

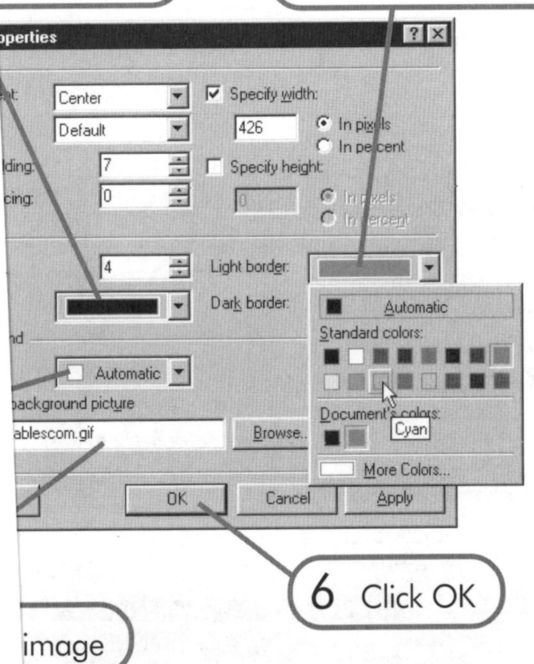

...operties
Center
Default
...dding:
...cing:
Specify width:
426
In pixels
In percent
Specify height:
In pixels
In percent
Light border:
Dark border:
Automatic
Standard colors:
Document's colors:
Cyan
More Colors...
...ackground picture
...ablescom.gif
Browse...
OK
Cancel
Apply


4 Set a Backgro...

...image

6 Click OK

| ... | Description | Price range |
|---|---|---|
| | ...plastic coffee tables | £10-£40 |
| | ...dining tables with tubular steel frame | £350-£600 |
| | ...ged forest mahogany dining tables | £4,995 + |

### Take note

**Different browsers have different ways of tiling background images.**

# Drawing tables

The **Table** toolbar in FrontPage 2000 holds tools for drawing tables from scratch as well as adjusting them. You draw the outer border first, then divide it up as you want it with horizontal and vertical lines. Tables built this way can take more complicated forms than the straight grids created using the standard method.

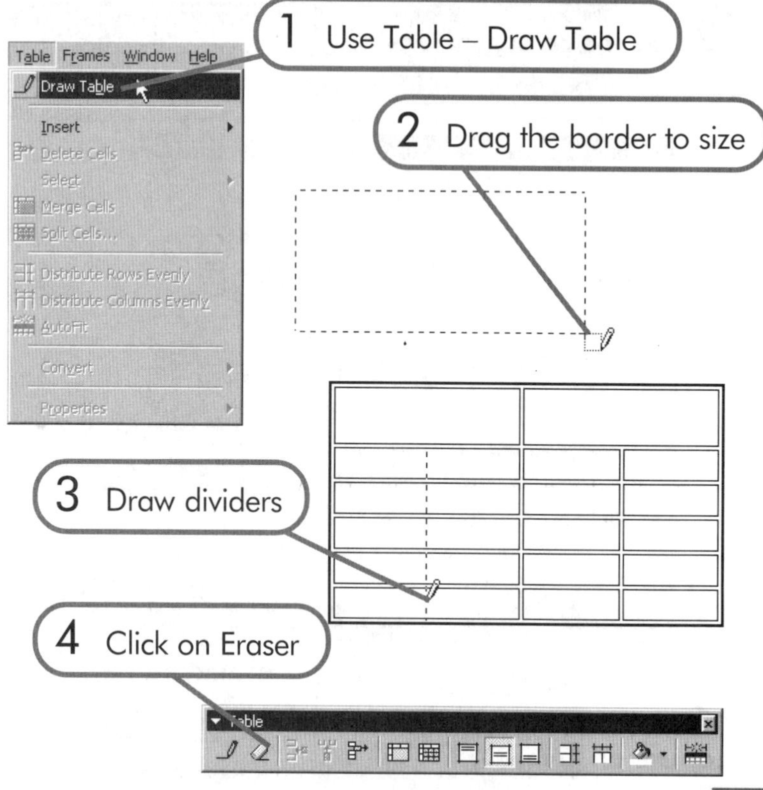
1 Use Table – Draw Table
Table Frames Window Help
Draw Table
Insert
Delete Cells
Select
Merge Cells
Split Cells...
Distribute Rows Evenly
Distribute Columns Evenly
AutoFit
Convert
Properties
2 Drag the border to size
3 Draw dividers
4 Click on Eraser

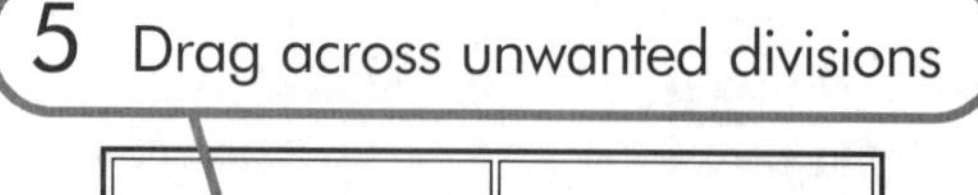
Table

5 Drag across unwanted divisions

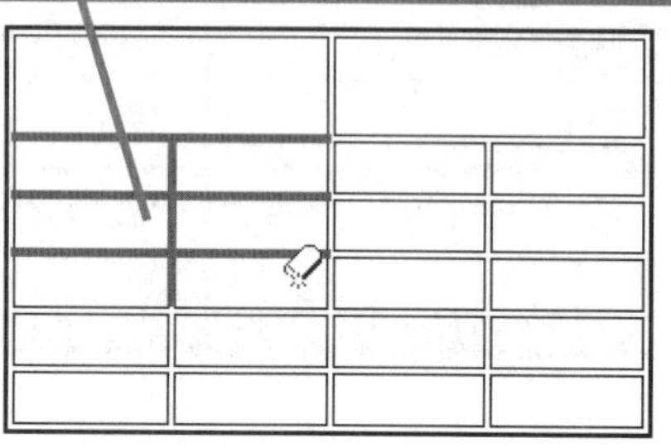

## Basic steps

1 Open the Table menu and select Draw Table. The Draw button should be selected.

2 Click and drag to create the table's outer border.

3 Click and drag to create horizontal and vertical divisions.

❑ To delete a division

4 Click on the Eraser button.

5 Click and drag *across* the division(s) – it/they will turn red.

6 Release the button to delete the line.

❑ To turn off Erase, click the Erase button again.

### Take note

**The divisions you draw will not necessarily appear exactly where you expect them to – don't worry, they can be adjusted later.**

## Basic steps

## Merging and splitting cells

❑ To Split Cells

1 Position the cursor in the cell to be split.

2 Click the Split Cells button.

3 Choose Rows or Columns.

4 Specify a number.

5 Click OK.

❑ To Merge Cells

6 Click and drag to highlight the cells to be merged.

7 Click the Merge Cells button.

Sometimes, instead of using the **Eraser** or **Draw Table** tools to divide cells up, you might find it quicker or easier to use the **Merge** and **Split Cells** tools. Suppose you have a table divided into two rows, and you have divided the bottom row into two columns. If you now try to divide the top row into three cells with the **Draw Table** tool, you will find that the first division aligns itself with the division in the bottom row. To avoid this, select the top cell and use the **Split Cells** tool to divide it into three.

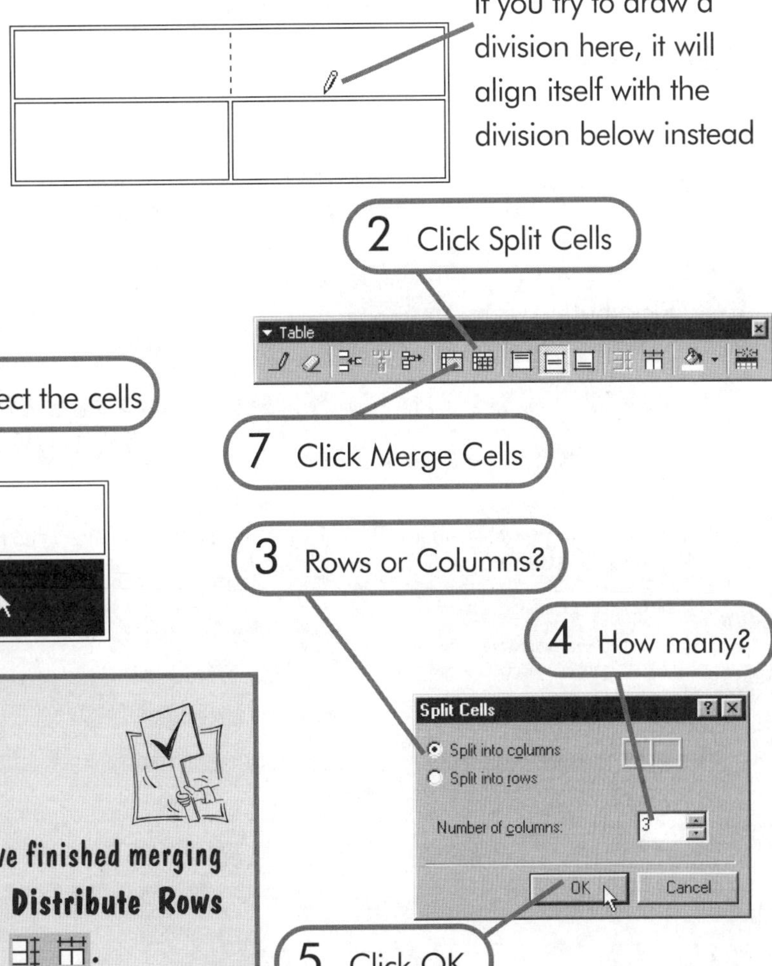

If you try to draw a division here, it will align itself with the division below instead
2 Click Split Cells
Table
7 Click Merge Cells
6 Select the cells
3 Rows or Columns?
4 How many?
Split Cells
Split into columns
Split into rows
Number of columns:
3
OK
Cancel
5 Click OK


### Tip

**To tidy up your table when you've finished merging and splitting cells, click the Distribute Rows and Columns Evenly buttons.**

# Importing table data

## Basic steps

FrontPage can convert Microsoft Excel spreadsheet data directly into tables – each worksheet is created as a separate table. Some of the formatting is lost, but that can be retouched from the Table Properties dialog box.

1 Place the cursor where you want the table.

2 Choose File... from the Insert menu.

3 Select the File of type from the list.

4 Select a file.

5 Click Open.

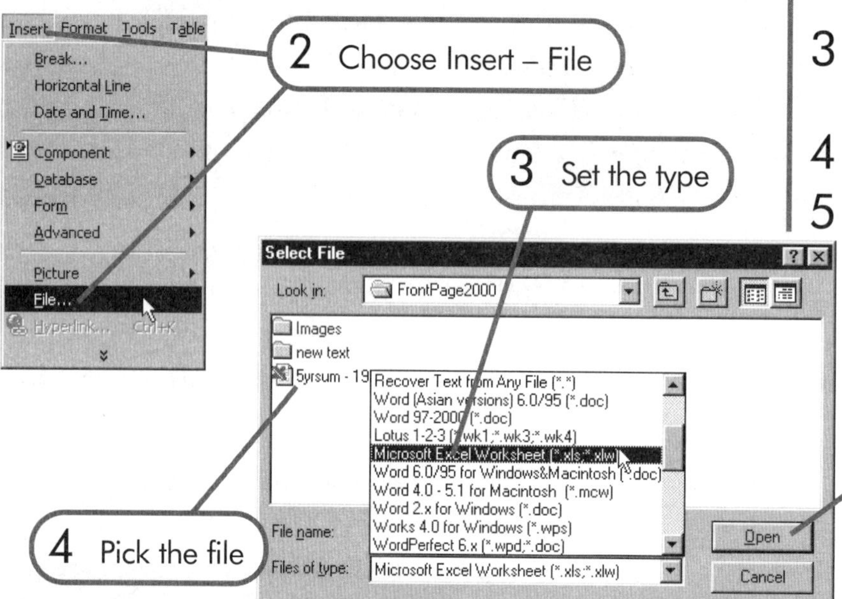

2 Choose Insert – File
3 Set the type
4 Pick the file
5 Open it
Insert Format Tools Table
Break...
Horizontal Line
Date and Time...
Component
Database
Form
Advanced
Picture
File...
Select File
Look in: FrontPage2000
Images
new text
5yrsum - 19
Recover Text from Any File (*.*)
Word (Asian versions) 6.0/95 (*.doc)
Word 97-2000 (*.doc)
Lotus 1-2-3 (*.wk1;*.wk3;*.wk4)
Microsoft Excel Worksheet (*.xls;*.xlw)
Word 6.0/95 for Windows&Macintosh (*.doc)
Word 4.0 - 5.1 for Macintosh (*.mcw)
Word 2.x for Windows (*.doc)
Works 4.0 for Windows (*.wps)
WordPerfect 6.x (*.wpd;*.doc)
File name:
Files of type: Microsoft Excel Worksheet (*.xls;*.xlw)
Open
Cancel


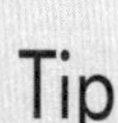

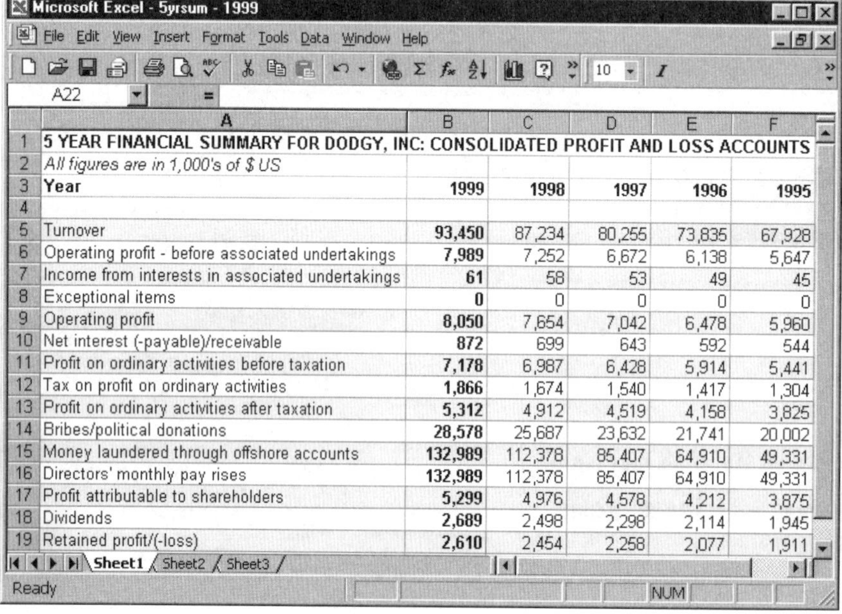

Microsoft Excel - 5yrsum - 1999
File Edit View Insert Format Tools Data Window Help
A22
Sheet1 Sheet2 Sheet3
Ready
NUM


| | A | B | C | D | E | F |
|---|---|---|---|---|---|---|
| 1 | 5 YEAR FINANCIAL SUMMARY FOR DODGY, INC: CONSOLIDATED PROFIT AND LOSS ACCOUNTS | | | | | |
| 2 | *All figures are in 1,000's of $ US* | | | | | |
| 3 | **Year** | **1999** | **1998** | **1997** | **1996** | **1995** |
| 4 | | | | | | |
| 5 | Turnover | **93,450** | 87,234 | 80,255 | 73,835 | 67,928 |
| 6 | Operating profit - before associated undertakings | **7,989** | 7,252 | 6,672 | 6,138 | 5,647 |
| 7 | Income from interests in associated undertakings | **61** | 58 | 53 | 49 | 45 |
| 8 | Exceptional items | **0** | 0 | 0 | 0 | 0 |
| 9 | Operating profit | **8,050** | 7,654 | 7,042 | 6,478 | 5,960 |
| 10 | Net interest (-payable)/receivable | **872** | 699 | 643 | 592 | 544 |
| 11 | Profit on ordinary activities before taxation | **7,178** | 6,987 | 6,428 | 5,914 | 5,441 |
| 12 | Tax on profit on ordinary activities | **1,866** | 1,674 | 1,540 | 1,417 | 1,304 |
| 13 | Profit on ordinary activities after taxation | **5,312** | 4,912 | 4,519 | 4,158 | 3,825 |
| 14 | Bribes/political donations | **28,578** | 25,687 | 23,632 | 21,741 | 20,002 |
| 15 | Money laundered through offshore accounts | **132,989** | 112,378 | 85,407 | 64,910 | 49,331 |
| 16 | Directors' monthly pay rises | **132,989** | 112,378 | 85,407 | 64,910 | 49,331 |
| 17 | Profit attributable to shareholders | **5,299** | 4,976 | 4,578 | 4,212 | 3,875 |
| 18 | Dividends | **2,689** | 2,498 | 2,298 | 2,114 | 1,945 |
| 19 | Retained profit/(-loss) | **2,610** | 2,454 | 2,258 | 2,077 | 1,911 |

## Tip

**You can save Excel spreadsheets as interactive Web pages. These can be added to your web as separate pages or inserted into existing pages. See *Excel 2000 Made Simple* for more about this.**

## Basic steps

# Tables in page design

1 Create a table.

2 Insert images and text into the cells.

❑ Highlighting

3 Click and insert a 1x1 table into a cell.

4 Edit the Table Properties to give it a border.

5 Insert into this inner table the images or text you want to draw attention to.

Besides arranging data, tables have another important function in FrontPage. Since most browsers do not recognise tab or multiple spaces between words and images, text and graphics are often arranged on a page using tables.

With their border thickness set to zero, the dashed lines which you can see in the editing window do not show up in browser windows.

If you want to highlight a particular element in the table, you can insert a table inside a cell and give this inner table a border.

2 Arrange text and images in the table

3 Insert a table into a cell

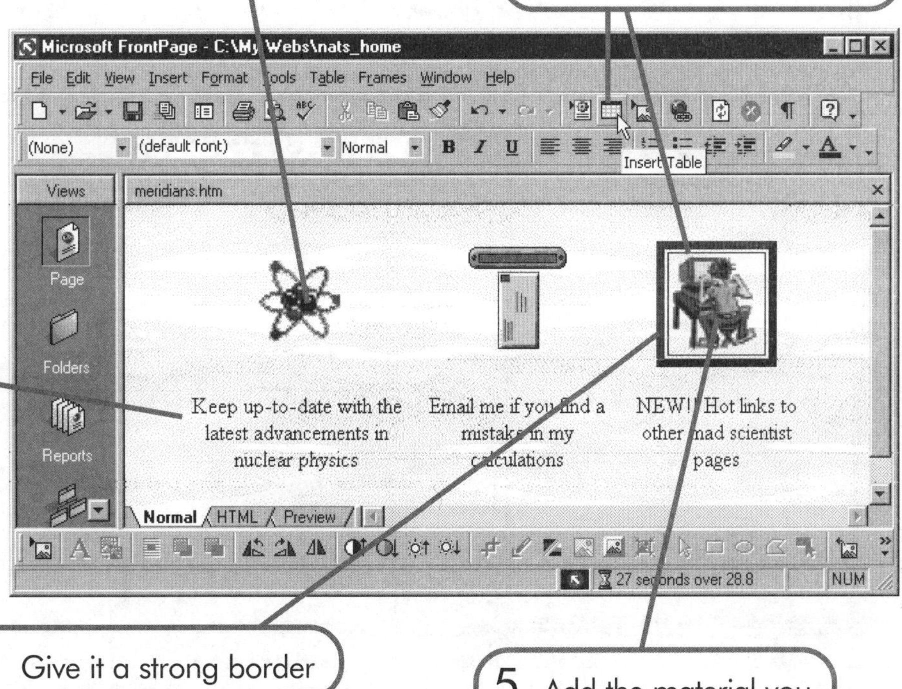
Microsoft FrontPage - C:\My Webs\nats_home
File Edit View Insert Format Tools Table Frames Window Help
(None)
(default font)
Normal
Insert Table
Views
meridians.htm
Page
Folders
Reports
Keep up-to-date with the latest advancements in nuclear physics
Email me if you find a mistake in my calculations
NEW! Hot links to other mad scientist pages
Normal
HTML
Preview
27 seconds over 28.8
NUM

Set the border width to 0 to hide the table outline

4 Give it a strong border

5 Add the material you want to highlight

# Complex designs

If your page layout is going to a bit more complicated, it is a good idea to sketch it out on paper and box the elements into a labelled grid to help you plan the table.

In the example below, the top banner needs to have one wide column in the centre with two small ones at either end for the pictures. Below this, the text needs to be set in three equal columns. The dotted lines show these divisions – now we can decide which cells need to be merged.

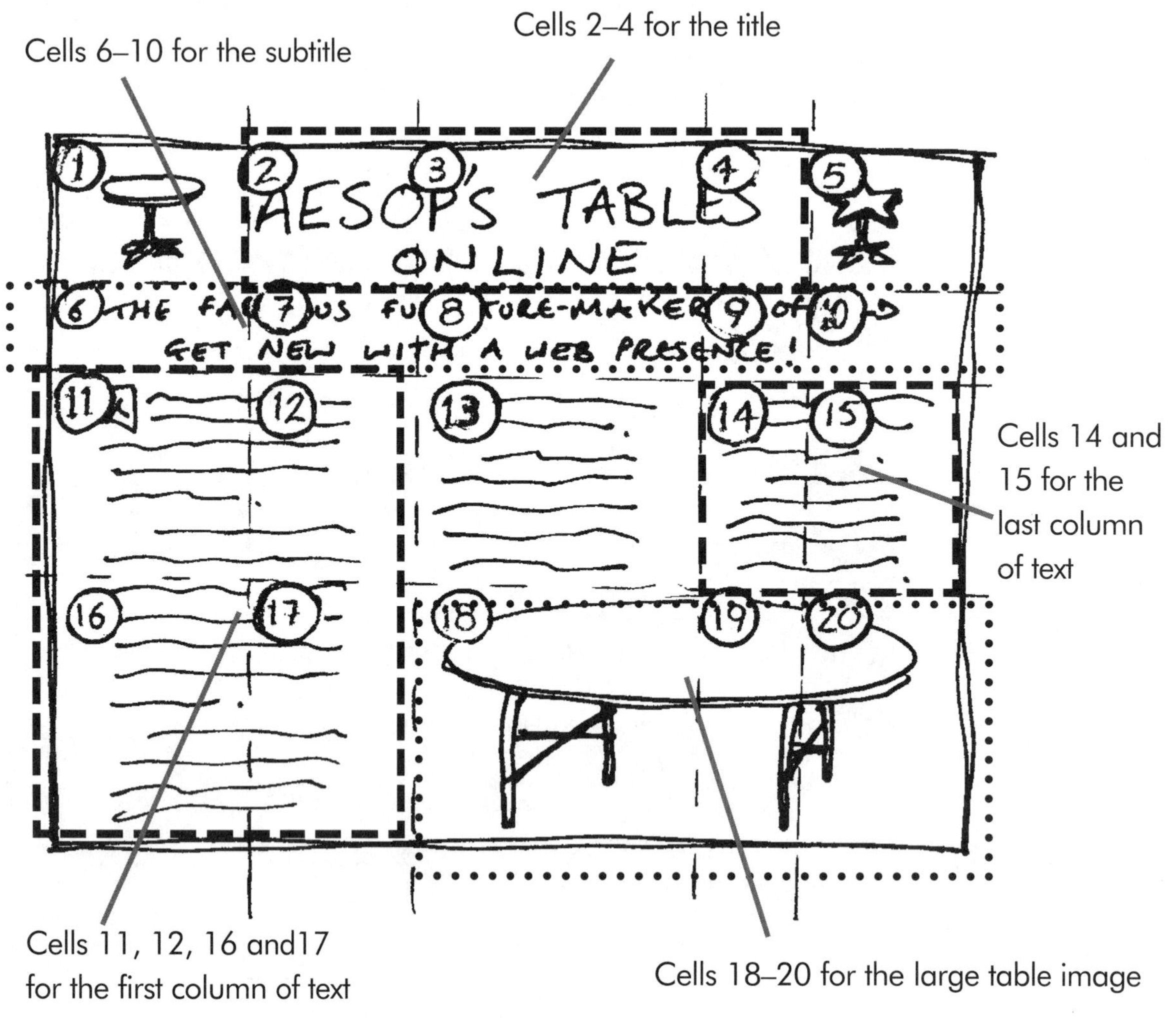
Cells 2–4 for the title
Cells 6–10 for the subtitle
AESOP'S TABLES
ONLINE
GET NEW WITH A WEB PRESENCE!
Cells 14 and 15 for the last column of text
Cells 11, 12, 16 and17 for the first column of text
Cells 18–20 for the large table image

## Basic steps

1 Click and drag the Insert Table button to create a 4 x 5 table.

2 In Table Properties, increase the table Width so you can see what you're doing.

3 Make sure the Table toolbar is turned on.

4 Select cells 2–4.

5 Click the Merge Cells button.

6 Do the same for the other cells to be merged.

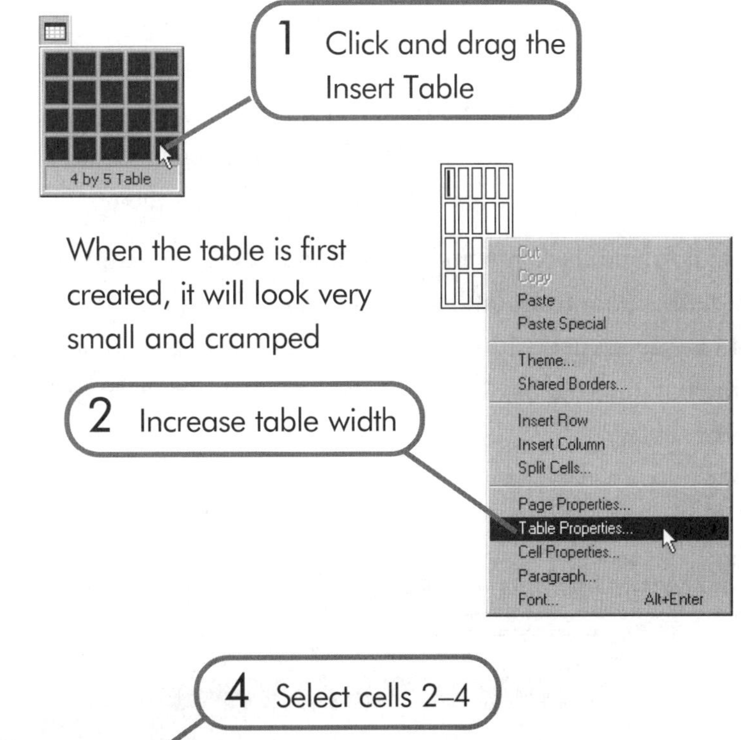
4 by 5 Table
1 Click and drag the Insert Table
When the table is first created, it will look very small and cramped
Cut
Copy
Paste
Paste Special
Theme...
Shared Borders...
Insert Row
Insert Column
Split Cells...
Page Properties...
Table Properties...
Cell Properties...
Paragraph...
Font... Alt+Enter
2 Increase table width
4 Select cells 2–4

3 Turn on the Table toolbar

Table

Merge Cells

5 Click Merge Cells

Aargh! The top corner cells are too big, because they've aligned themselves with the columns below! Back to the drawing board... (read the next page!)

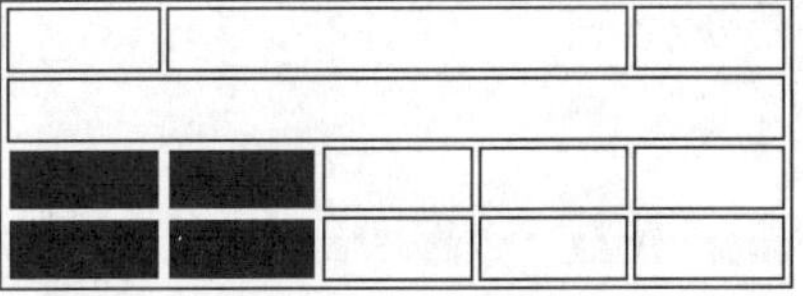

## Troubleshooting

When working with tables, you will often come across problems which don't seem to make any sense. For instance, in this case, no matter how much I fiddle with the table, specifying cell widths, or merging and splitting them, I can't get the two top corner cells to be nice and small the way I want them.

This is where there are no hard and fast rules, unfortunately – but with a little lateral thinking and a fair bit of patience you'll find a way around it! In this case, one solution is to start from scratch with *two* tables – one for the banner and one for the rest of the table.

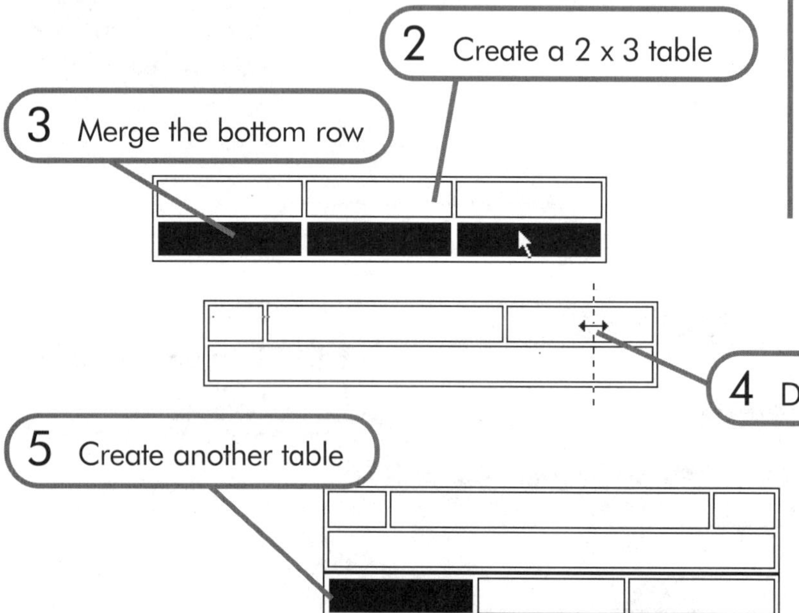

2 Create a 2 x 3 table
3 Merge the bottom row
4 Drag to resize the cells
5 Create another table


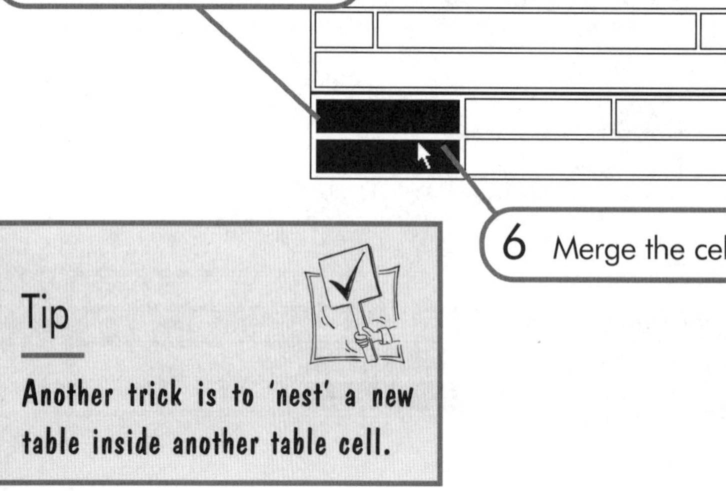

6 Merge the cells


### Tip

**Another trick is to 'nest' a new table inside another table cell.**

## Basic steps

1. Take a deep breath and put that monkey wrench down.
2. Create a new 2 x 3 table.
3. Merge the bottom row into one cell.
4. Click and drag on the divisions to resize the top cells.
5. Below that table, create another 2 x 3 table.
6. Merge cells as before to get the right layout.

### Tip

**Don't be surprised if it doesn't turn out the way it should! You may well find you have to go back to the drawing board once or twice...**

## Filling in the table

**Take note**

**Transparent images are simple to create – but the way you do it depends on the image editing program you use. If you're not sure how to do it on yours, try the program's Help files.**

You'll find that when you start dropping text and images into your table, the cell sizes change wildly, and don't always end up the way you planned.

A useful tool for this kind of problem is a spacer image – a small GIF image of solid colour which has been set as transparent. This can be inserted into the table, and the height and width set to whatever necessary to force a cell into the right size. To ensure my text columns were of equal width, for instance, I put a spacer 187 pixels long by 1 pixel high at the top of each one. As the image is transparent, it is invisible when the page is displayed in a browser.

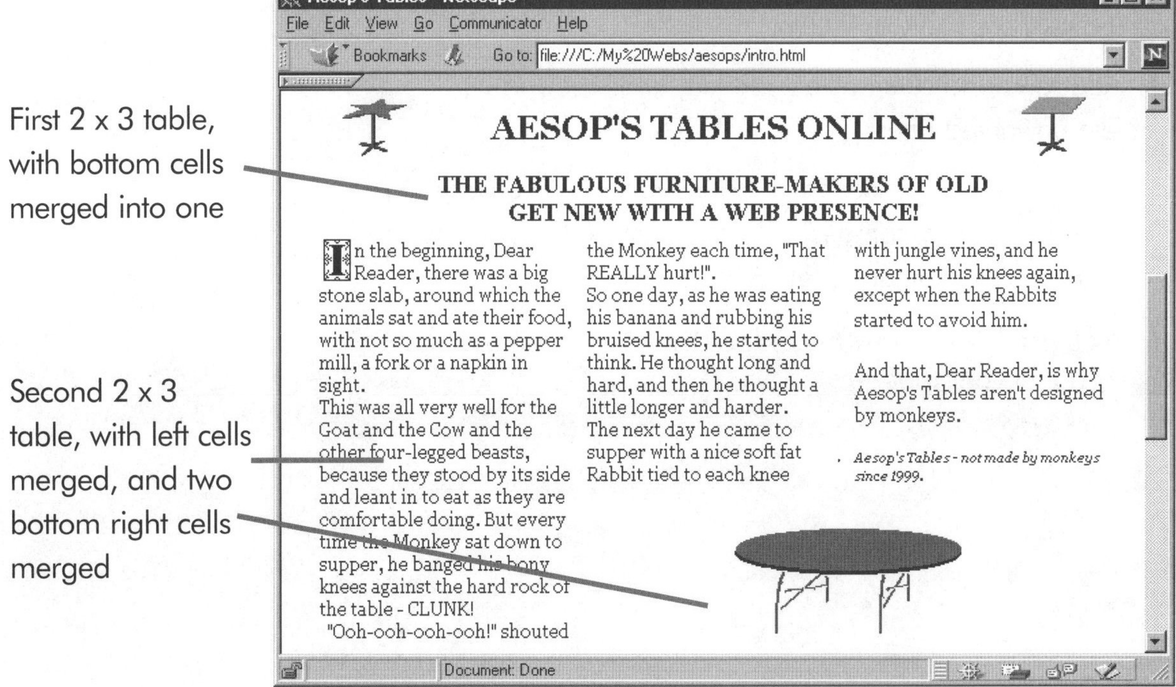
First 2 x 3 table, with bottom cells merged into one
Second 2 x 3 table, with left cells merged, and two bottom right cells merged
Aesop's Tables - Netscape
File Edit View Go Communicator Help
Bookmarks
Go to: file:///C:/My%20Webs/aesops/intro.html
AESOP'S TABLES ONLINE
THE FABULOUS FURNITURE-MAKERS OF OLD GET NEW WITH A WEB PRESENCE!
In the beginning, Dear Reader, there was a big stone slab, around which the animals sat and ate their food, with not so much as a pepper mill, a fork or a napkin in sight.
This was all very well for the Goat and the Cow and the other four-legged beasts, because they stood by its side and leant in to eat as they are comfortable doing. But every time the Monkey sat down to supper, he banged his bony knees against the hard rock of the table - CLUNK!
"Ooh-ooh-ooh-ooh!" shouted the Monkey each time, "That REALLY hurt!".
So one day, as he was eating his banana and rubbing his bruised knees, he started to think. He thought long and hard, and then he thought a little longer and harder.
The next day he came to supper with a nice soft fat Rabbit tied to each knee with jungle vines, and he never hurt his knees again, except when the Rabbits started to avoid him.
And that, Dear Reader, is why Aesop's Tables aren't designed by monkeys.
Aesop's Tables - not made by monkeys since 1999.
Document: Done

# Summary

- ❑ Use tables to present data or to arrange text and graphics on the page.
- ❑ Add text and pictures to the table in the same way as you would add them to the main page.
- ❑ Text in tables can be formatted as normal.
- ❑ Configure the table's properties from the Table properties... dialog box.
- ❑ Change individual Cell properties to highlight areas of the table.
- ❑ Use the Table toolbar to 'draw' the table directly on screen.
- ❑ Merge and Split cells to position the contents of the table where you want them.
- ❑ Add rows and columns as needed, or select and Delete unwanted ones.
- ❑ You can import spreadsheet data directly onto a page. FrontPage will automatically create a table for it, which you can then edit as usual.
- ❑ Be patient and think creatively when perfecting the layout of your tables!

# 5 Bookmarks and links

the flag icon in it at the top of the window.

3 Type a Name for the Bookmark.

4 Click OK.

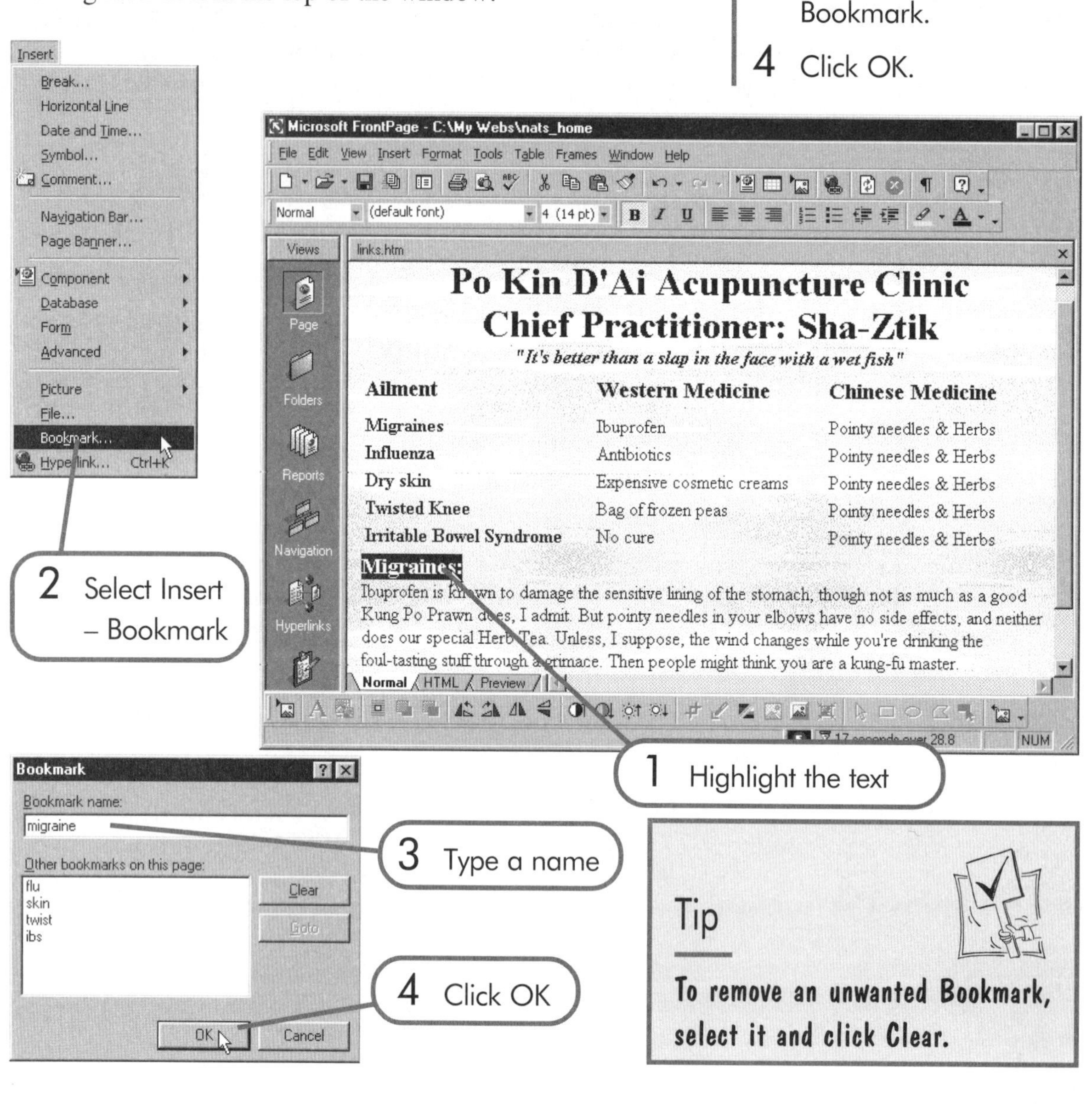
Insert
Break...
Horizontal Line
Date and Time...
Symbol...
Comment...
Navigation Bar...
Page Banner...
Component
Database
Form
Advanced
Picture
File...
Bookmark...
Hyperlink... Ctrl+K
2 Select Insert – Bookmark
Microsoft FrontPage - C:\My Webs\nats_home
Po Kin D'Ai Acupuncture Clinic
Chief Practitioner: Sha-Ztik
"It's better than a slap in the face with a wet fish"
Ailment
Western Medicine
Chinese Medicine
Migraines
Ibuprofen
Pointy needles & Herbs
Influenza
Antibiotics
Dry skin
Expensive cosmetic creams
Twisted Knee
Bag of frozen peas
Irritable Bowel Syndrome
No cure
Migraines:
1 Highlight the text
Bookmark
Bookmark name:
migraine
Other bookmarks on this page:
flu
skin
twist
ibs
Clear
Goto
OK
Cancel
3 Type a name
4 Click OK

## Tip

**To remove an unwanted Bookmark, select it and click Clear.**

## Basic steps

1. Highlight the text which you want to use as a link.
2. Click the Hyperlink button.
3. Ignore the URL field – the default is the current page.
4. Select a Bookmark from the drop-down menu.
5. Click OK.

## Tip

**If you have a long page, add a Bookmark at the top and provide links back to it at regular intervals further down the page.**

## Links to Bookmarks

Having links to different parts of a page is useful if it is much longer than a screen's height. Being able to jump from a directory at the top to something which interests you and back again saves a lot of tedious scrolling up and down.

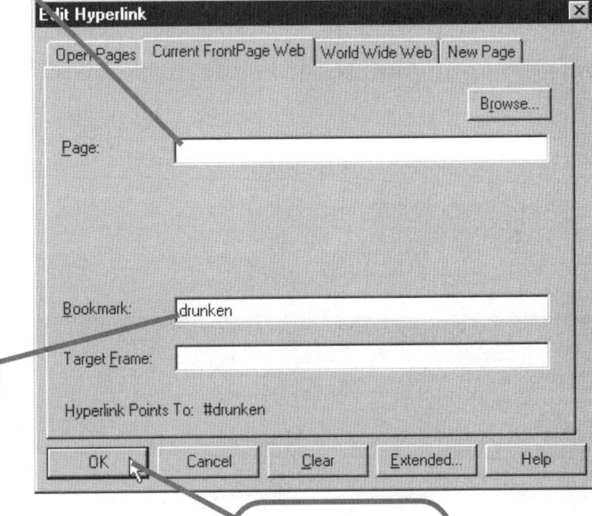
3 Leave URL blank
Edit Hyperlink
Open Pages
Current FrontPage Web
World Wide Web
New Page
Browse...
Page:
Bookmark:
drunken
Target Frame:
Hyperlink Points To: #drunken
OK
Cancel
Clear
Extended...
Help
4 Choose a Bookmark
5 Click OK

## Navigating with Bookmarks

You can use Bookmarks to move around a page as you edit. In the Bookmark dialog box, select a Bookmark from the list and click Goto. To follow hyperlinks between pages, point to the linked text or image, hold **[Ctrl]** and click the left mouse button.

Bookmark
Bookmark Name:
firststrike
Clear
Other Bookmarks on this Page:
drunken
armour
jeetkdo
firststrike
dragon
Goto
OK
Cancel
Help
Go to the Bookmark

# Links to other pages

## Basic steps

Links turn a collection of files into a web. Think about your material, and decide which pages should be linked, and where those links should fit.

It's often a good idea to link your pages as you construct them. The drop-down **URL** menu has a list of pages you've been working on recently, so you can use this.

You can create a link to a specific part of another page by choosing a **Bookmark** from the drop-down list of Bookmark (make sure that you have selected the page first).

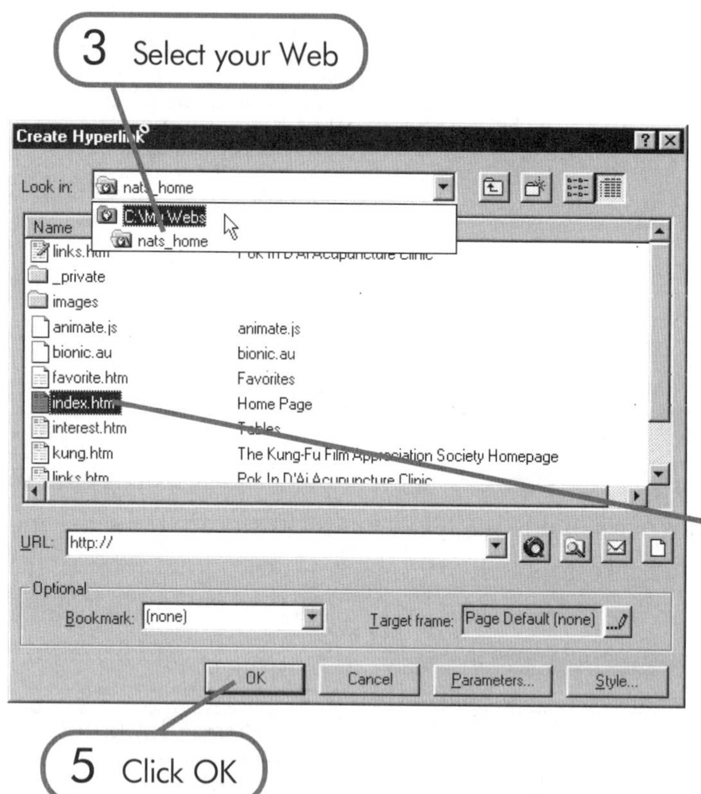

3 Select your Web
Create Hyperlink
Look in:
nats_home
Name
links.htm
_private
images
animate.js
bionic.au
favorite.htm
index.htm
interest.htm
kung.htm
animate.js
bionic.au
Favorites
Home Page
The Kung-Fu Film Appreciation Society Homepage
URL:
http://
Optional
Bookmark:
(none)
Target frame:
Page Default (none)
OK
Cancel
Parameters...
Style...
5 Click OK


4 Select the page

1. Highlight the text you want to use as a link.
2. Click the Hyperlink button.
3. Use the Current Web tab and browse your Web folders for a file.
4. Select the page.

*Or*

5. Select a page from the URL list.
6. Select Bookmark from the list if you want the link to be more specific.
7. Click OK.

## Tip

**To ensure that all your pages are linked, include a navigation bar (see page 127) or give each page a link back to a home page or table of contents page.**

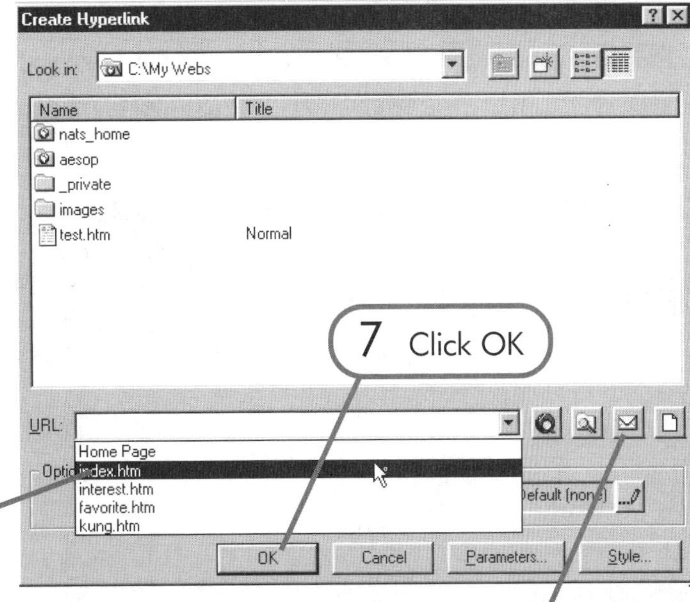

Create Hyperlink
Look in: C:\My Webs
Name
Title
nats_home
aesop
_private
images
test.htm
Normal
7 Click OK
URL:
Home Page
index.htm
interest.htm
favorite.htm
kung.htm
Default (none)
6 Select a page
OK
Cancel
Parameters...
Style...


Create an e-mail link (see below)

### Basic steps

1. Click the e-mail button [e-mail button icon].
2. Type your e-mail address.
3. Click OK.

## E-mail links

E-mail links call up a message window with your e-mail address pre-typed in it so that people can send you comments easily.

1 Click the e-mail button

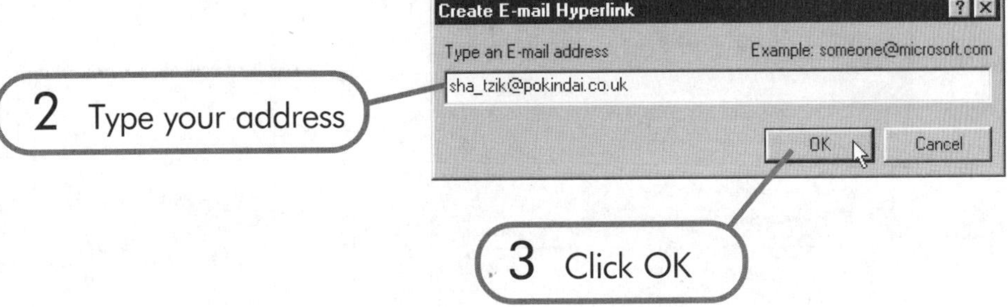

Create E-mail Hyperlink
Type an E-mail address
Example: someone@microsoft.com
sha_tzik@pokindai.co.uk
2 Type your address
OK
Cancel
3 Click OK

# Links to a new page

If you want something to have a page of its own, you can set up a link to a page which does not exist yet. FrontPage will create a new page, which you can edit immediately, or add to the **Tasks List** as a job for another day.

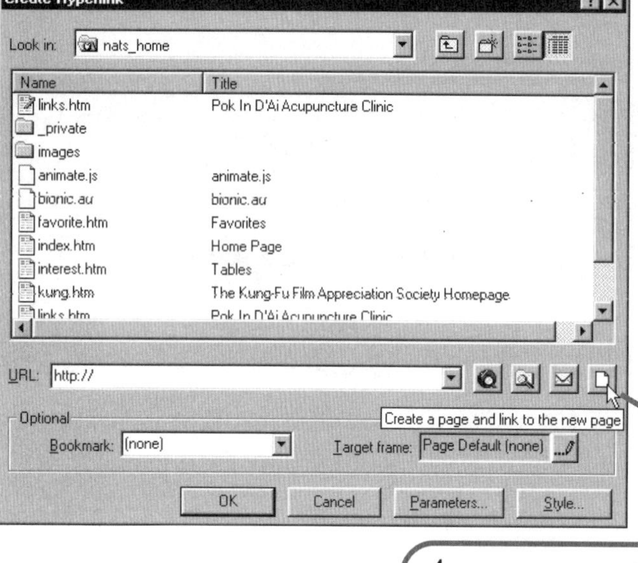

Create Hyperlink
Look in: nats_home
Name
Title
links.htm
Pok In D'Ai Acupuncture Clinic
_private
images
animate.js
animate.js
bionic.au
bionic.au
favorite.htm
Favorites
index.htm
Home Page
interest.htm
Tables
kung.htm
The Kung-Fu Film Appreciation Society Homepage
URL: http://
Create a page and link to the new page
Optional
Bookmark: (none)
Target frame: Page Default (none)
OK
Cancel
Parameters...
Style...


3 Create New Page

4 Choose a template

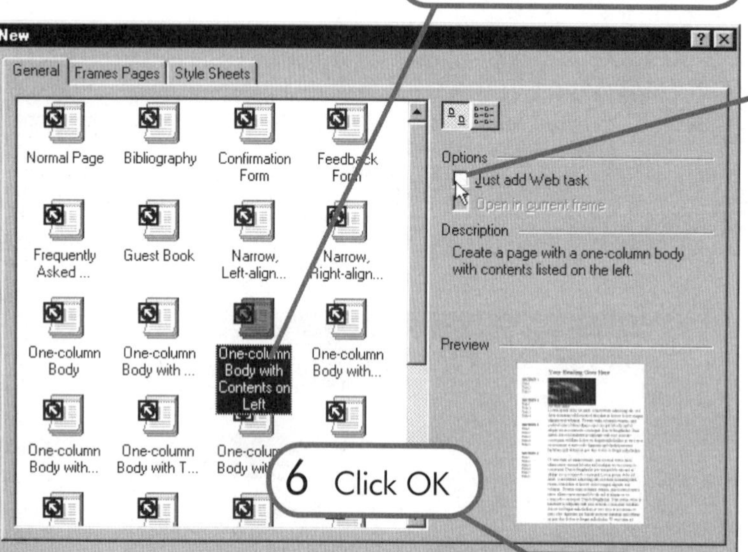

New
General
Frames Pages
Style Sheets
Normal Page
Bibliography
Confirmation Form
Feedback Form
Frequently Asked ...
Guest Book
Narrow, Left-align...
Narrow, Right-align...
One-column Body
One-column Body with ...
One-column Body with Contents on Left
One-column Body with...
One-column Body with...
One-column Body with T...
Options
Just add Web task
Open in current frame
Description
Create a page with a one-column body with contents listed on the left.
Preview
6 Click OK
OK
Cancel


## Basic steps

1 Highlight the text you want to use as a link.

2 Click the Hyperlink button on the main toolbar.

3 Click on the New Page button.

4 Choose a template.

5 Tick Just add Web task if you want to add it to the Tasks list for later editing.

6 Click OK.

5 Edit it later?

The description and preview give you an idea of what kind of page will be created

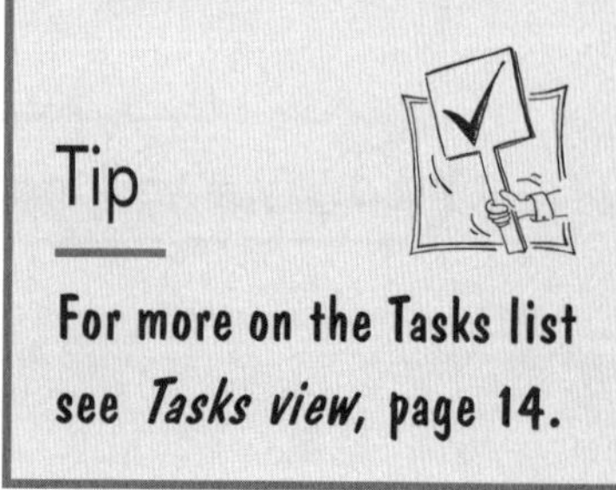

**Tip**

**For more on the Tasks list see *Tasks view*, page 14.**

## Basic steps

# Links to Web pages

1 Highlight the text to use as a link and click the Hyperlink button.
2 Type the URL into the field.

*Or*

3 Click the Web button.
4 Surf to the page.
5 Switch back to Front-Page – the URL is there.
6 Click OK.

External hyperlinks are very important – many organisations increase the number of visitors to their sites by establishing reciprocal links with other sites.

Browse the Internet to find a site you want to link to, then switch back to FrontPage and the URL of the site will be entered for you.

## Other World Wide Web locations

Links can be created to other types of World Wide Web locations – to an FTP site so that visitors can download software, for example, or to a newsgroup.

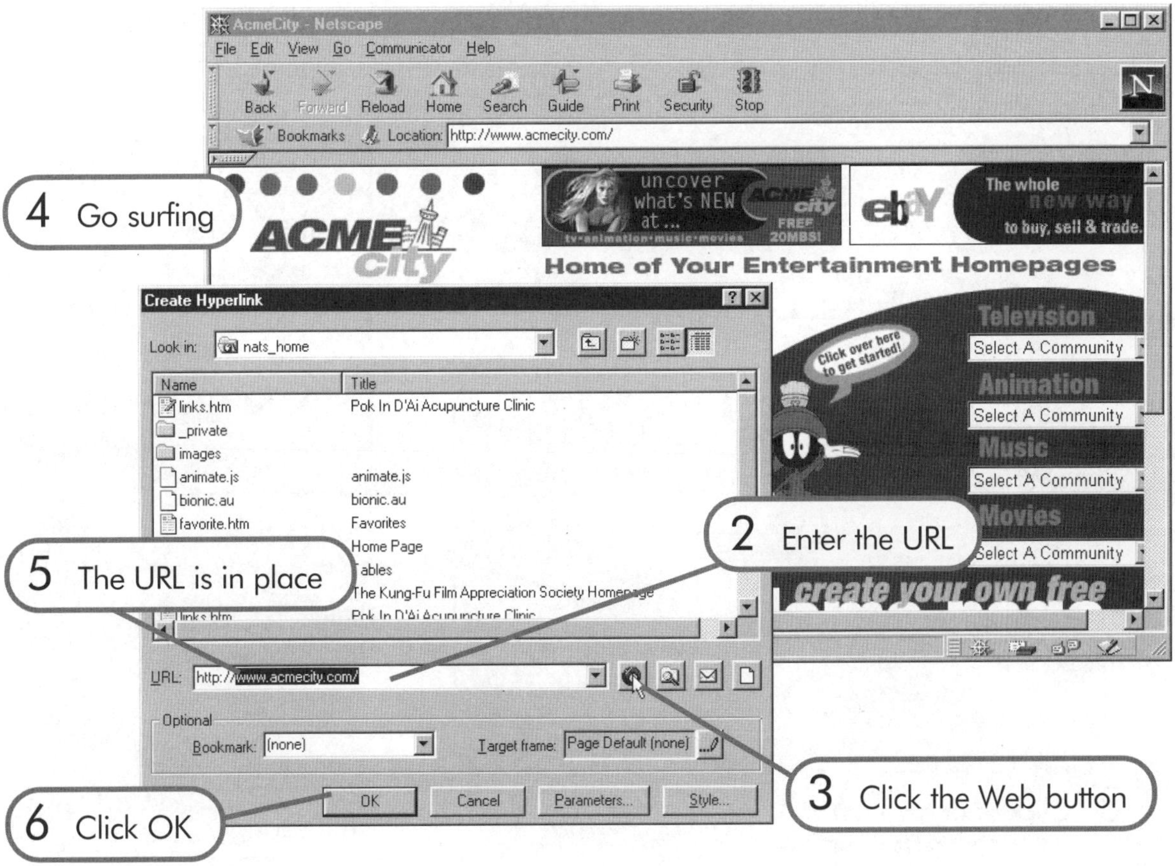

4 Go surfing

2 Enter the URL

5 The URL is in place

3 Click the Web button

6 Click OK

# Using images as links

## Basic steps

- ❑ To create an image map
1. Click on the image to select it.
2. Click the Rectangle button on the Picture toolbar.
3. Position the cursor at one corner of the area you want to be a hotspot.
4. Drag to the opposite corner of the area.

There are two ways of using images as links. In the first case, the whole picture acts as a link, so you just highlight the image and create a link as you would for text.

## Image maps

The second way of using images is to designate different areas of a picture (**hotspots**) as links to different locations. FrontPage makes light work of these **image maps**, and allows you to adjust the hotspots after you have created them.

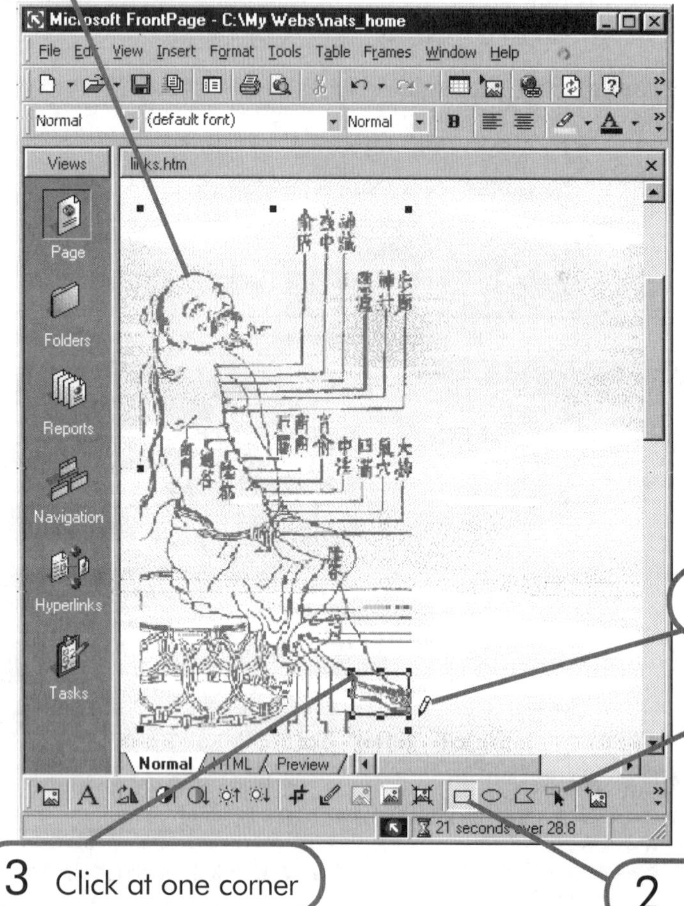
1 Select the image
Microsoft FrontPage - C:\My Webs\nats_home
File Edit View Insert Format Tools Table Frames Window Help
Views
links.htm
Page
Folders
Reports
Navigation
Hyperlinks
Tasks
Normal HTML Preview
21 seconds over 28.8
3 Click at one corner

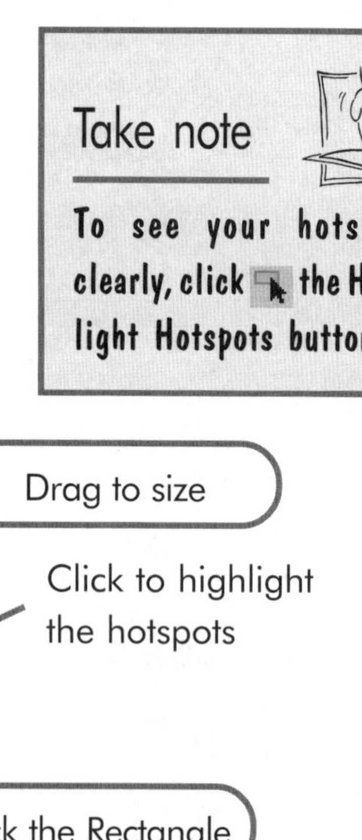

### Take note

**To see your hotspots clearly, click the Highlight Hotspots button.**

4 Drag to size
Click to highlight the hotspots
2 Pick the Rectangle

❑ Circle hotspots

1 Click the Circle button.

2 Point at the *centre* of the hotspot.

3 Drag to expand the circle to the size you want.

❑ Polygon hotspots

4 Click the Polygon button.

5 Move around the hotspot, clicking once to create each vertex.

6 Double-click to end.

Microsoft FrontPage - C:\My Webs\nats_home
File Edit View Insert Format Tools Table Frames Window Help
Normal
(default font)
Normal
3 Drag to size
2 Click at the centre
6 Double-click to end
5 Click the vertices
Page
Folders
Reports
Navigation
Hyperlinks
Tasks
Normal
HTML
Preview
21 seconds over 28.8
1 Pick the Circle
4 Pick the Polygon

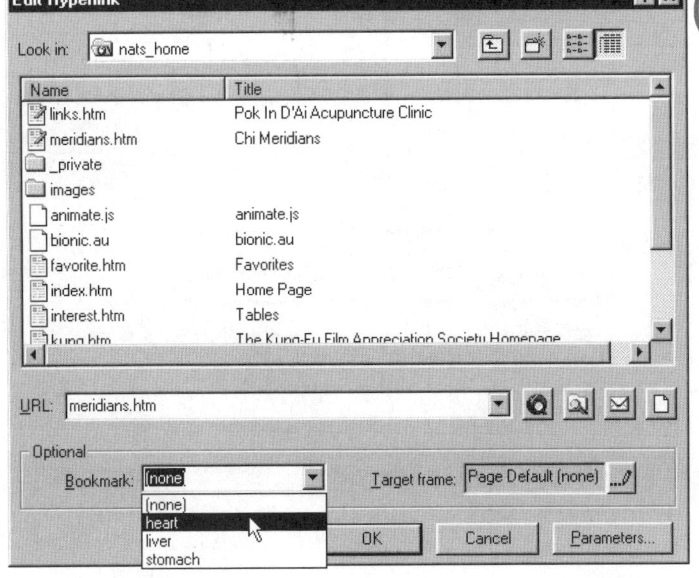
Edit Hyperlink
Look in: nats_home
Name
Title
links.htm
Pok In D'Ai Acupuncture Clinic
meridians.htm
Chi Meridians
_private
images
animate.js
animate.js
bionic.au
bionic.au
favorite.htm
Favorites
index.htm
Home Page
interest.htm
Tables
URL: meridians.htm
Optional
Bookmark: (none)
Target frame: Page Default (none)
(none)
heart
liver
stomach
OK
Cancel
Parameters...

The Edit Hyperlink dialog box opens when you have created a hotspot – enter or browse for the URL or Bookmark as usual and click OK

# Editing hotspots

Once you have created a hotspot, you can change the destination of its link, move it, or adjust its shape.

## Background links

As well as creating hotspots on an image, you can set the rest of it (the 'cold background', as it were) to be a link. This is done by selecting the image as a whole and giving it a hyperlink as normal.

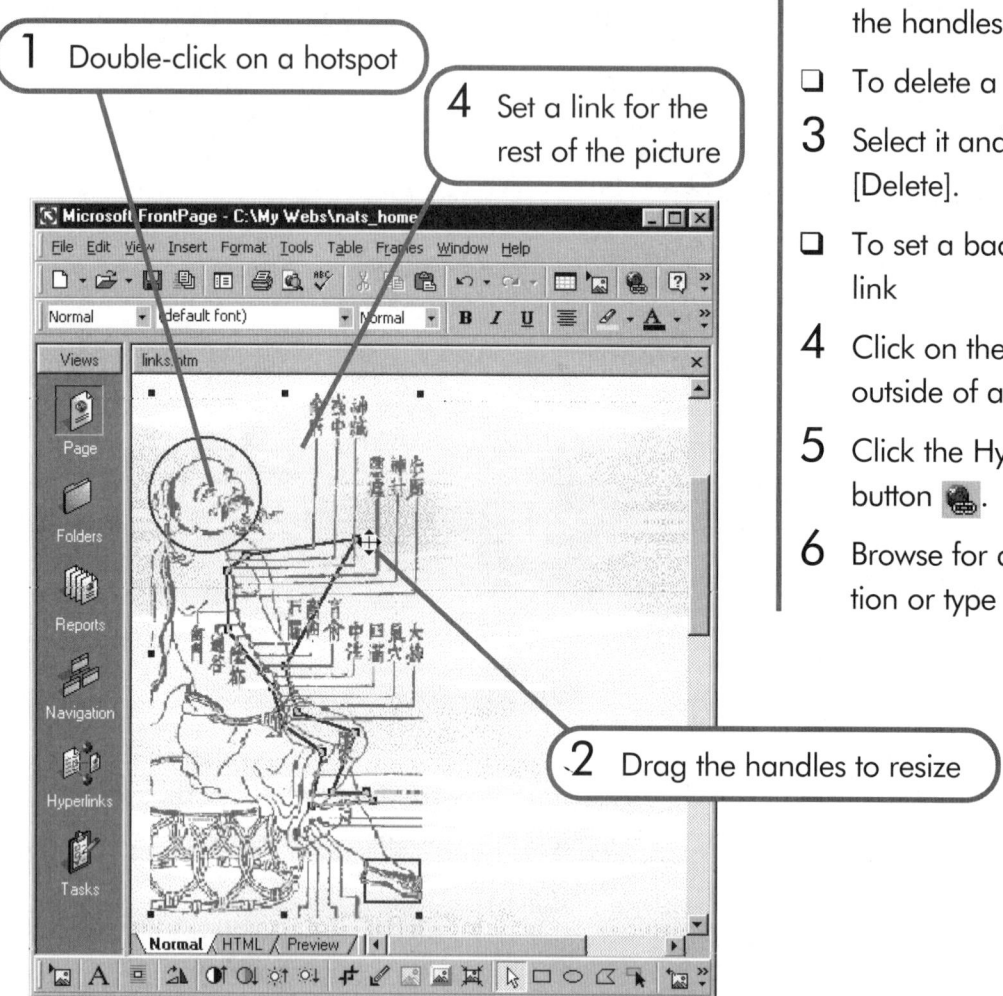

1 Double-click on a hotspot

4 Set a link for the rest of the picture

2 Drag the handles to resize

## Basic steps

- To edit the link

1 Double-click on the hotspot to reopen the Create Hyperlink dialog box.

- To edit the hotspot

2 Click once and drag the handles.

- To delete a hotspot

3 Select it and press [Delete].

- To set a background link

4 Click on the image outside of any hotspots.

5 Click the Hyperlink button.

6 Browse for a destination or type an URL.

## Basic steps

1 Choose Recalculate Hyperlinks… from the Tools menu.

2 Click Yes – unless your web is really huge, it doesn't take that long!

# Recalculating hyperlinks

When FrontPage recalculates your hyperlinks it performs two functions. It goes through every file in your web to:

- make sure that the automatically-generated parts of the web structure are up-to-date – if an **Include Page** (see page 120) component is moved, for instance, any page containing it may need updating.
- update the text index which a **Search** (see page 129) component uses.

Recalculating your hyperlinks only deals with links which are generated automatically be FrontPage. To check for broken links, see the next page.

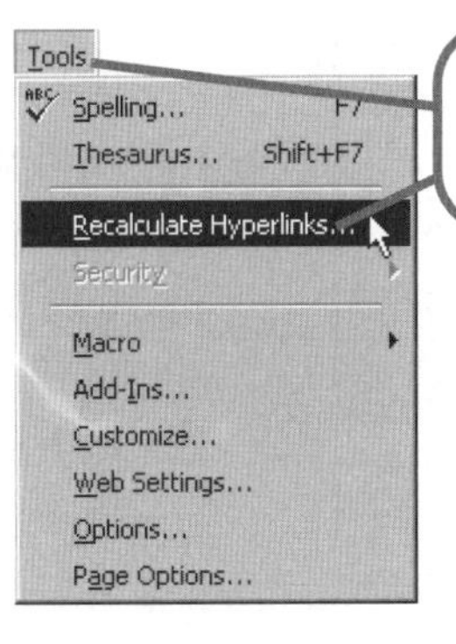
Tools
Spelling… F7
Thesaurus… Shift+F7
Recalculate Hyperlinks…
Security
Macro
Add-Ins…
Customize…
Web Settings…
Options…
Page Options…

1 Use Tools – Recalculate Hyperlinks…

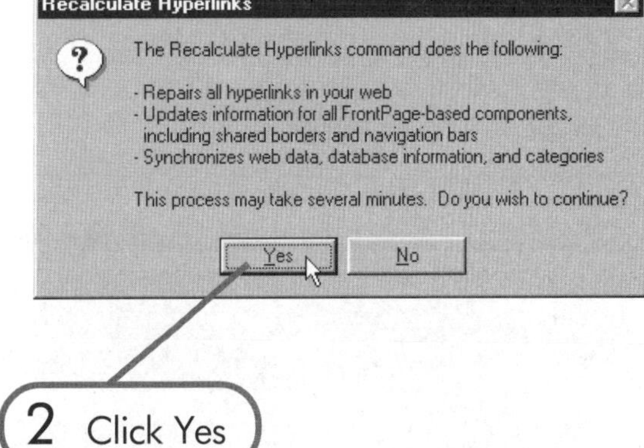
Recalculate Hyperlinks
The Recalculate Hyperlinks command does the following:
- Repairs all hyperlinks in your web
- Updates information for all FrontPage-based components, including shared borders and navigation bars
- Synchronizes web data, database information, and categories
This process may take several minutes. Do you wish to continue?
Yes
No

2 Click Yes

## Take note

**One of FrontPage's automatic functions is to create links between your pages according to the navigation structure which you determine using the Navigation view (see page 126).**

# Checking hyperlinks

To make sure that all your hyperlinks are working, look in the **Reports** view for a **Site Summary**. Remember to save any pages you have been working on, otherwise recent changes will not be picked up by FrontPage. If you are not connected to the internet, all external links are marked as **Unverified**; you will need to go online to check these.

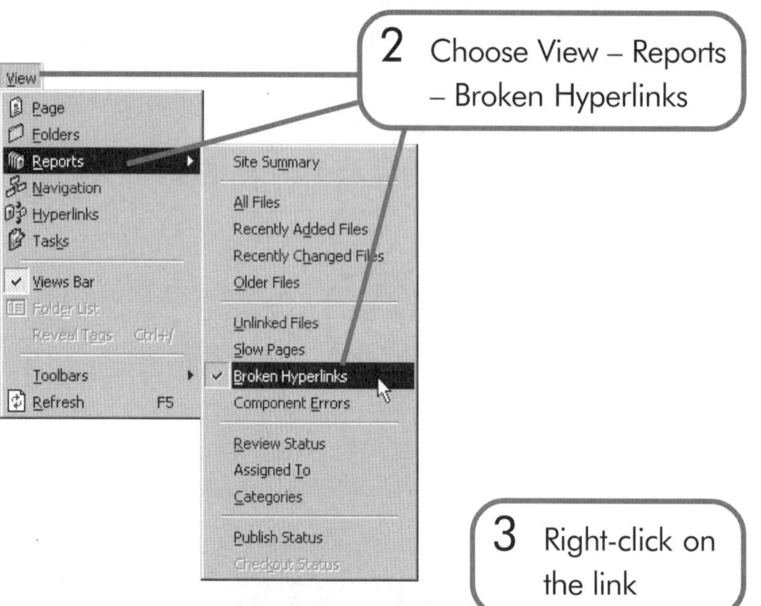

2 Choose View – Reports – Broken Hyperlinks
View
Page
Folders
Reports
Navigation
Hyperlinks
Tasks
Views Bar
Folder List
Reveal Tags Ctrl+/
Toolbars
Refresh F5
Site Summary
All Files
Recently Added Files
Recently Changed Files
Older Files
Unlinked Files
Slow Pages
Broken Hyperlinks
Component Errors
Review Status
Assigned To
Categories
Publish Status
Checkout Status
3 Right-click on the link


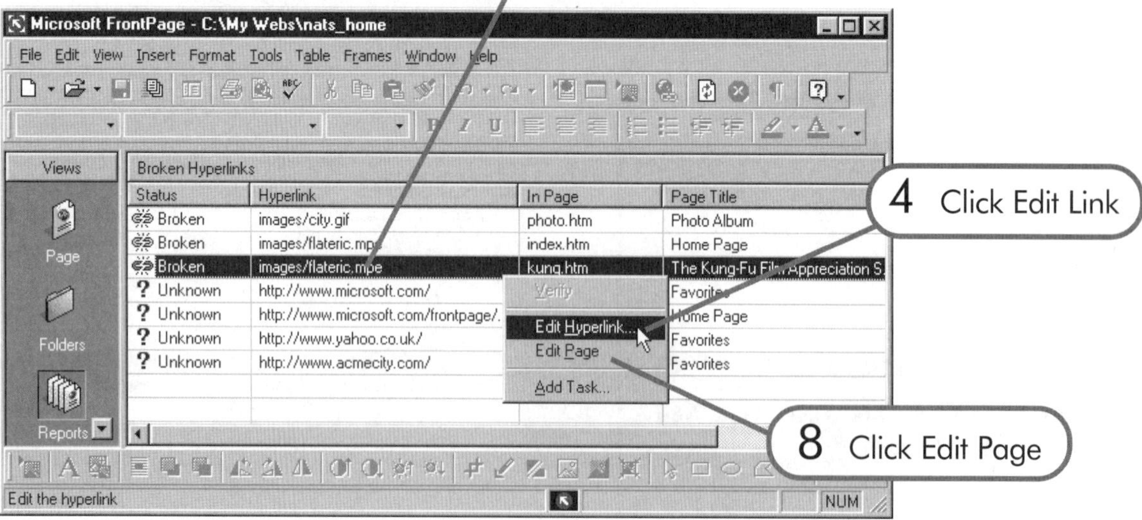

Microsoft FrontPage - C:\My Webs\nats_home
File Edit View Insert Format Tools Table Frames Window Help
Views
Page
Folders
Reports
Broken Hyperlinks
Status
Hyperlink
In Page
Page Title
Broken
images/city.gif
photo.htm
Photo Album
Broken
images/flateric.mpe
index.htm
Home Page
Broken
images/flateric.mpe
kung.htm
The Kung-Fu Film Appreciation S
Unknown
http://www.microsoft.com/
Unknown
http://www.microsoft.com/frontpage/
Unknown
http://www.yahoo.co.uk/
Unknown
http://www.acmecity.com/
Verify
Edit Hyperlink...
Edit Page
Add Task...
Favorites
Home Page
Favorites
Favorites
Edit the hyperlink
NUM
4 Click Edit Link
8 Click Edit Page


## Basic steps

1. Save any open pages.
2. Choose Reports… Broken hyperlinks from the View menu.
3. Right-click on a broken link.
4. Choose Edit Hyperlink.
5. Type the correct URL for the target.
6. The default is to update all pages containing the broken link. Leave this option selected.
7. Click Replace.

*Or*

8. Choose Edit Page to change or remove the link on that page only.

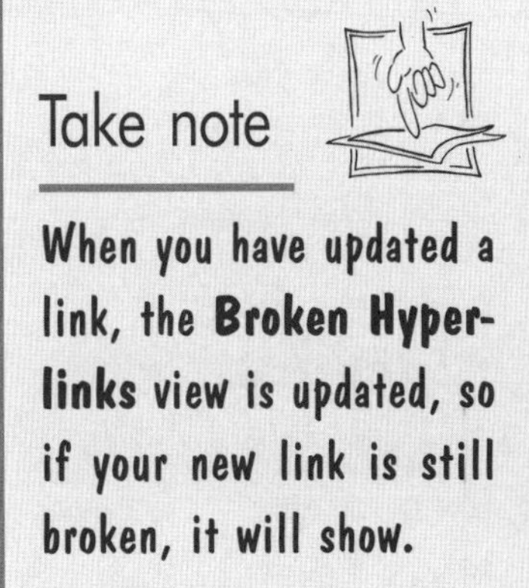

## Take note

**When you have updated a link, the Broken Hyperlinks view is updated, so if your new link is still broken, it will show.**

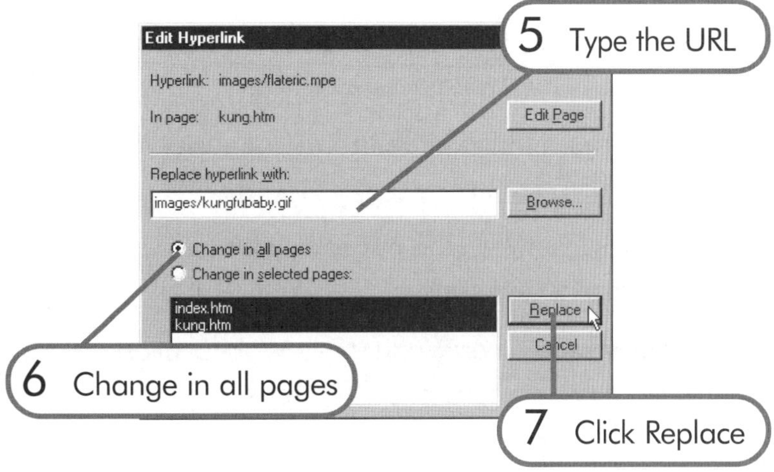

Edit Hyperlink
Hyperlink: images/flateric.mpe
In page: kung.htm
Edit Page
Replace hyperlink with:
images/kungfubaby.gif
Browse...
Change in all pages
Change in selected pages:
index.htm
kung.htm
Replace
Cancel
5 Type the URL
6 Change in all pages
7 Click Replace


## Basic steps

1. Select all your Unverified Hyperlinks.
2. Right-click and choose Verify.
3. You will be prompted to connect to the Internet – give Front-Page a few moments to check the links.
4. Select any links which are still broken.
5. Edit Hyperlink or Edit Page as before.
6. Click Replace.

## External links

When you check any external links, FrontPage connects briefly to each web site you have linked to, to make sure that it does exist. Those links which are found to be OK are marked with a green tick, any which point to non-existent URLs are given a broken link icon.

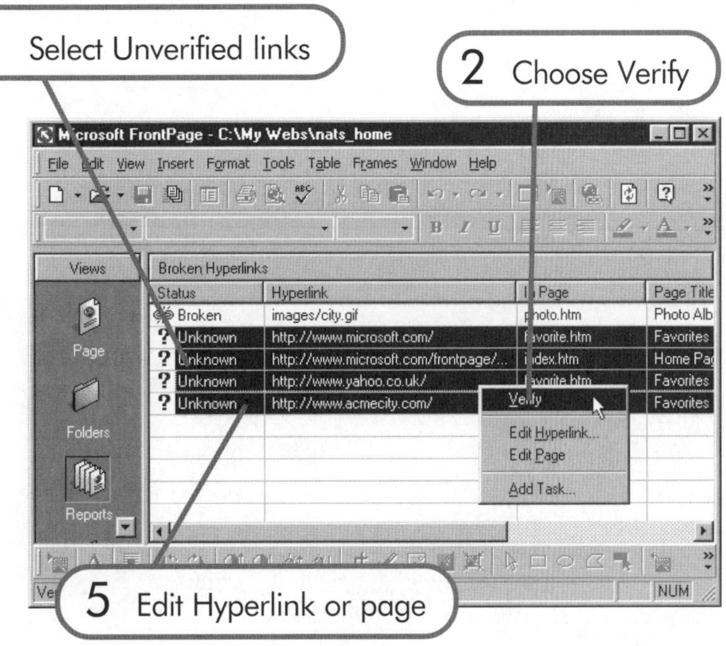

1 Select Unverified links
2 Choose Verify
Microsoft FrontPage - C:\My Webs\nats_home
File Edit View Insert Format Tools Table Frames Window Help
Views
Broken Hyperlinks
Status
Hyperlink
Page Title
Broken
images/city.gif
Unknown
http://www.microsoft.com/
http://www.microsoft.com/frontpage/...
http://www.yahoo.co.uk/
http://www.acmecity.com/
Photo Alb
Favorites
Verify
Edit Hyperlink...
Edit Page
Add Task...
Page
Folders
Reports
NUM
5 Edit Hyperlink or page

# Summary

- Use Bookmarks to define specific sections of a page as destinations for hyperlinks.
- Create links within a page to make it easier to find your way around it.
- Set up links between the pages in your web to make it an interconnected site.
- Create links to other World Wide Web locations, including newsgroups and FTP sites.
- Use an e-mail hyperlink to launch a new message window addressed to you.
- Use text, images or image hotspots as links.
- Recalculate Hyperlinks to update the parts of your web which relate to special FrontPage components.
- Make sure your hyperlinks are working with the Reports:Broken Hyperlinks... command.
- Add a navigation bar to your pages to make it easy to browse through your web.

# 6 Frames

# What are frames?

Frames are a way of breaking up the browser window into sections, each of which has a separate page displayed in it. When a new page is displayed in a frame, other frames in the set– the whole browser window – are not changed.

Typically, a frame set might consist of a main frame in which new pages are displayed, and a contents page which remains unchanged so that visitors can always use it to navigate around your web.

## Take note

**Some old browsers do not support frames, so you may want to construct a frameless alternative page with the same information and links.**

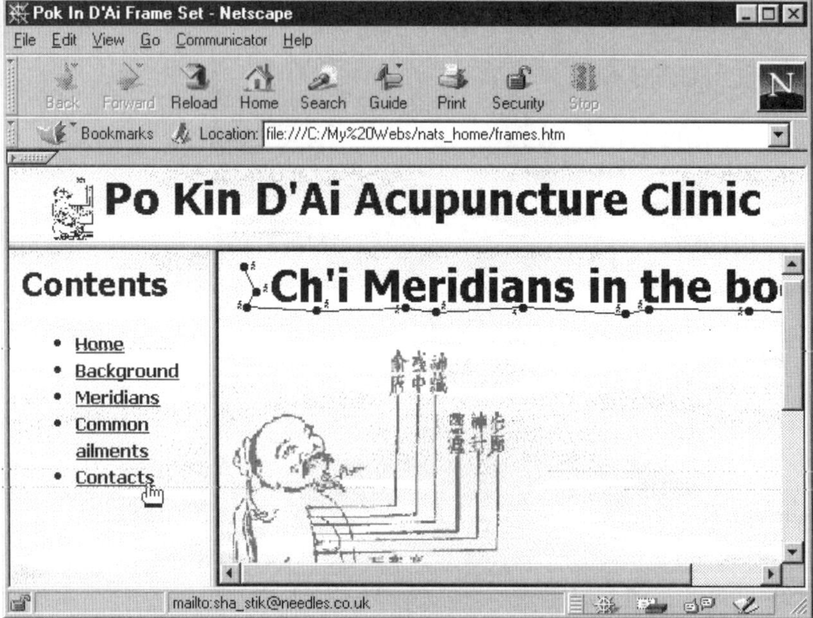
Pok In D'Ai Frame Set - Netscape
File Edit View Go Communicator Help
Back Forward Reload Home Search Guide Print Security Stop
Bookmarks Location: file:///C:/My%20Webs/nats_home/frames.htm
Po Kin D'Ai Acupuncture Clinic
Contents
Home
Background
Meridians
Common ailments
Contacts
Ch'i Meridians in the bo
mailto:sha_stik@needles.co.uk

## Tip

**When a page is loaded into a frame, the frame is treated as a screen in its own right, so text is wrapped around to fit within the margins. Images which fit comfortably on a full screen may fall off the edge of a frame, as with the Ch'i Meridians banner above. To avoid this, specify the width of large images as a percentage.**

# Working with frames

Tip

**If you have a frame for your logo, make sure that it is a small one. A large frame may well fix your name in visitors' minds – but it will be associated with an irritating waste of space!**

Frames can make navigating a web more user-friendly, but don't overcomplicate things by having too many of them. Besides being potentially confusing, they actually take up quite a lot of space – imagine trying to read anything in the three shallow frames in the example screen below.

Remember to take into account the blank margins around a page's contents, and the scrollbars which will probably be needed in a browser window.

Also, when using frames, hyperlinks have to specify which frame to put the new page in. With more than a handful of frames, you will find it difficult to keep track of which page is to be displayed in which frame at which time!

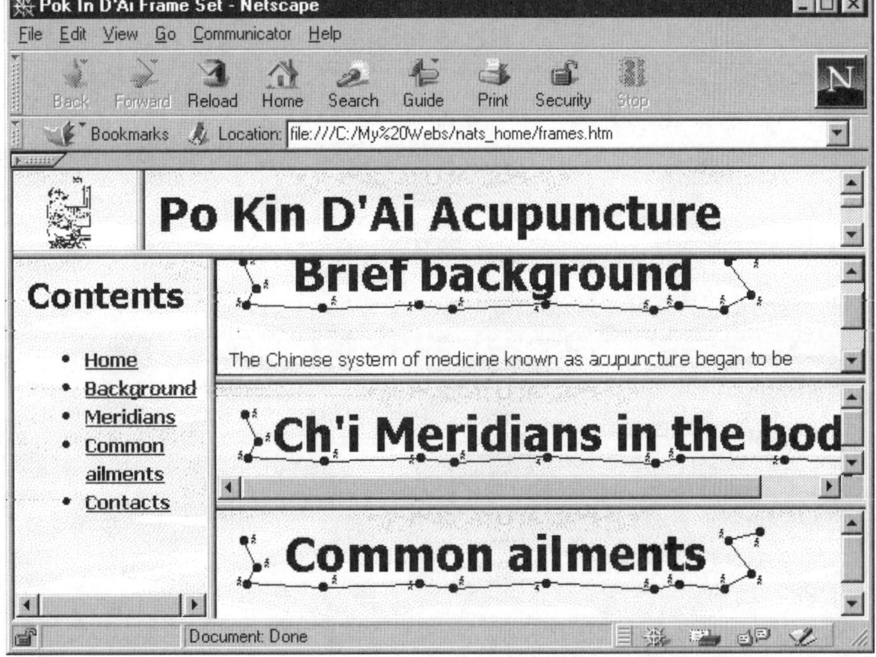
Pok In D'Ai Frame Set - Netscape
File Edit View Go Communicator Help
Back Forward Reload Home Search Guide Print Security Stop
Bookmarks Location: file:///C:/My%20Webs/nats_home/frames.htm
Po Kin D'Ai Acupuncture
Contents
Home
Background
Meridians
Common ailments
Contacts
Brief background
The Chinese system of medicine known as acupuncture began to be
Ch'i Meridians in the bod
Common ailments
Document: Done

Don't overdo the sub-division into frames!

# Creating a frame set

When you divide a web page into frames, you are actually dividing the browser window up rather than the page. Each frame contains a separate page, and a small document called a *frame set* tells the browser how to lay out the frames and which page to display in each frame.

FrontPage has a number of frame set templates to choose from. Usually one of these will do the job, but if necessary you can customise it by adding or deleting frames.

## Basic steps

1 Choose New… Page… from the File menu.

2 Click on the Frames Pages.

3 Choose a template.

4 Click OK.

1 Use File – New – Page…

2 Go to Frames Pages

The Description and Preview will help you decide which to use.

3 Choose a template

4 Click OK

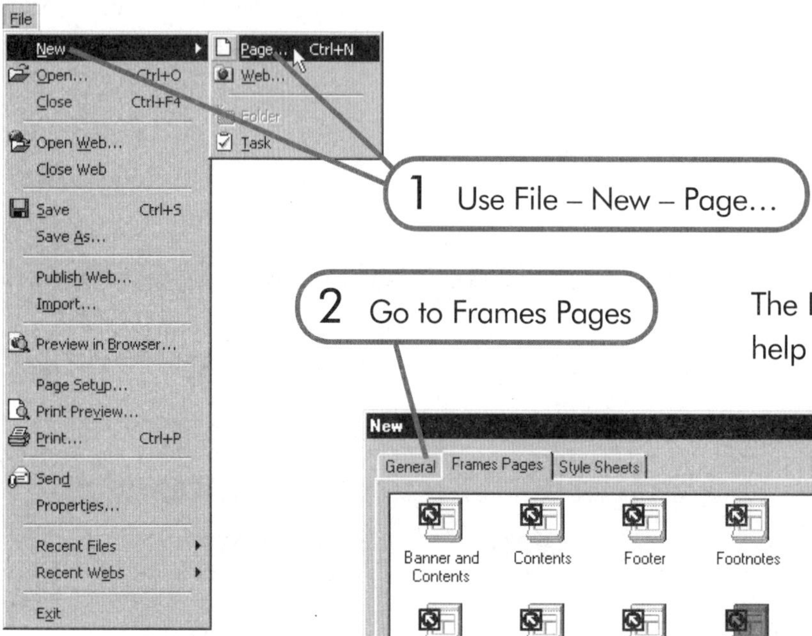

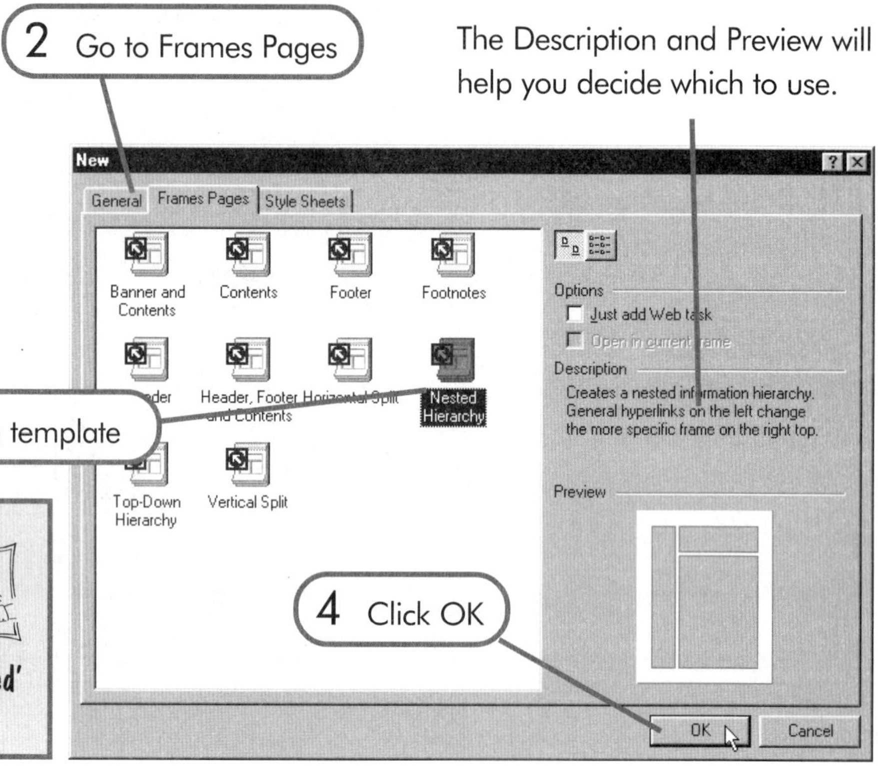

**Tip**

**For an example of 'nested' frames, see page 98.**

## Basic steps

# Setting initial pages

1 Select the frame – it will then have a blue border.

2 Right-click and click on Frame Properties…

3 Browse for an Initial Page.

4 Set other options – see page 96 for more.

5 Click OK.

The **Initial Page** for each frame is the page which is displayed when the frame set is first loaded. These pages may change later as your visitors browse through your site.

You can use the **Set Initial Page** button to locate this page, but I find it better to do it through the **Frame Properties** dialog box. This gives you the chance to set the size, margins and other options at the same time.

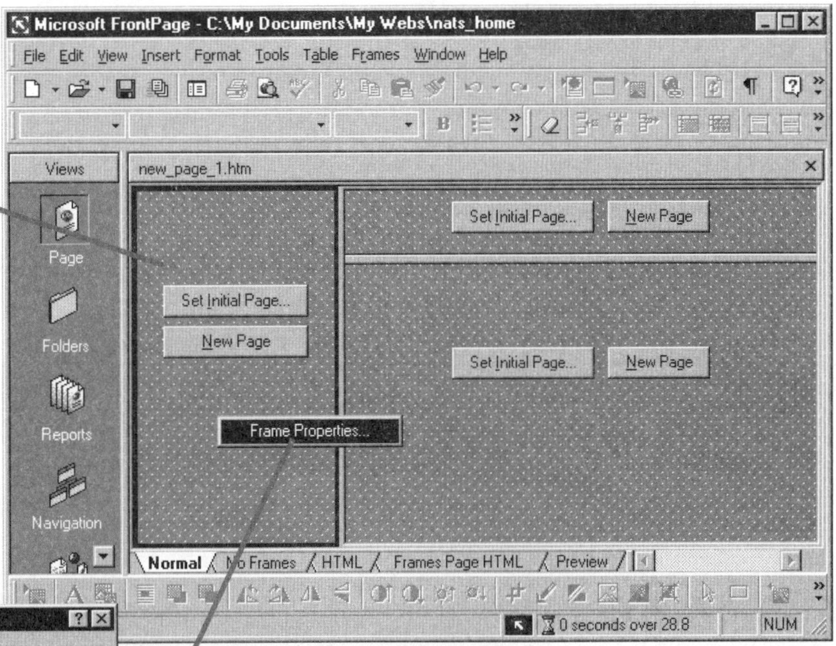

1 Select a frame

2 Click Frame Properties

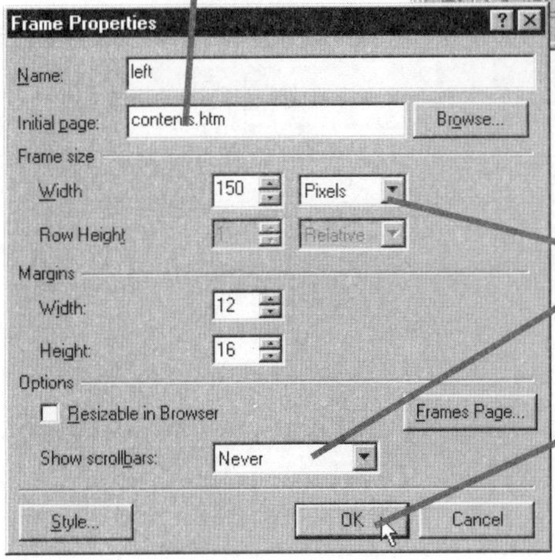

3 Browse for an Initial page

4 Set other options

5 Click OK

### Tip

**If you don't have a page for the frame, click New Page to create one from scratch.**

# Editing frames

## Basic steps

To change the size of each frame, you can just click and drag on the frame borders. Other **Frame Properties** can be changed from a dialog box:

- **Name** – used when specifying targets for hyperlinks (see page 100);
- **Initial Page** – set the default page displayed;
- **Frame size** – the dimensions can be set here instead of clicking and dragging the frame borders;
- **Margins** – set the distance in pixels between the edge of a frame and its contents;
- **Resizable in Browser** – choose whether or not to let your visitors resize the frames;
- **Show scrollbars** – *If needed* puts scroll bars in if necessary (safest option); *Always* and *Never* turn them on or off absolutely.

1. Right-click in a frame and choose Frame Properties…
2. Give the frame a new Name.
3. Change the Initial Page.
4. Set the Width and Height of the Frame.
5. Set the Margin Width and Height.
6. Set Resizable and Scrollbars options.
7. Click OK.

If a frame runs the whole width or height of the browser window, only one option will available

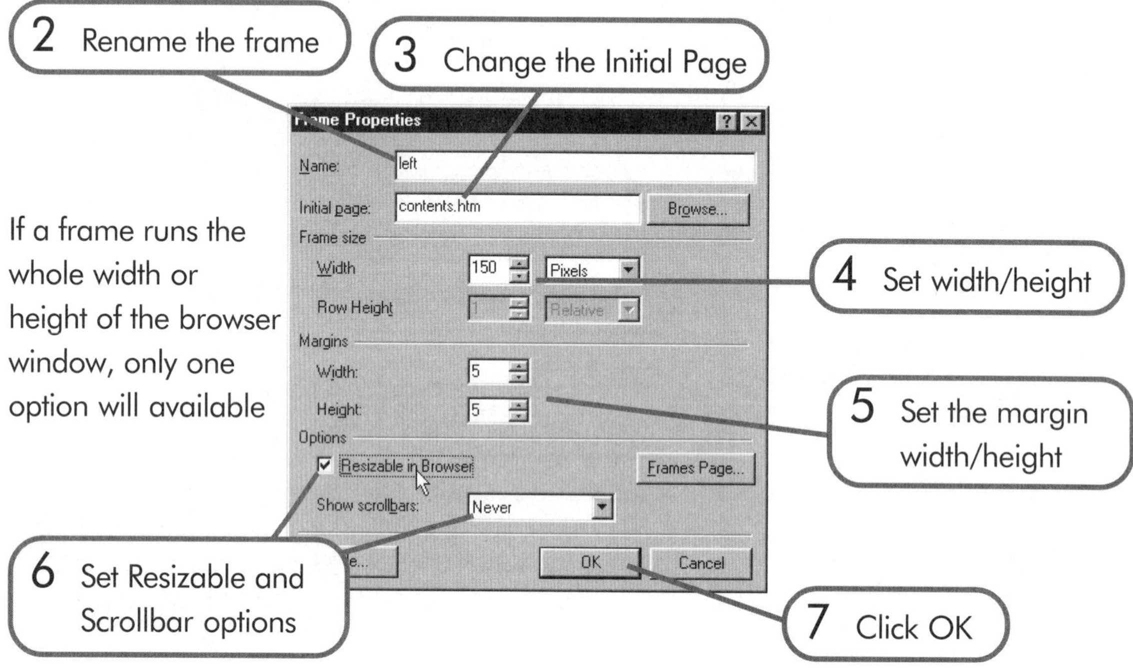
2 Rename the frame
3 Change the Initial Page
Frame Properties
Name:
left
Initial page:
contents.htm
Browse...
Frame size
Width
150
Pixels
Row Height
1
Relative
Margins
Width:
5
Height:
5
Options
Resizable in Browser
Frames Page...
Show scrollbars:
Never
OK
Cancel
4 Set width/height
5 Set the margin width/height
6 Set Resizable and Scrollbar options
7 Click OK

## Basic steps

1. Open the Frame Properties dialog box.
2. Click Frames Page…
3. Set the Frame Spacing to 0.
4. Uncheck the Show Borders box.
5. Click OK.

## Invisible frames

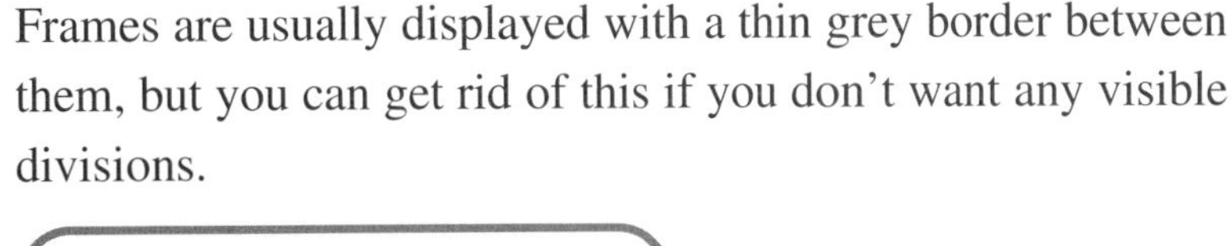

Frames are usually displayed with a thin grey border between them, but you can get rid of this if you don't want any visible divisions.

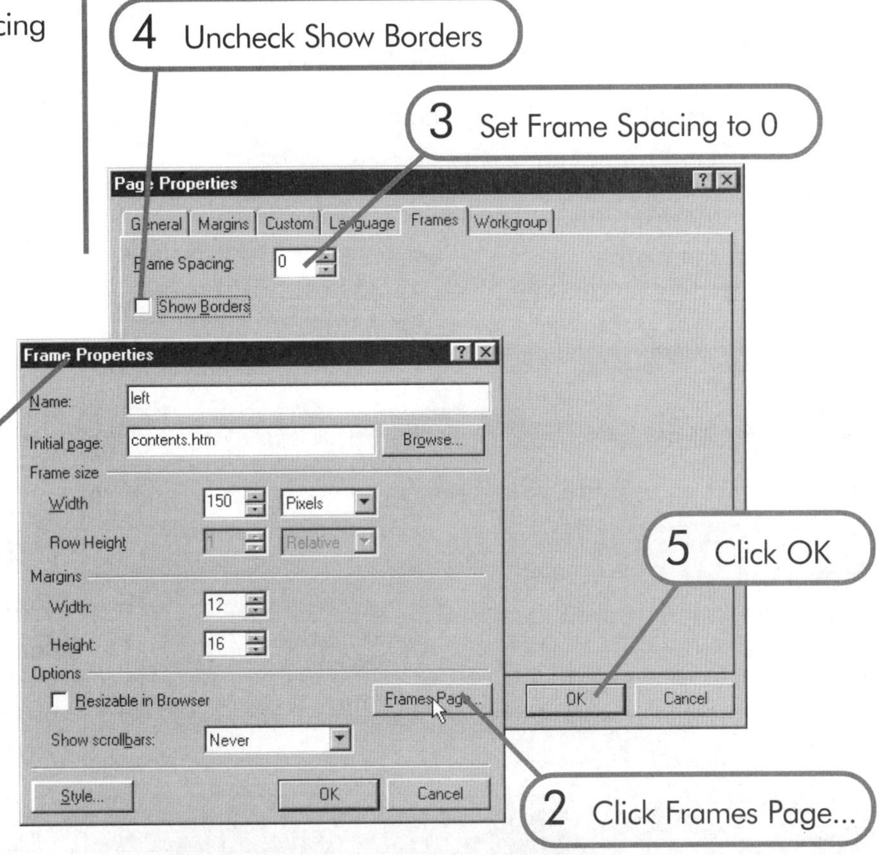
4 Uncheck Show Borders
3 Set Frame Spacing to 0
Page Properties
General
Margins
Custom
Language
Frames
Workgroup
Frame Spacing:
0
Show Borders
Frame Properties
Name:
left
Initial page:
contents.htm
Browse...
Frame size
Width
150
Pixels
Row Height
Relative
Margins
Width:
12
Height:
16
Options
Resizable in Browser
Frames Page...
Show scrollbars:
Never
Style...
OK
Cancel
1 Open Frame Properties...
5 Click OK
2 Click Frames Page...

### Tip

**When you resize by clicking and dragging on the frame borders, make sure you check that it looks right in a browser, because sometimes it doesn't seem to be picked up properly by FrontPage. If this happens, specify the Width and Height in the Frame Properties dialog box.**

# Customised frame sets

If the frame layout you have in mind is not amongst the templates, you can pick one which is close, and then split the frames as necessary to create the divisions you want.

Frames can be split before or after you have created or linked a page into them. Each split creates one new frame.

If the frame layout has too many frames – or you split one by mistake – excess frames are easily deleted.

## Basic steps

1. Create a new frame set.
2. Select the frame.

❑ To split a frame

3. Open the Frames menu and select Split Frame.
4. Choose Split into columns or rows.
5. Click OK.

❑ To delete a frame

6. Open the Frames menu and select Delete Frame.

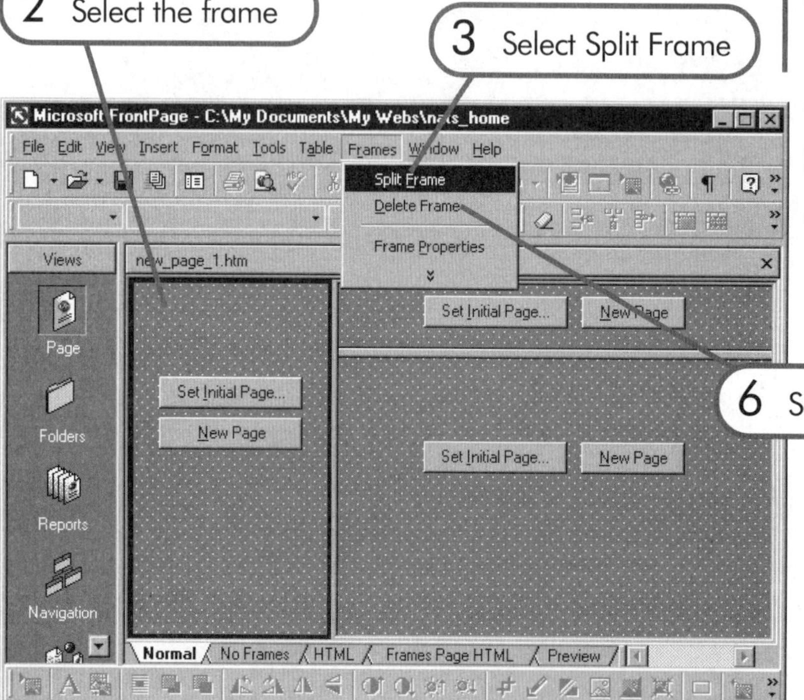
2 Select the frame
3 Select Split Frame
6 Select Delete Frame
Microsoft FrontPage - C:\My Documents\My Webs\nats_home
File Edit View Insert Format Tools Table Frames Window Help
Split Frame
Delete Frame
Frame Properties
Views
Page
Folders
Reports
Navigation
new_page_1.htm
Set Initial Page...
New Page
Normal
No Frames
HTML
Frames Page HTML
Preview
0 seconds over 28.8
NUM

In this example, the window is split vertically into two frames, then the right-hand frame is split horizontally to give a 'nested' frame set.

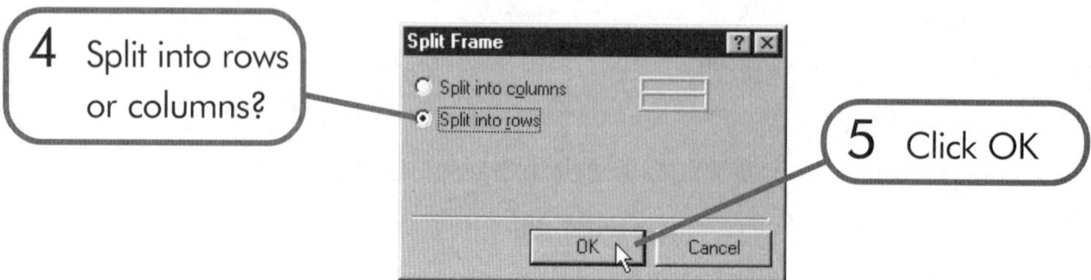
4 Split into rows or columns?
Split Frame
Split into columns
Split into rows
OK
Cancel
5 Click OK

## Basic steps

1 Click on the No Frames tab.

2 Edit the page to display your no-frames message.

*Or*

3 Begin to create your no-frames alternative pages.

## No frames page

You may have noticed while working with frames that at the bottom of the window there is a new tab, labelled **No Frames**. Some older browsers cannot handle frames, so you may want to create an alternative page, which will automatically be displayed instead. The No Frames tab opens a window where you can edit this alternative page.

There are two ways of going about no frames pages. The polite way is to build an alternative structure to your site which caters for non-frames browsers, using a navigation bar on every page instead of a frame. This could be a fair bit of work though, so you might want to display a brief message like this instead:

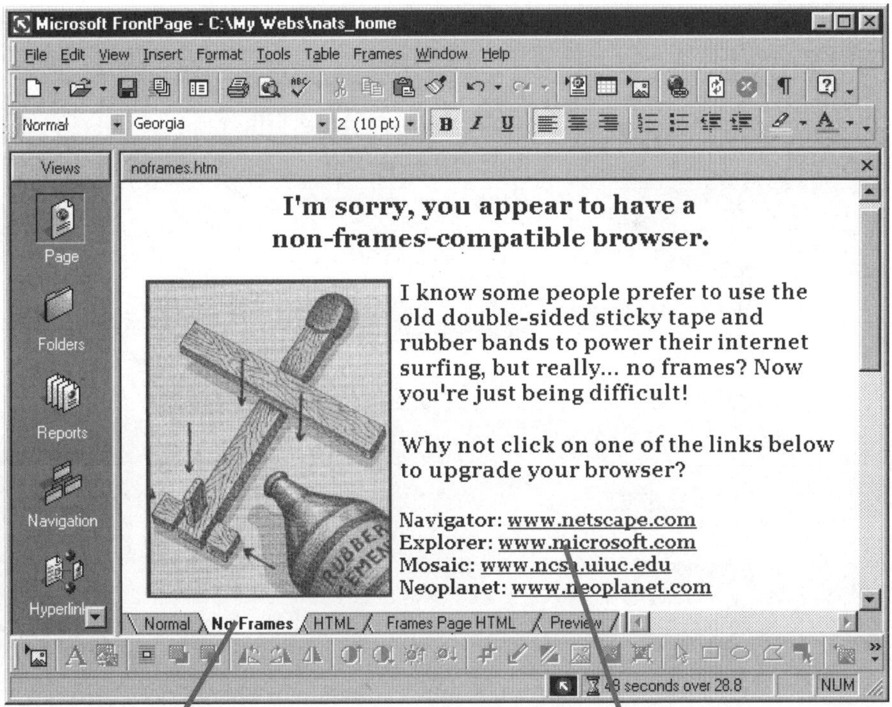

Microsoft FrontPage - C:\My Webs\nats_home
File Edit View Insert Format Tools Table Frames Window Help
Normal
Georgia
2 (10 pt)
Views
Page
Folders
Reports
Navigation
Hyperlinks
noframes.htm
I'm sorry, you appear to have a non-frames-compatible browser.
I know some people prefer to use the old double-sided sticky tape and rubber bands to power their internet surfing, but really... no frames? Now you're just being difficult!
Why not click on one of the links below to upgrade your browser?
Navigator: www.netscape.com
Explorer: www.microsoft.com
Mosaic: www.ncsa.uiuc.edu
Neoplanet: www.neoplanet.com
Normal
No Frames
HTML
Frames Page HTML
Preview
48 seconds over 28.8
NUM
1 Click No Frames
3 Edit the page for the no-frames message

### Tip

**You might like to provide a link to a browser download source along with your message.**

# Target frames

When you are working with frames, you need to specify **target frames** for your hyperlinks. These tell the browser where to display the new page. If you don't specify a target, the browser will normally open the new page in the frame which contained the link, replacing its contents.

A default target frame can be set for each page, and this will apply to all links on the page unless otherwise specified. Contents pages, for instance, often use a default so that all linked pages are displayed in the main frame.

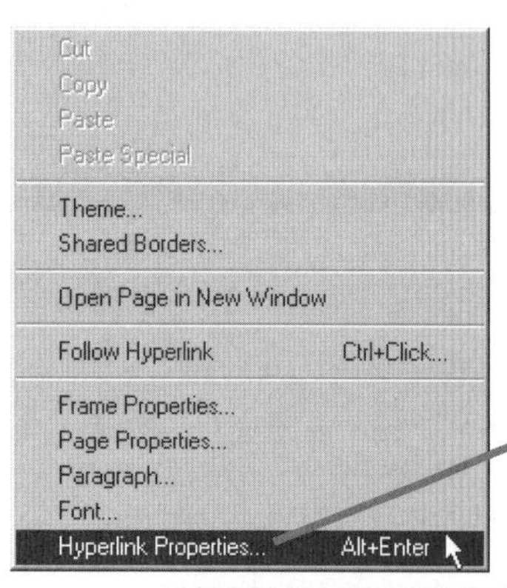

Cut
Copy
Paste
Paste Special
Theme...
Shared Borders...
Open Page in New Window
Follow Hyperlink Ctrl+Click...
Frame Properties...
Page Properties...
Paragraph...
Font...
Hyperlink Properties... Alt+Enter


2 Right-click on a link for the menu

3 Select Hyperlink Properties

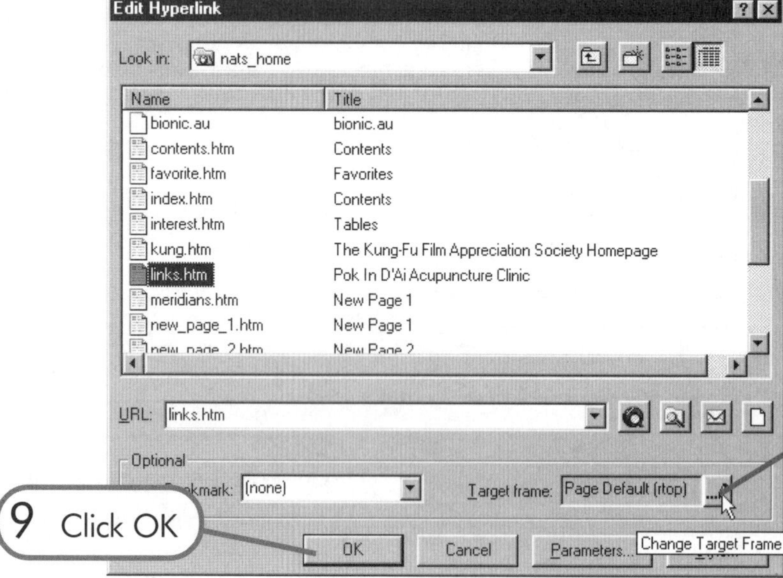

Edit Hyperlink
Look in: nats_home
Name
Title
bionic.au
bionic.au
contents.htm
Contents
favorite.htm
Favorites
index.htm
Contents
interest.htm
Tables
kung.htm
The Kung-Fu Film Appreciation Society Homepage
links.htm
Pok In D'Ai Acupuncture Clinic
meridians.htm
New Page 1
new_page_1.htm
New Page 1
URL: links.htm
Optional
(none)
Target frame: Page Default (rtop)
OK
Cancel
Parameters...
Change Target Frame


4 Click the Target frame button

9 Click OK

## Basic steps

1 Create a hyperlink.

*Or*

2 Right-click on an existing hyperlink for the context menu.

3 Choose Hyperlink Properties...

4 Click the Change Target Frame... button.

5 In the Current frames page pane, click on the frame you want the page displayed in.

❑ To set a default target

6 Check the Set as page default box.

❑ To set a special target

7 Choose one of the Common targets.

8 Click OK.

9 Click OK again.

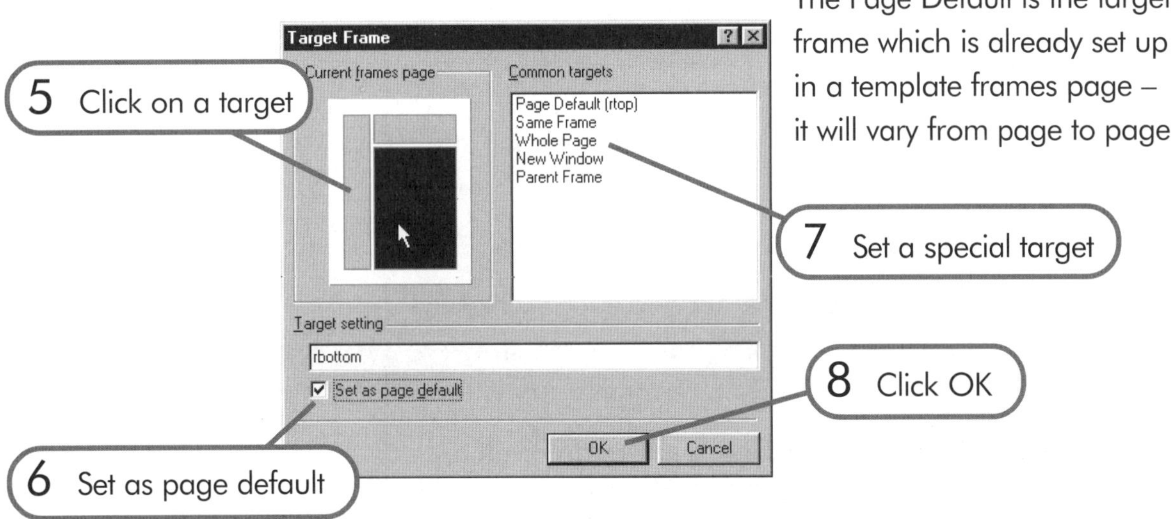
Target Frame
Current frames page
Common targets
Page Default (rtop)
Same Frame
Whole Page
New Window
Parent Frame
Target setting
rbottom
Set as page default
OK
Cancel
5 Click on a target
6 Set as page default
7 Set a special target
8 Click OK

The Page Default is the target frame which is already set up in a template frames page – it will vary from page to page

## Special targets

There are five pre-defined targets which have special functions. They are listed in the **Common targets** window of the **Target Frame** dialog box.

When you select one, you will see that the **Target setting** (the **Name** of the target frame) changes to one beginning with an _underscore. Note that these names should not be used when renaming frames (see page 96), or you'll confuse the browser!

- **Same Frame** (**_self**) tells the browser to display the new page in the same frame as the hyperlink.
- **Whole Page** (**_top**) removes all frames from the browser window and replaces them with the new page.
- **New Window** (**_blank**) opens a new browser window to display the page in.
- When you create a frame set with both horizontal and vertical divisions, you are actually creating one frame set within another, because a frame set can only be made up of *either* rows *or* columns. **Parent Frame** (**_parent**) tells the browser to replace an inner frame set with the new page. It sounds complicated, but have a go and you'll soon see how it works!

# Summary

- ❑ Use frames to divide the browser window into independent sections.
- ❑ You can create a frame set from one of the FrontPage templates.
- ❑ Click and drag on a frame's border to resize it.
- ❑ Choose the Initial Page as the page or image which is called up into a frame when the frame set is first loaded.
- ❑ Edit a frame's margins, turn the Scrolling on or off or make it Not resizable in the Edit Frame Attributes dialog box.
- ❑ You can create a customised frame set by splitting a template into as many frames as you want.
- ❑ Set the Frame Spacing to 0 and turn off the Show Borders option for invisible frames.
- ❑ Create a No frames page – or a full matching set of pages – for people with older browsers.
- ❑ Specify Target Frames for hyperlinks so that browsers know where to display a new page.

# 7 Forms and feedback

# What are forms?

Forms are sections of a page which request information from visitors to your web. Visitors type answers to your prompts or questions into the blank spaces on the page, and the form is then sent back to your web server where you can access the results.

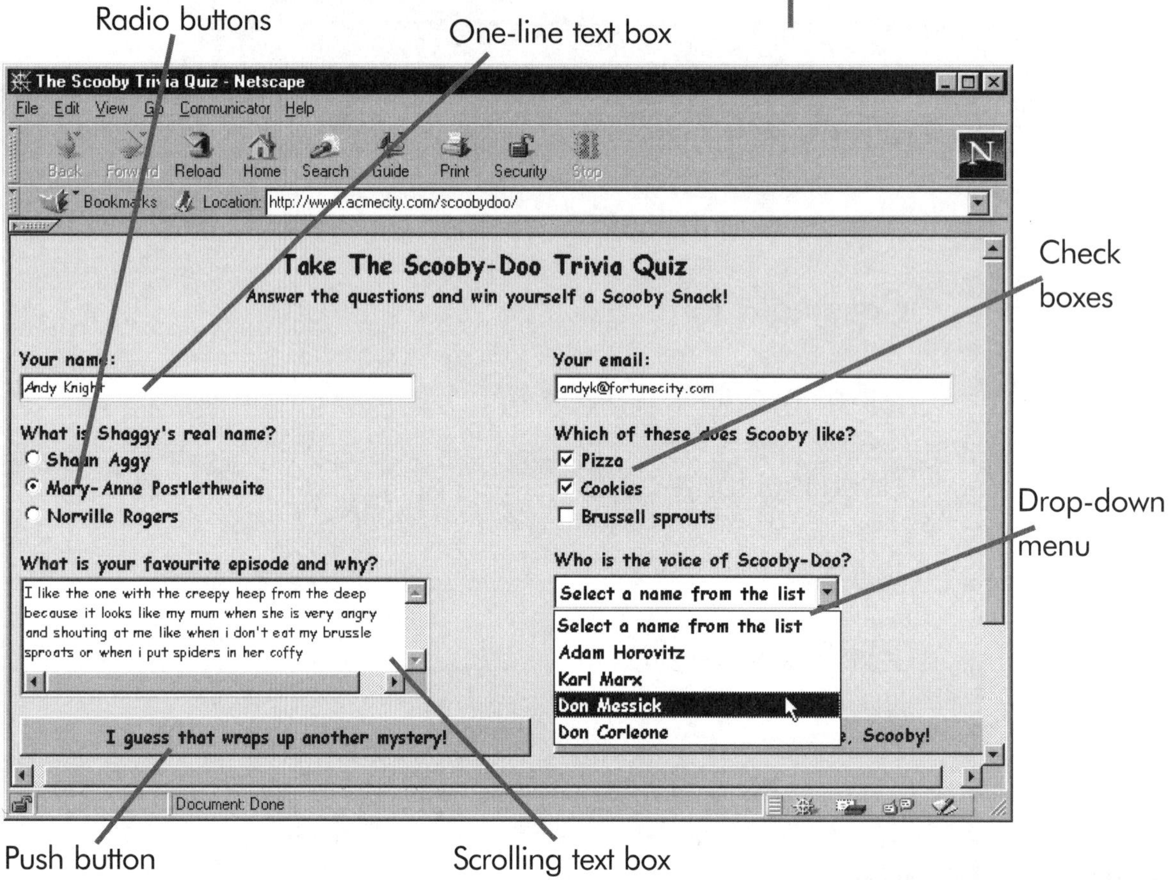

Radio buttons

One-line text box

Check boxes

Drop-down menu

Push button

Scrolling text box

## How do they work?

If your Internet Service Provider (ISP) supports FrontPage Extensions, the data sent by visitors is collated by the Extensions on your ISP's server into a database or HTML file. If your ISP does not support the Extensions, you will need a CGI script, to handle incoming data. These also run on your ISP's server. Talk to your ISP about this.

### Tip

**Use forms to gather data about visitors, to invite them to send you feedback, or just for fun.**

# Names and values

Items of information submitted from a form have two main attributes:

- a **name**, which identifies the items when you access the results file where returned form data is stored.
- a **value**, which is the information itself. Sometimes, this will be whatever the user types in; in other cases, you will set the values for *either/or* responses. Some values can be returned automatically, such as the time and date that the form was submitted.

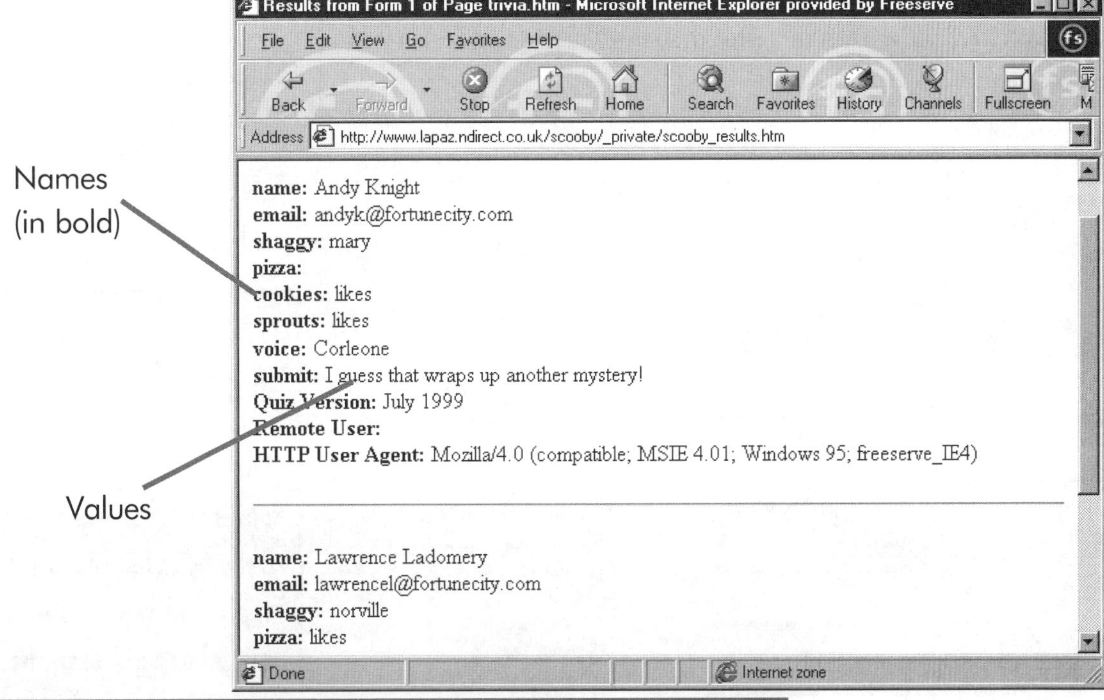

Results from Form 1 of Page trivia.htm - Microsoft Internet Explorer provided by Freeserve
File Edit View Go Favorites Help
Back Forward Stop Refresh Home Search Favorites History Channels Fullscreen M
Address http://www.lapaz.ndirect.co.uk/scooby/_private/scooby_results.htm
Names (in bold)
name: Andy Knight
email: andyk@fortunecity.com
shaggy: mary
pizza:
cookies: likes
sprouts: likes
voice: Corleone
submit: I guess that wraps up another mystery!
Quiz Version: July 1999
Remote User:
HTTP User Agent: Mozilla/4.0 (compatible; MSIE 4.01; Windows 95; freeserve_IE4)
Values
name: Lawrence Ladomery
email: lawrencel@fortunecity.com
shaggy: norville
pizza: likes
Done
Internet zone


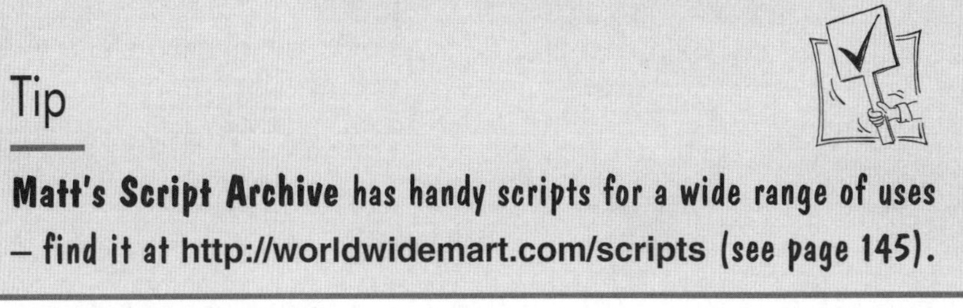

## Tip

**Matt's Script Archive** has handy scripts for a wide range of uses – find it at http://worldwidemart.com/scripts (see page 145).

# Creating a form

## Basic steps

When you add a form field or a button to a page, an area containing it is designated as a form. Both the form field and the form itself are inserted with standard default properties. Once a form and its elements are on the page, you can then configure them to suit your purposes.

Every form has to have a **Submit** button to send the information, and usually you would provide a **Reset** button to clear the form. Whenever you insert a form field, these two are automatically included in the form.

However, if you are going to use a table to lay out your form, you will need to create a form area first, then insert a table and add form fields to it.

1 Position the cursor where you want a form field.

2 Open the Insert menu and point to Form...

3 Point to [»] at the bottom, or wait a moment.

4 When the full submenu opens choose Form...

5 Set out your form inside the form area.

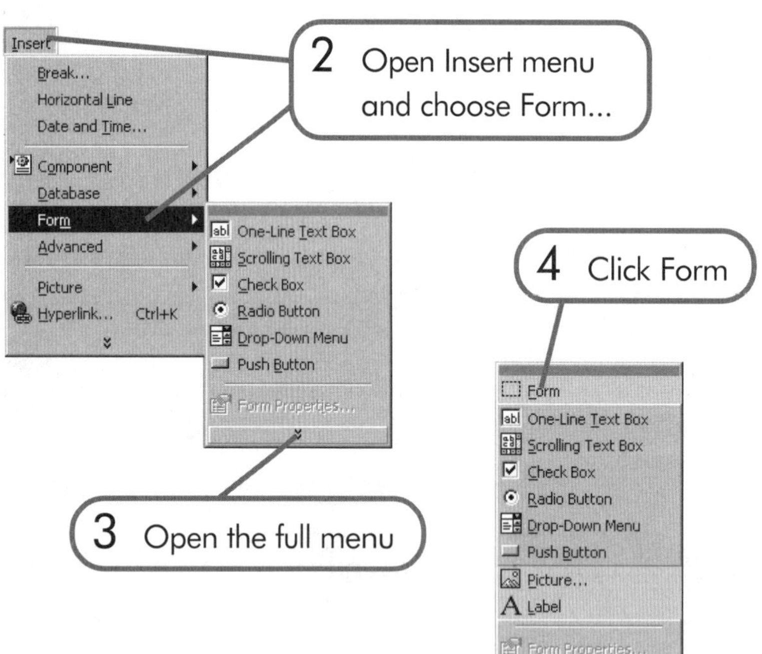
Insert
Break...
Horizontal Line
Date and Time...
Component
Database
Form
Advanced
Picture
Hyperlink... Ctrl+K
One-Line Text Box
Scrolling Text Box
Check Box
Radio Button
Drop-Down Menu
Push Button
Form Properties...
2 Open Insert menu and choose Form...
3 Open the full menu
4 Click Form
Form
One-Line Text Box
Scrolling Text Box
Check Box
Radio Button
Drop-Down Menu
Push Button
Picture...
Label
Form Properties...

## Tip

**You can make a form stand out from the rest of the page by inserting it into a table and then giving it a border or a different background colour.**

## Basic steps

1. Create a form area.
2. Create a two-column table inside this area.
3. Type a prompt for information into a cell.
4. Position the cursor in the adjacent cell.
5. Select a Form Field from the Insert – Form menu.

# Form layout

If you want your form to look like a form, it is probably best to arrange the elements in a table so that your prompts for information are aligned comfortably with the fields for users to type into.

- Set the table border to zero if you don't want it to show.

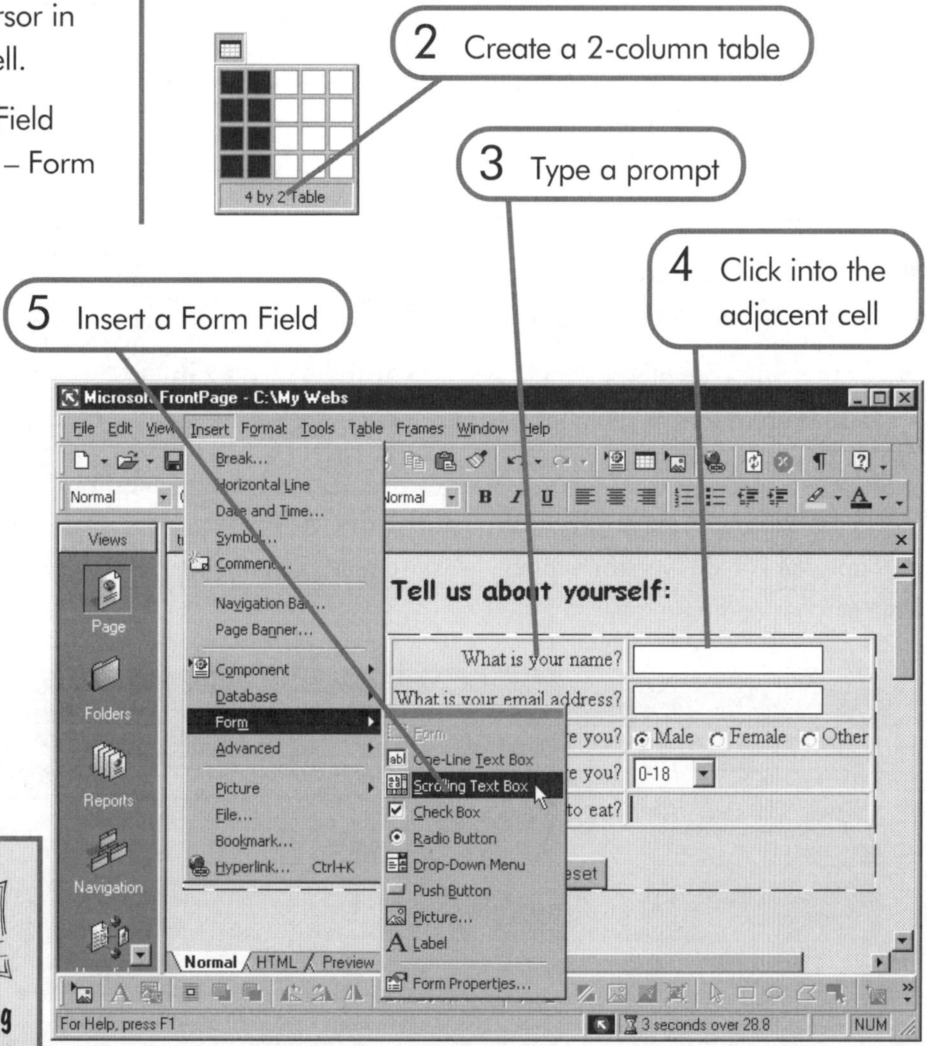

2 Create a 2-column table

3 Type a prompt

4 Click into the adjacent cell

5 Insert a Form Field

**Tip**

**See the following pages for details of each field type.**

# Handling form data

## Basic steps

By default, form results – the data entered by visitors – are handled by FrontPage's own form handler. Using this, you can save data in various file formats when it is submitted. The results can either be accessed later through FrontPage, or you can have them e-mailed to you:

- **HTML** – the default style, which collates information and displays it as ordinary text in an HTML page.
- **Formatted text** – preserves tabs and spaces as they were entered by the user (HTML does not recognise tabs or multiple spaces). This creates a text file unless you select **Formatted text within HTML**.
- **HTML List** – creates an HTML page with Name/Value pairs set as a **Definition** or **Bulleted** list.
- **Text file** – creates a simple text file, using **Tabs**, **Commas** or **Spaces** as separators between the values. This can be imported into a database or spreadsheet.

You can choose to have the results stored in two formats – perhaps one HTML version which is easy to read, and one text fiel for your database.

1 Right-click on the form and choose Form Properties…

2 Edit the suggested File name if you want.

3 Click Options…

4 Choose a File format for the results.

❑ To get results by e-mail

5 Click on the E-mail Results tab.

6 Type an E-mail address.

7 Enter a Subject line.

8 Click OK.

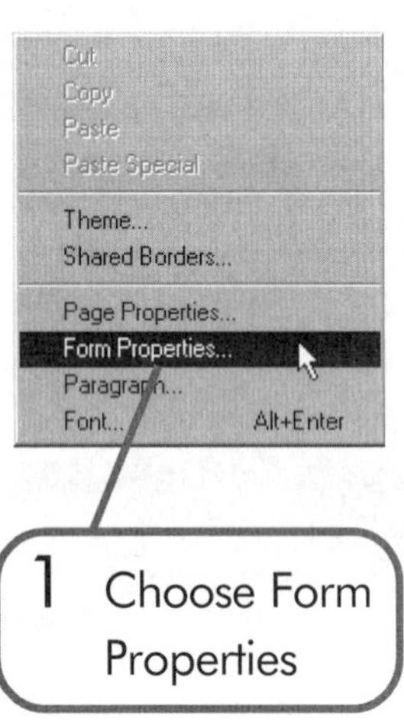
Cut
Copy
Paste
Paste Special
Theme...
Shared Borders...
Page Properties...
Form Properties...
Paragraph...
Font... Alt+Enter
1 Choose Form Properties

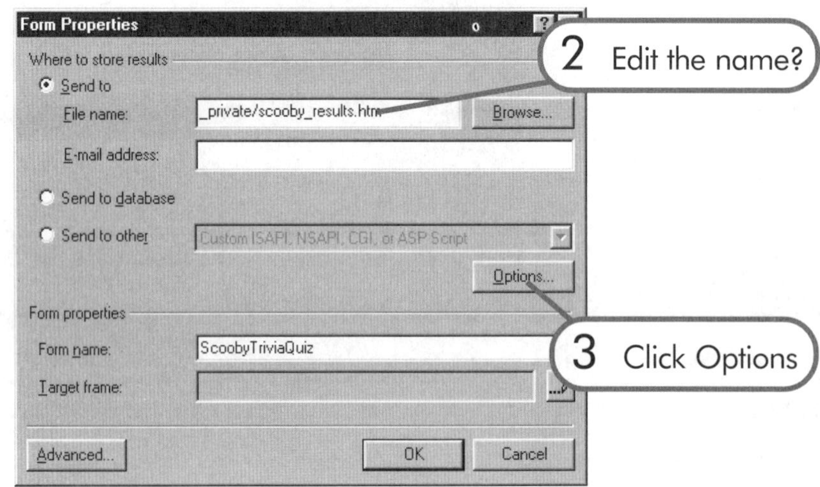
Form Properties
Where to store results
Send to
File name:
_private/scooby_results.htm
Browse...
E-mail address:
Send to database
Send to other
Custom ISAPI, NSAPI, CGI, or ASP Script
Options...
Form properties
Form name:
ScoobyTriviaQuiz
Target frame:
Advanced...
OK
Cancel
2 Edit the name?
3 Click Options

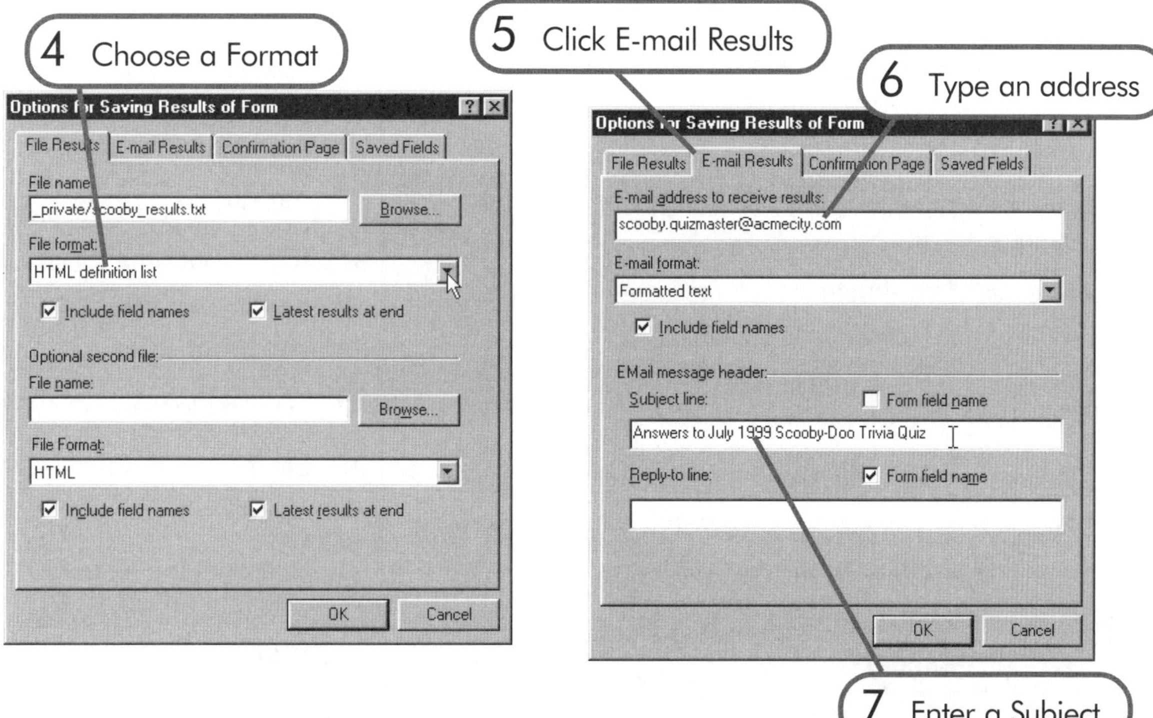
4 Choose a Format
5 Click E-mail Results
6 Type an address
Options for Saving Results of Form
File Results
E-mail Results
Confirmation Page
Saved Fields
File name:
_private/scooby_results.txt
Browse...
File format:
HTML definition list
Include field names
Latest results at end
Optional second file:
File name:
Browse...
File Format:
HTML
Include field names
Latest results at end
OK
Cancel
Options for Saving Results of Form
File Results
E-mail Results
Confirmation Page
Saved Fields
E-mail address to receive results:
scooby.quizmaster@acmecity.com
E-mail format:
Formatted text
Include field names
EMail message header:
Subject line:
Form field name
Answers to July 1999 Scooby-Doo Trivia Quiz
Reply-to line:
Form field name
OK
Cancel
7 Enter a Subject

## Basic steps

1 In the Form Properties... dialog box, click Advanced...
2 Click Add...
3 Enter a Name and Value.
4 Click OK.

# Hidden fields

To help you identify the information when you access your results page, you can set Hidden fields which cannot be seen by the user, but which are returned with each submitted form.

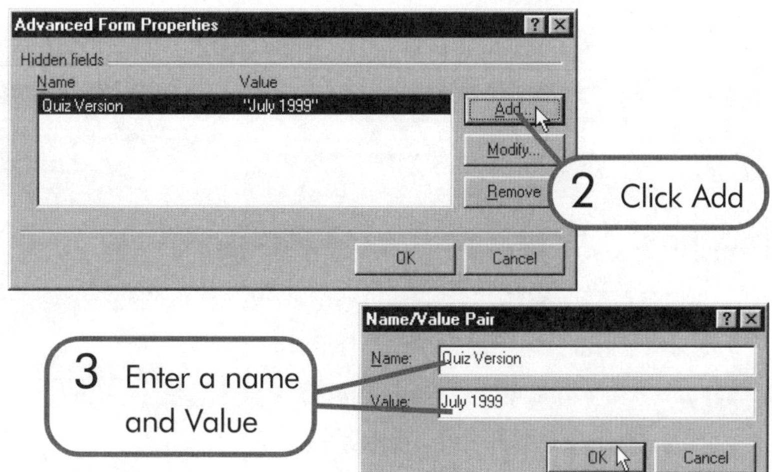
Advanced Form Properties
Hidden fields
Name
Value
Quiz Version
"July 1999"
Add...
Modify...
Remove
OK
Cancel
2 Click Add
Name/Value Pair
Name:
Quiz Version
Value:
July 1999
OK
Cancel
3 Enter a name and Value

# Text Boxes

## Basic steps

Text Boxes collect data from visitors. There are two kinds.

## One-line Text Box

This used for entering simple information such as names, job titles, e-mail addresses, and so on. You can specify the Width, and set it as a password field, which means that any characters the visitor types are displayed as asterisks.

## Scrolling Text Boxes

These are larger areas – addresses, questions or feedback. As for a one line text box, you can vary the width to suit its purpose, and also specify the number of lines deep it is.

1. Choose One-Line or Scrolling Text Box from the Insert – Form menu.
2. Right-click on it for its menu and pick Form Field Properties...
3. Type a Name.
4. Set the Width in characters.
5. In a one-line text box, set it as a Password field if it is part of an access control routine.
6. In a scrolling text box set the Number of lines.
7. Click OK.

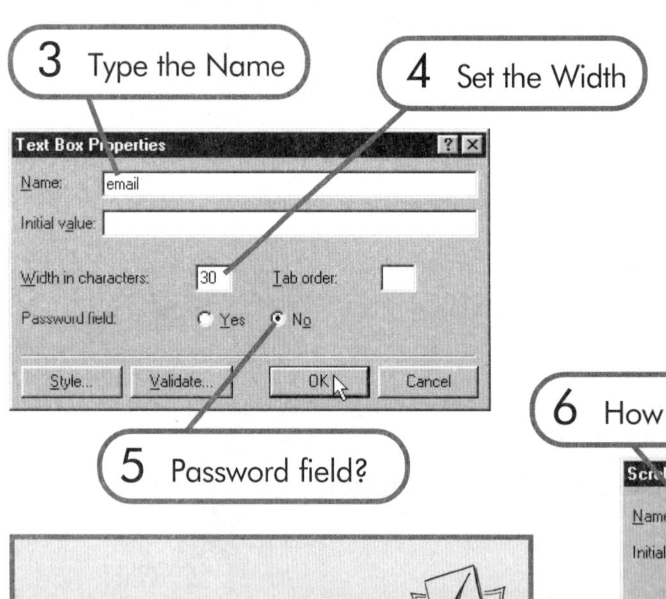
3 Type the Name
4 Set the Width
Text Box Properties
Name: email
Initial value:
Width in characters: 30
Tab order:
Password field: Yes No
Style... Validate... OK Cancel
5 Password field?

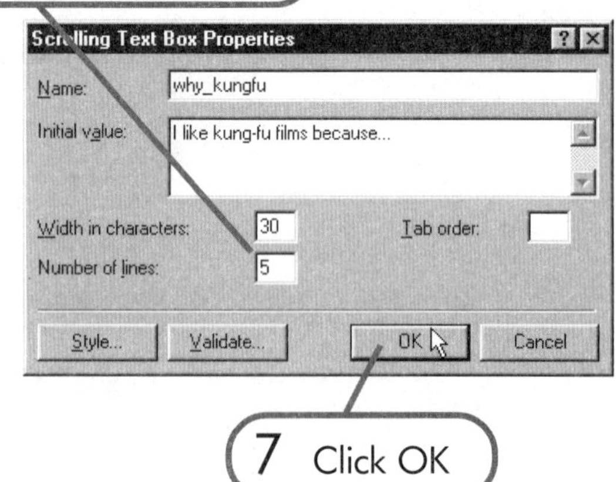
6 How many lines?
Scrolling Text Box Properties
Name: why_kungfu
Initial value: I like kung-fu films because...
Width in characters: 30
Tab order:
Number of lines: 5
Style... Validate... OK Cancel
7 Click OK

### Tip

**You can enter 'Initial value' text to appear before the visitor starts typing – perhaps for a competition tie-breaker.**

# Text Box validation

Text Boxes can have certain constraints imposed on the kind of information users enter into them. This might be to stop typing mistakes slipping through – imposing an upper limit of 110 on an 'age' field, for example. It might be to ensure that the right sort of information is supplied – setting a minimum of 11 characters in a telephone field ensures that a full national code is given.

The Text Box Validation dialog box gives you several ways of restricting the kind of information you are sent:

Take note

**To allow characters other than letters, numerals and blank spaces in a field, you must click the Other field and type them into it. This includes all punctuation marks.**

- **Data Type** – choose *Text*, *Number* or *Integer* (whole numbers only). Each type has a set of more specific restrictions:
  - *Text Format* – Letters, Digits, Whitespace or specified Others can be allowed or disallowed. Check the options you want to allow.
  - *Numeric Format* – the default is commas for grouping and full stops for decimal points (4,364.99), but you can switch to Continental-style numbering (4.364,99).
- **Data Length** – click *Required* and set a minimum and/or maximum number of characters.
- **Data Value** – using the comparisons 'greater/less than' and 'equal to', you can set upper and/or lower limits for a number entered. However, it also works on an alphabetical basis with words: 'greater than' meaning 'further towards Z than' and 'less than' meaning 'closer to A than'.

## Basic steps

When a visitor tries to submit data which is not within the defined range, a message will tell them what is acceptable.

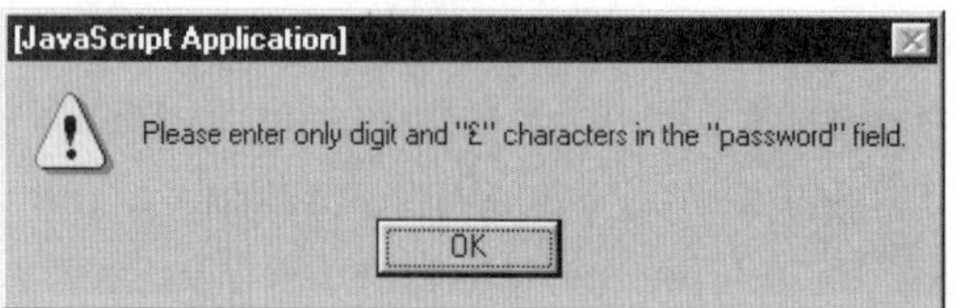
[JavaScript Application]
Please enter only digit and "£" characters in the "password" field.
OK

Alternatively, you can create a page to explain what sort of information is required, and set this to be displayed:

- Open the **Form properties** dialog box, click **Settings...** and then click the **Confirm** tab.
- Type the address into the **Validation failure page** field or Browse... for it.

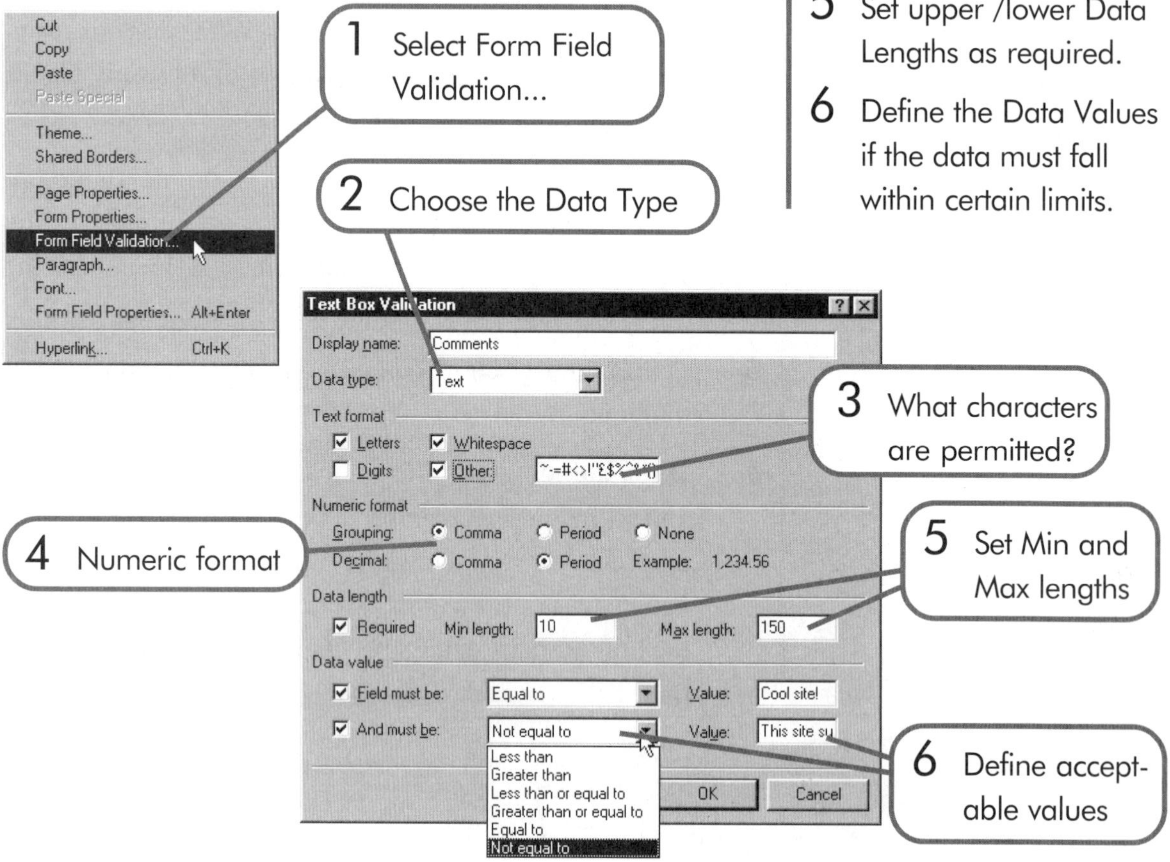

1 Select Form Field Validation...

2 Choose the Data Type

3 What characters are permitted?

4 Numeric format

5 Set Min and Max lengths

6 Define acceptable values

1 Right-click on a text box and choose Form Field Validation...

2 Choose a Data Type to permit (*No constraints* allows any characters).

3 If you chose *Text*, click on a Text Format option to allow it.

4 If you chose *Number*, pick a Numeric Format.

5 Set upper /lower Data Lengths as required.

6 Define the Data Values if the data must fall within certain limits.

## Basic steps

# Push buttons

1. Select Push Button from the Form menu.
2. Right-click on the push button and choose Form Field Properties...
3. Type a Name for it.
4. Type the word(s) you want to appear on the button in the Value/ Label field.
5. Decide whether it is a Submit, Reset, or Normal (custom) button.
6. Click OK.

There are three types of Push Buttons:

- **Submit**, sends the form information to the server when clicked by the visitor.
- **Reset** clears the contents of the form, so that the visitor can start again.
- **Normal** buttons can be customised to perform different functions by attaching JavaScript code, or associating them with CGI scripts, but this is a little beyond the scope of this book. If you want to learn JavaScript, try *JavaScript Made Simple*. For information on CGI scripts, talk first to your ISP.

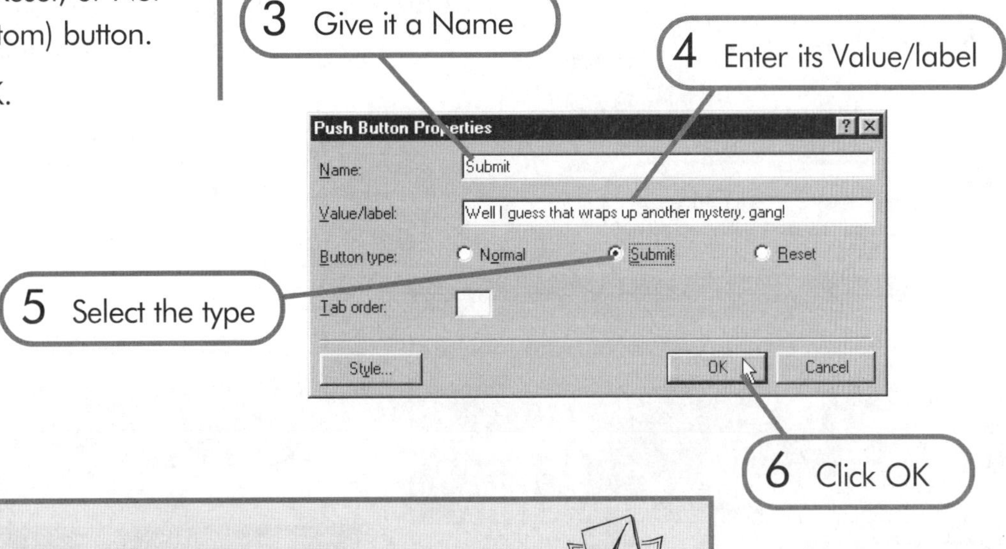
3 Give it a Name
4 Enter its Value/label
Push Button Properties
Name:
Submit
Value/label:
Well I guess that wraps up another mystery, gang!
Button type:
Normal
Submit
Reset
Tab order:
Style...
OK
Cancel
5 Select the type
6 Click OK

### Tip

**Instead of a plain text Submit button, you can use a picture instead. Just delete the Submit button which was automatically inserted, then select Picture... from the Form menu, and browse for an image.**

# Radio buttons

Radio buttons are usually grouped into sets of two or more. They are used when you want visitors to select only one of a range of possibilities, because only one in a set can be on at any time.

Radio buttons are grouped by giving all members the same **Group Name**; this is returned along with the **Value** of the button which was turned on by the visitor.

## Validation

You can set the **Validate...** feature to insist that at least one of a group of radio buttons be selected (**Data required**). In this dialog box you are prompted to supply a Display name, which is what visitors will see in an error message when they do not select any button.

## Basic steps

1 Right-click on the radio button and choose Form Field Properties…

2 Type the Group name.

3 Enter a Value to return if selected.

4 Decide whether this button is Selected or Not to begin with (use this to set a default option).

❑ Validation

5 Click Validate...

6 Type a Display Name.

7 Check Data Required.

8 Click OK.

2 Type the Group Name

3 Type a Value

Radio Button Properties

Group name: shaggy

Value: norville

Initial state: Selected / Not selected

Tab order:

Style... | Validate... | OK | Cancel

4 Selected at the start?

5 Click Validate...

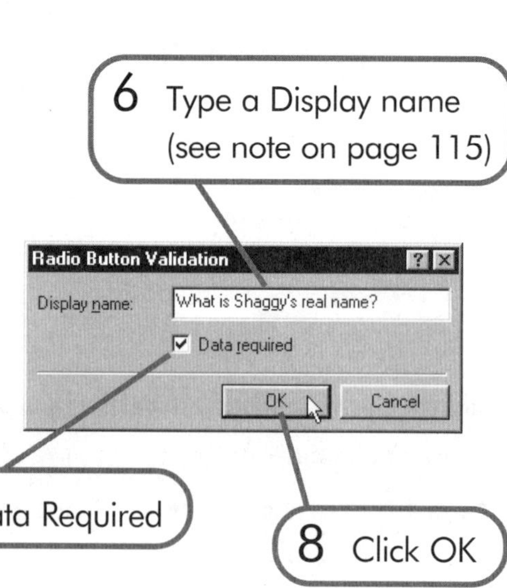
6 Type a Display name (see note on page 115)
Radio Button Validation
Display name: What is Shaggy's real name?
Data required
OK
Cancel
7 Check Data Required
8 Click OK

Basic steps

1 Type a prompt for the Check Box.

2 Select the Check Box from the Form menu.

3 Right-click on the Check Box and choose Form Field Properties...

4 Type a Name for the Check Box.

5 Enter a Value to be returned if checked.

6 Decide whether the box is Checked or Not when first loaded.

7 Click OK.

# Check Boxes

These are for simple Yes/No responses to the questions or prompts you give. The Value you specify for the field will appear alongside its Name on your results page if the box is checked; if it is left unchecked, then no value is returned (see picture on page 105). Check Boxes cannot be given validation requirements.

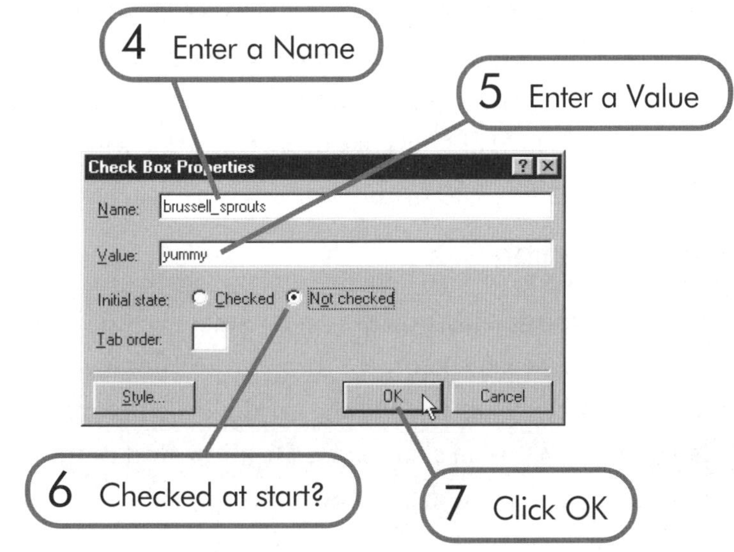
4 Enter a Name
5 Enter a Value
Check Box Properties
Name: brussell_sprouts
Value: yummy
Initial state: Checked Not checked
Tab order:
Style...
OK
Cancel
6 Checked at start?
7 Click OK

## Take note

**The Radio Button Validation Display names you have chosen for your reference may be confusing if you're not careful!**

**Make sure that you enter Display names that will make sense to your visitors:**

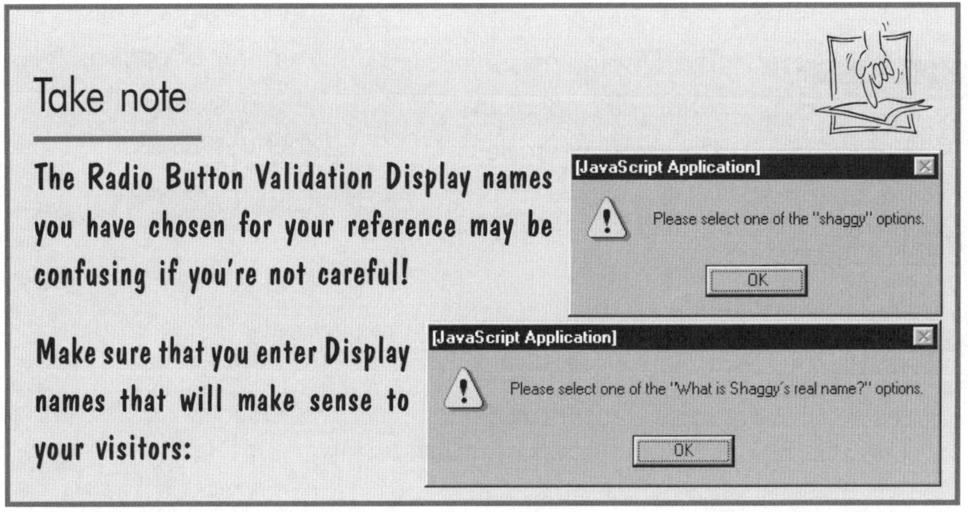
[JavaScript Application]
Please select one of the "shaggy" options.
OK
[JavaScript Application]
Please select one of the "What is Shaggy's real name?" options.
OK

# Drop-down menus

These are exactly like the menus on a toolbar, and are useful when you have a lot of options which would take up too much room to display as radio buttons or check boxes.

When a menu is first inserted, it is empty, so you will have to add the items which will appear in it, and their corresponding values, which will be returned to you in the form results file.

**Height** controls how the menu items are displayed. A height of 1 gives one item visible to begin with, and an arrow icon which 'drops-down' the menu. Any other height value, (e.g. 4) displays that number (4) of items in a deeper window with a set of scroll bars along the side.

## Menu validation

As with other form fields, you can require that at least one item be selected from a menu before the form can be submitted. Click **Validate...** to bring up the Validation dialog box, and click **Data required**. You can also choose **Disallow first item** – this allows you to use the item which is initially visible to write a helpful prompt, such as 'Click for a list of options'.

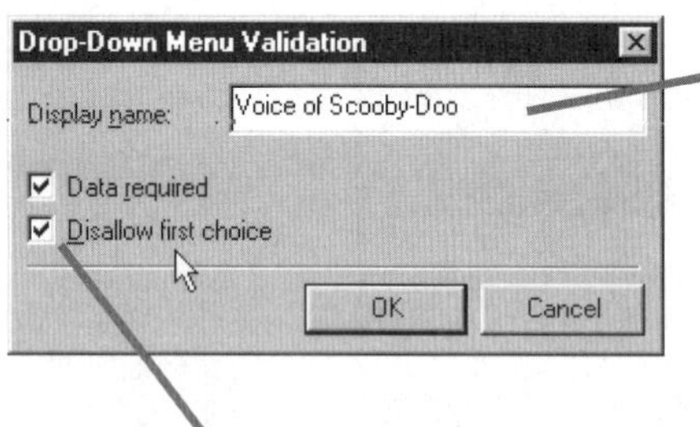

Drop-Down Menu Validation
Display name:
Voice of Scooby-Doo
Data required
Disallow first choice
OK
Cancel


The Display name is what will appear in the error message

Use if you want to write a prompt at the top of the menu display

## Basic steps

1 Select Drop-Down Menu from the Form menu.
2 Right-click on the menu and choose Form Field Properties…
3 Type a Name for the menu.
4 Click Add… to open the Add Choice dialog box.
5 Type a menu item.
6 Click Specify Value if you want to change the suggested one.
7 Choose whether this option is Selected or Not to begin with.
8 Set a Height – this is the number of options showing when the menu is closed.
9 Click OK.

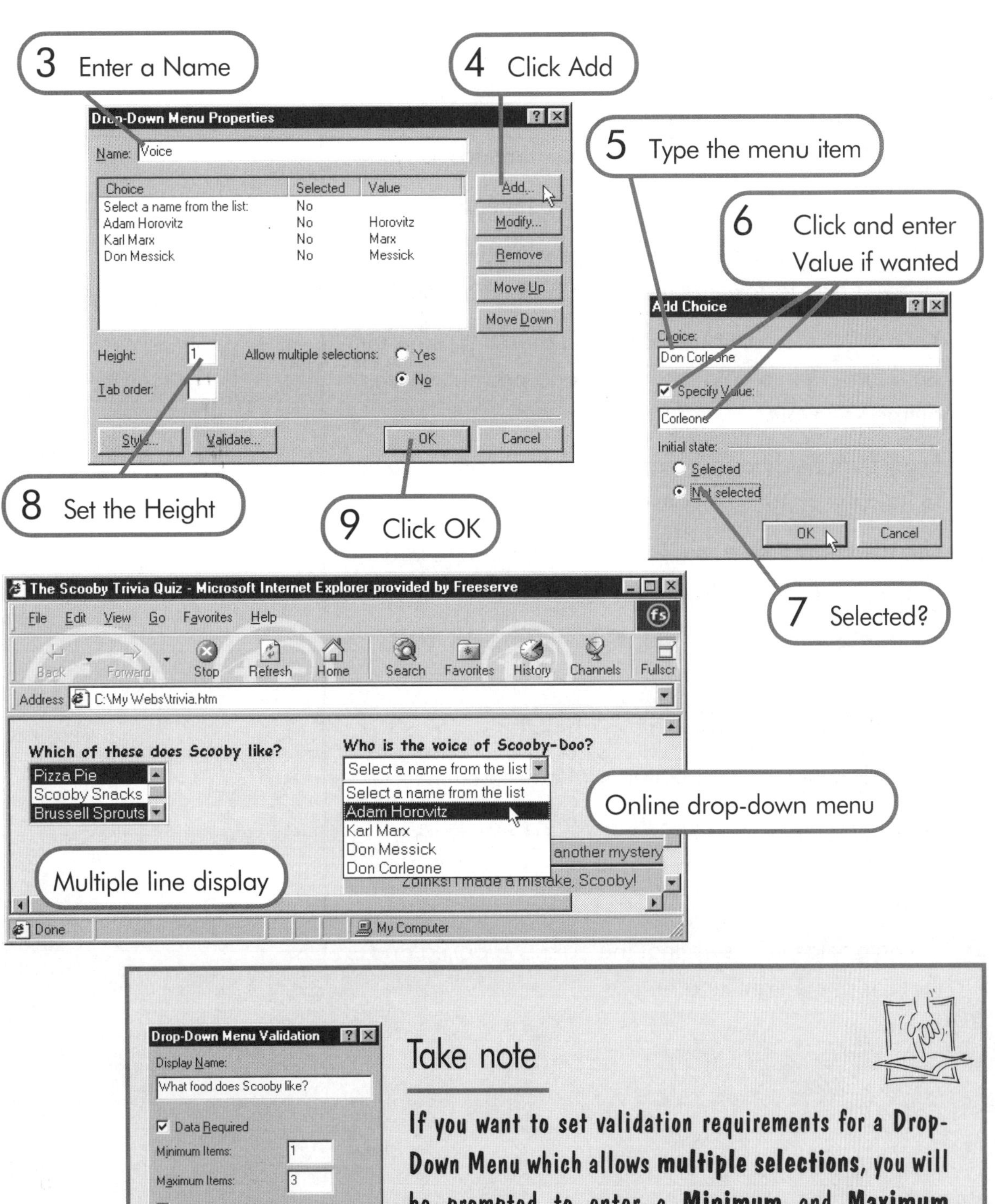
3 Enter a Name
4 Click Add
5 Type the menu item
6 Click and enter Value if wanted
7 Selected?
8 Set the Height
9 Click OK
Online drop-down menu
Multiple line display

## Take note

**If you want to set validation requirements for a Drop-Down Menu which allows multiple selections, you will be prompted to enter a Minimum and Maximum number of selections which a user can make.**

# Summary

- ❑ Use forms to collect information about visitors and to allow them to submit feedback and questions to you.
- ❑ Insert fields through the Insert – Forms menu.
- ❑ Inserting any form field into a page will automatically create a new form with Submit and Reset buttons.
- ❑ You can also create an empty form area first, then set up a table in it to hold your fields and prompts in an atttractive layout.
- ❑ Every form field has a name, to identify it, and a value to hold the visitor's response.
- ❑ Use the Form Properties dialog box to organise your form.
- ❑ Use text boxes to ask for complex information from visitors.
- ❑ Submit or Reset the form with push buttons.
- ❑ Replace the text Submit button with a Picture.
- ❑ Specify Values to be returned to you as simple responses to radio buttons, check boxes and drop-down menus.
- ❑ Validate fields to ensure that the data is supplied and that it is of the right kind.

# 8 Components

# Include Page

## Basic steps

FrontPage has several small program scripts called **Components** which perform various functions. Some are used essentially as labour-saving devices in the construction of FrontPage webs, such as **Include**, **Table of Contents, Substitution, Shared Borders** and **Navigation Bars**.

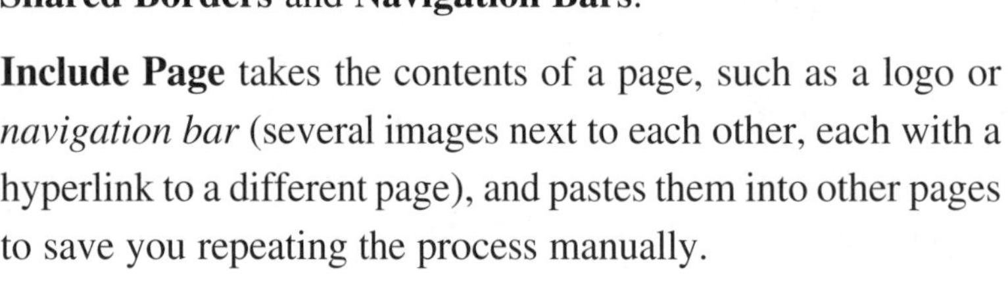

**Include Page** takes the contents of a page, such as a logo or *navigation bar* (several images next to each other, each with a hyperlink to a different page), and pastes them into other pages to save you repeating the process manually.

A page of included elements is not a web page in its own right – or rather, it is not one you want people to have access to – so save it in the *_private* folder.

1. Create a New Page.
2. Write into it the elements that you want to include on other pages.
3. Save the page in the _private folder.
4. Position the cursor where you want the included elements.
5. Choose Component – Include Page ... from the Insert menu.
6. Browse... for the page to include.
7. Click OK.

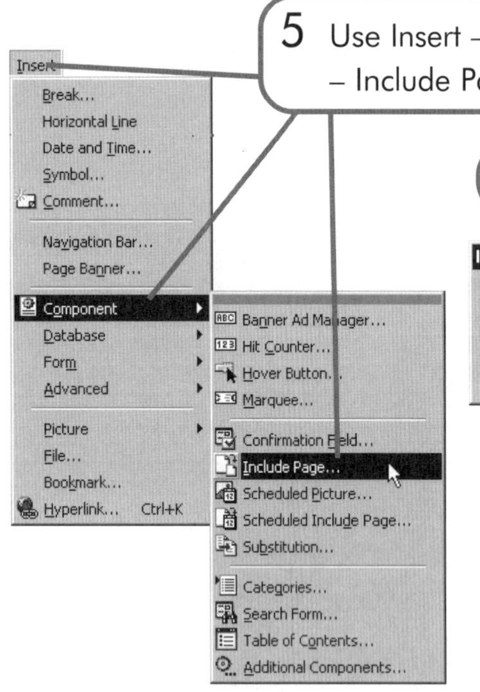
5 Use Insert – Component – Include Page
Insert
Break...
Horizontal Line
Date and Time...
Symbol...
Comment...
Navigation Bar...
Page Banner...
Component
Database
Form
Advanced
Picture
File...
Bookmark...
Hyperlink... Ctrl+K
Banner Ad Manager...
Hit Counter...
Hover Button...
Marquee...
Confirmation Field...
Include Page...
Scheduled Picture...
Scheduled Include Page...
Substitution...
Categories...
Search Form...
Table of Contents...
Additional Components...

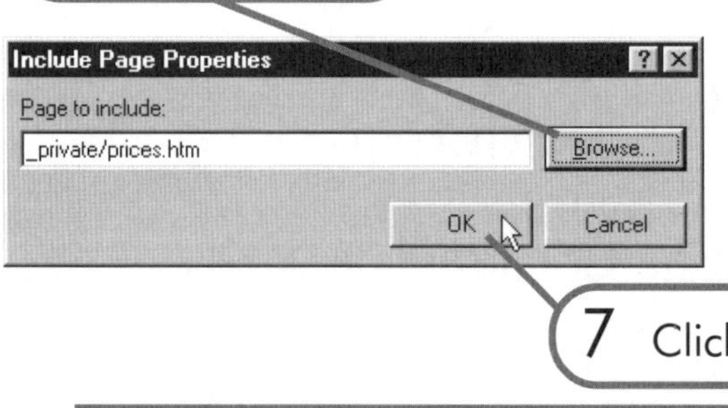
6 Get the page
Include Page Properties
Page to include:
_private/prices.htm
Browse...
OK
Cancel
7 Click OK

### Take note

**When you update or alter the contents of an 'included' page and save it to your web, all pages containing it are supplied with the new version.**

Basic steps

# Table of contents

1 Open the Insert – Component menu.

2 Choose Table of Contents.

3 Browse... for a starting page (usually index.htm or default.htm).

4 Set the Heading Size.

5 Set the options you want.

6 Click OK.

Creates a table of contents with hyperlinks to all the pages on your web. There are three options for tables of contents:

- **Show each page only once** – prevents FrontPage displaying a page every time it finds a link into it.
- **Show pages with no incoming hyperlinks** – displays pages even if they have no links from other pages to them.
- **Recompute table of contents when any other page is edited** – makes sure that it remains up to date when you edit your web.

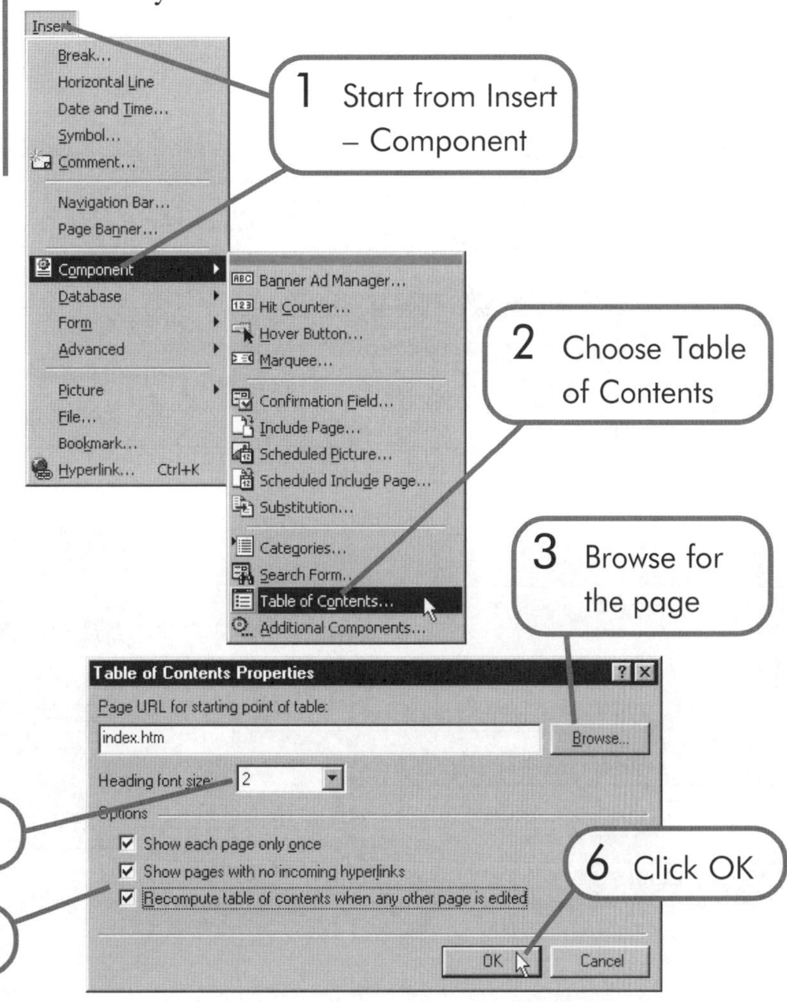
1 Start from Insert – Component
2 Choose Table of Contents
3 Browse for the page
4 Set the Heading Size
5 Set options
6 Click OK
Insert
Break...
Horizontal Line
Date and Time...
Symbol...
Comment...
Navigation Bar...
Page Banner...
Component
Database
Form
Advanced
Picture
File...
Bookmark...
Hyperlink... Ctrl+K
Banner Ad Manager...
Hit Counter...
Hover Button...
Marquee...
Confirmation Field...
Include Page...
Scheduled Picture...
Scheduled Include Page...
Substitution...
Categories...
Search Form...
Table of Contents...
Additional Components...
Table of Contents Properties
Page URL for starting point of table:
index.htm
Browse...
Heading font size: 2
Options
Show each page only once
Show pages with no incoming hyperlinks
Recompute table of contents when any other page is edited
OK
Cancel

**Take note**

**Don't worry if the table of contents appears to be stuck. It always looks the same in the FrontPage, but if you Preview the page in a browser, you will see how it works.**

# Substitutions

## Basic steps

Names, addresses, slogans – anything which is used regularly can be assigned as a parameter, which can then be pasted into a page as a Substitution component, acting much as AutoText in Word. Parameters are set from the Web Settings dialog box.

1 Choose Web Settings… from the Tools menu.
2 Click on the Parameters tab.
3 Click Add…
4 Type a Name to identify the substitution.
5 Type a Value – the text to be substituted.
6 Click OK.
7 Click Apply.
8 Click OK.


1 Choose Tools – Web Settings
2 Go to Parameters
3 Click Add
4 Enter a Name
5 Type the Value to substitute

**Web Settings**

General | Parameters | Advanced | Language | Navigation | Database

| Name | Value |
|------|-------|
| Slogan | You won't get a cheaper table unless y... |
| Discount | 50% discount available to the over-90's ... |
| Contact | For sales details, call Mr Aesop on 0465... |
| Address | Aesop's Tables, 4 Leggid Place, Wobbl... |

Add...
Modify...
Remove

OK    Cancel    Apply

**Add Name and Value**

Name: quality

Value: This table is made from the finest quality materials available from demolition yards, and tested to rigorous standards, some of which it may even have passed.

OK    Cancel

6 Click OK
7 Click Apply
8 Click OK

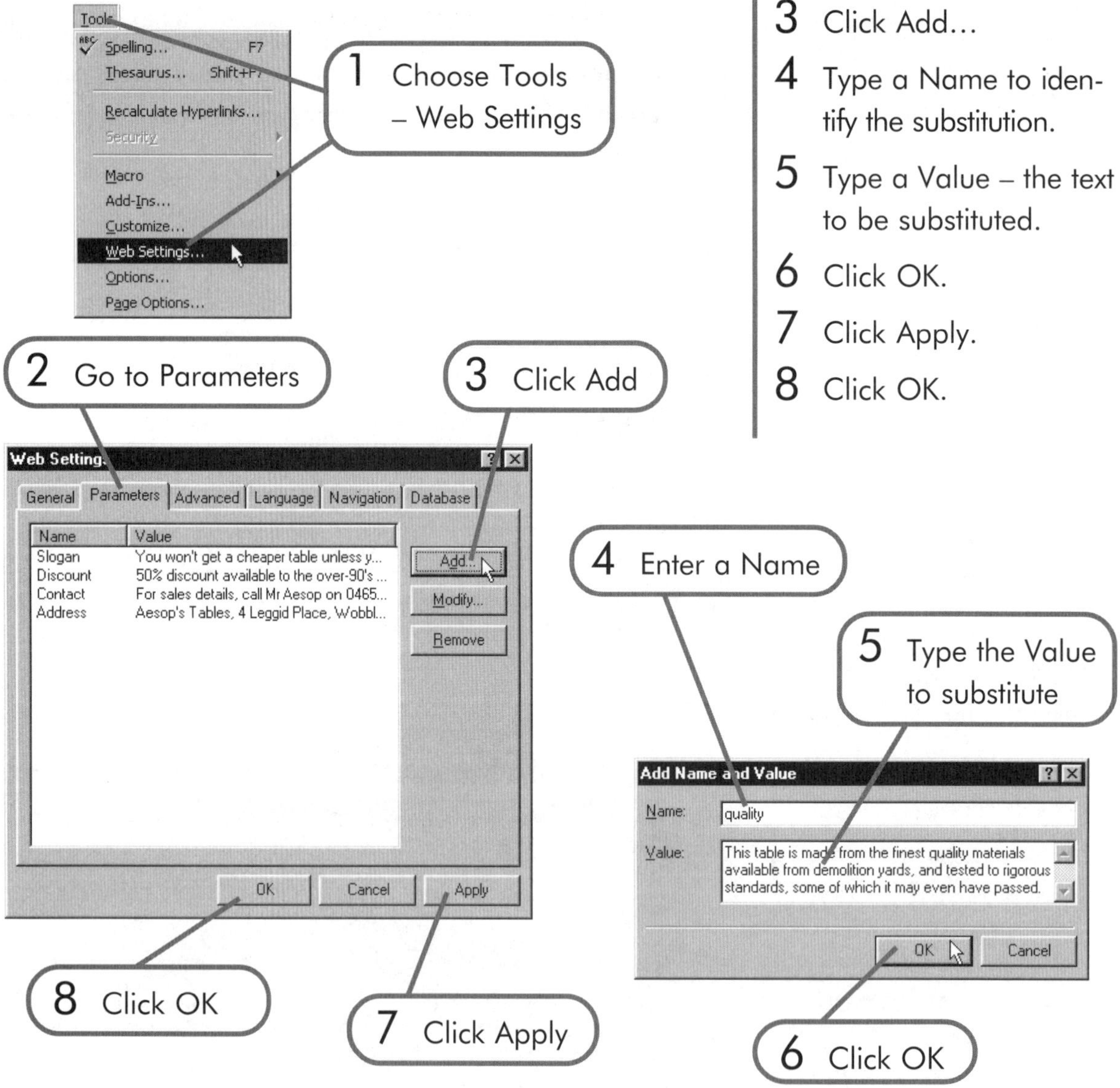

## Basic steps

1. Position the cursor where you want the substituted text.
2. Open the Insert – Component menu.
3. Select Substitution.
4. Choose a variable from the drop-down menu.
5. Click OK.

## Using substitutions

While the process of inserting substitutions is simple, it takes long enough to render itself rather pointless if the substituted text is only a few words – by the time you have taken your hands off the keyboard and worked through a couple of dialog boxes with the mouse, you might as well have carried on typing.

Substitutions are perhaps most useful when they are done by FrontPage – when you generate a web from a template, various details such as your name and address are made into parameters and substituted into your pages automatically.

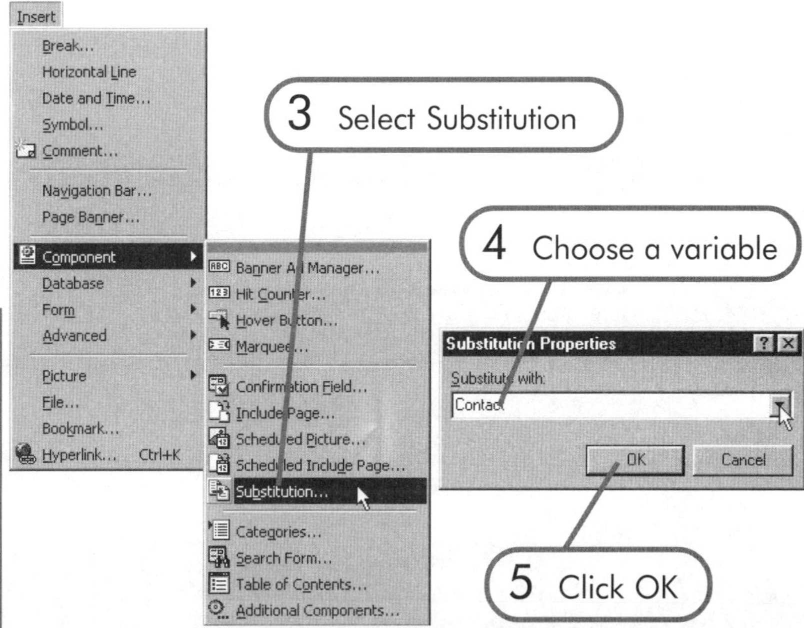
3 Select Substitution
4 Choose a variable
5 Click OK
Insert
Break...
Horizontal Line
Date and Time...
Symbol...
Comment...
Navigation Bar...
Page Banner...
Component
Database
Form
Advanced
Picture
File...
Bookmark...
Hyperlink... Ctrl+K
Hit Counter...
Confirmation Field...
Substitution...
Categories...
Search Form...
Table of Contents...
Additional Components...
Substitution Properties
Contact
OK
Cancel

### Take note

**Some Components, such as stamping the date and time of the last update, or organising responses from forms, run on the server which hosts your web. These require your ISP to support FrontPage Extensions, and not many do at present. Talk to your ISP before adding any of these.**

### Tip

**Substitution are not quite like Include components – they are a cut-down version, with the disadvantage of only substituting text, not images, but an Include takes up the whole width of the page, whereas a substitution will slot in anywhere.**

# Scheduled components

## Basic steps

These display a **Picture**, or the contents of an **Include page**, between certain dates and times, and not any other time. You might use these to ensure that a 'Sale Ends 6th January' sign doesn't outlive its usefulness, for instance. A scheduled component can be replaced by an alternative image or page when its time is up, or simply removed.

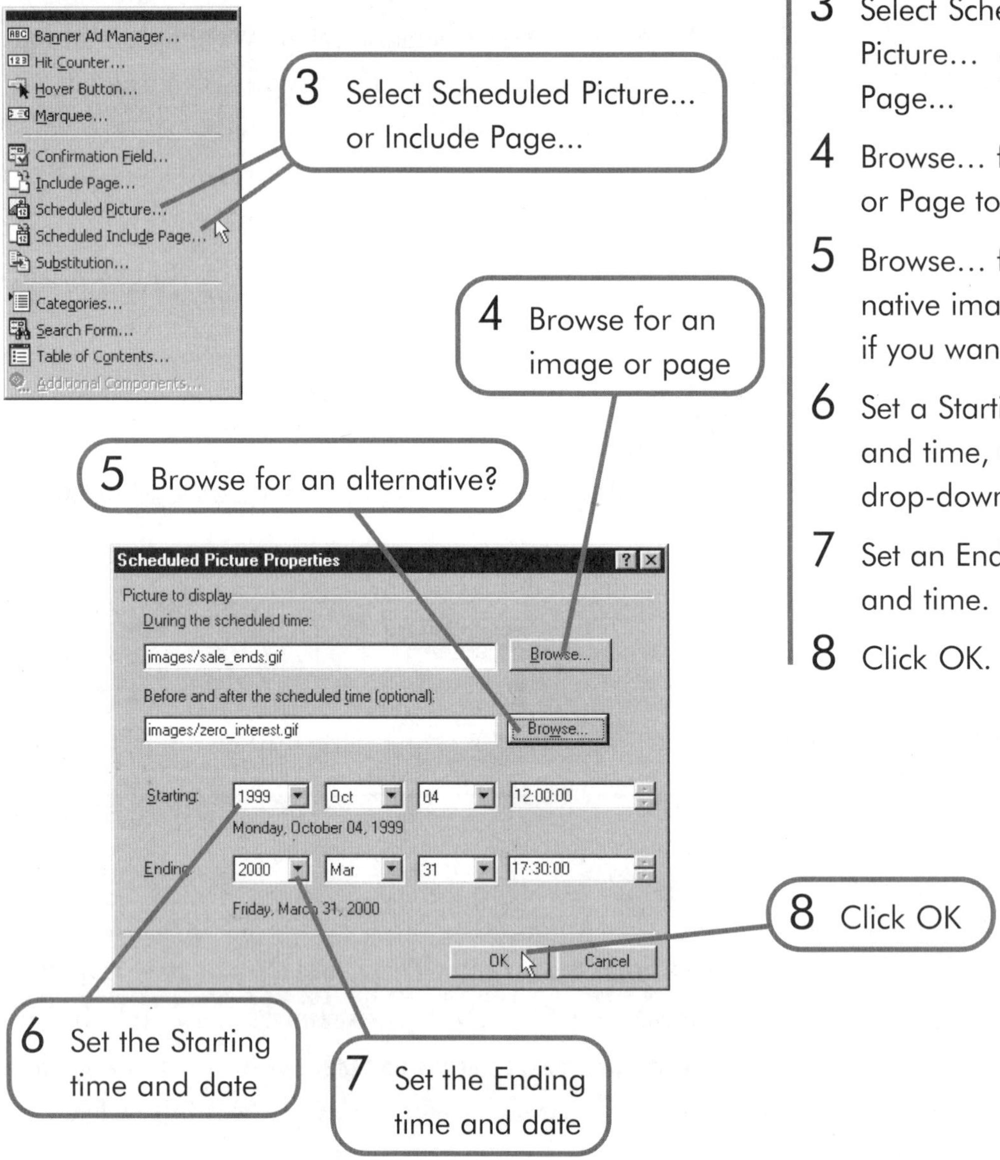

1 Position the cursor where you want the Picture/Include Page.

2 Open the Insert - Component menu.

3 Select Scheduled Picture... or Include Page...

4 Browse... for a Picture or Page to include.

5 Browse... for an alternative image or page if you want one.

6 Set a Starting date and time, using the drop-down menus.

7 Set an Ending date and time.

8 Click OK.

Banner Ad Manager...
Hit Counter...
Hover Button...
Marquee...
Confirmation Field...
Include Page...
Scheduled Picture...
Scheduled Include Page...
Substitution...
Categories...
Search Form...
Table of Contents...
Additional Components...

3 Select Scheduled Picture... or Include Page...

4 Browse for an image or page

5 Browse for an alternative?

Scheduled Picture Properties
Picture to display
During the scheduled time:
images/sale_ends.gif
Browse...
Before and after the scheduled time (optional):
images/zero_interest.gif
Browse...
Starting: 1999 Oct 04 12:00:00
Monday, October 04, 1999
Ending: 2000 Mar 31 17:30:00
Friday, March 31, 2000
OK Cancel

8 Click OK

6 Set the Starting time and date

7 Set the Ending time and date

Basic steps

# Shared borders

1 Select Shared Borders... from the Format menu.

2 Apply the borders to All pages or just the Current page.

3 Tick the ones to share.

4 Tick Include navigation buttons if required (only with All pages).

5 Click OK.

6 Click inside the dotted border areas and edit as required.

These are set up in the margins of pages to contain information which you want on many of your web's pages; e.g. a footer with copyright information, or a panel of navigation buttons (see the next pages). When you change a shared border on one page, it is automatically updated on all other pages which share it.

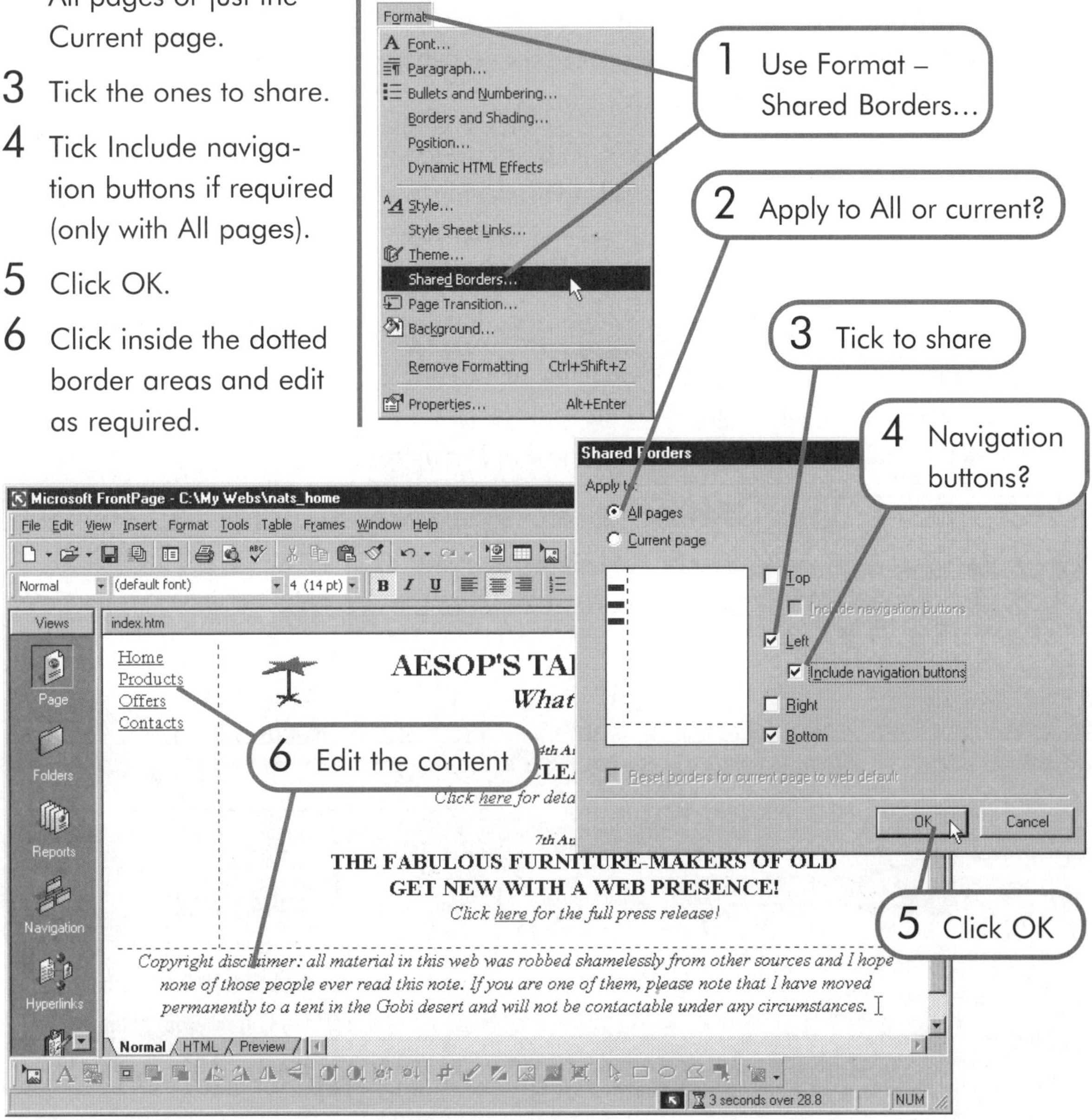

1 Use Format – Shared Borders...

2 Apply to All or current?

3 Tick to share

4 Navigation buttons?

5 Click OK

6 Edit the content

# Navigation structure

## Basic steps

Navigation bars link a web together in a hierarchical structure – and FrontPage will create and maintain the links for you. Before you create a Navigation bar, you must set up a hierarchy for the navigation bar generator to follow. This is done in **Navigation view**: files from the **Folder List** are dragged into the main window, and moved around until a line joins the right pages. The line shows that a link will be created between those pages when you use the **Navigation bar** feature.

The structure is arranged visually in levels, and uses the terms 'parent' and 'child' to describe the relationship between pages. A 'parent' page might be a category such as *Products.* Beneath that you would want to list its 'children': *Products1*, *2*, *3*, etc.These may have lower level pages, with further details.

You might then have a new category of the same importance as *Products*, such as *News*, and arranged on the same level. Child pages of *News* would be on the same level as those of *Products*.

1 Click the Navigation view button.

2 Make sure the Folders List is open.

3 Click on a file and drag it into the main window, moving it near a page until the dotted line joins them.

4 Release the mouse button.

5 Repeat for other files.

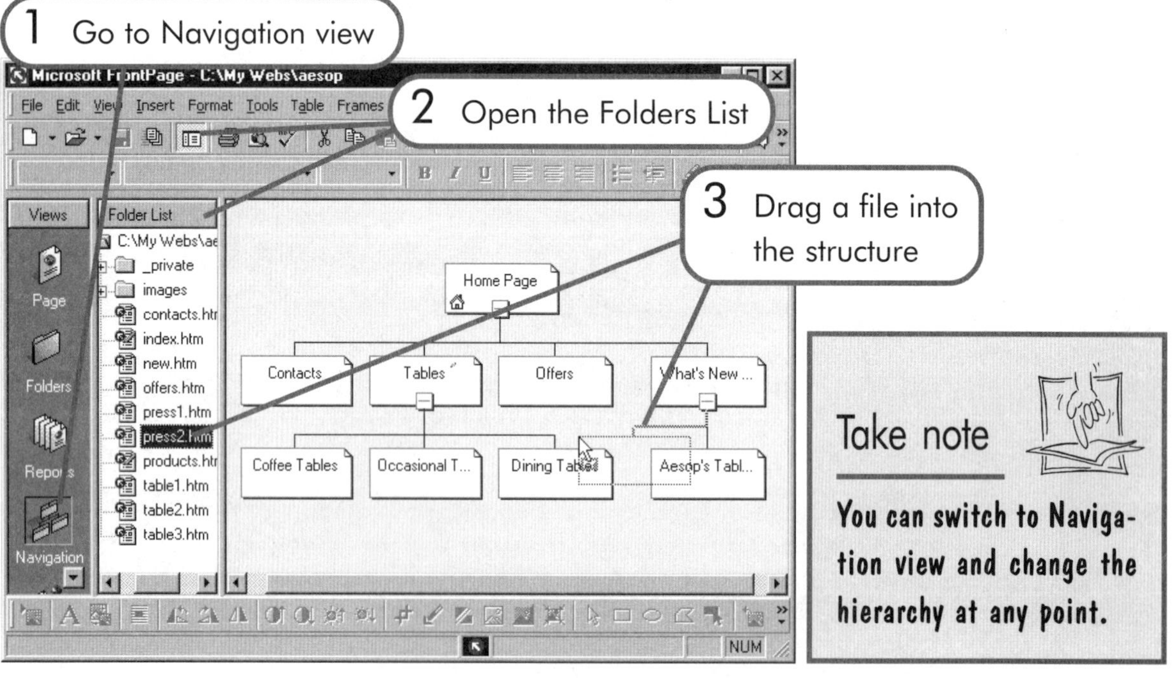
1 Go to Navigation view
2 Open the Folders List
3 Drag a file into the structure
Microsoft FrontPage - C:\My Webs\aesop
File Edit View Insert Format Tools Table Frames
Views
Page
Folders
Reports
Navigation
Folder List
C:\My Webs\ae
_private
images
contacts.htm
index.htm
new.htm
offers.htm
press1.htm
press2.htm
products.htm
table1.htm
table2.htm
table3.htm
Home Page
Contacts
Tables
Offers
What's New ...
Coffee Tables
Occasional T...
Dining Tables
Aesop's Tabl...
NUM

### Take note

**You can switch to Navigation view and change the hierarchy at any point.**

## Basic steps

1 Open your home page in Page view.
2 Create a shared border – check All pages and Include navigation buttons.
3 Right-click the prompt and choose Navigation Bar Properties…
4 Choose a structure.
5 Specify Additional pages to include.
6 Set the Orientation and appearance.
7 Click OK.

## Navigation bars

Navigation bars use the hierarchy set up in Navigation view to create a set of links for each page. The bar can be created in a Shared border, and you have a choice of structures based on the various levels and parent/child relationships. Click on one to see which pages will be included using that structure.

Navigation links can be buttons if using a **Theme** (see page 39), or plain text. In either case, the text used is the name on the page in Navigation view, and can only be changed in Navigation view.

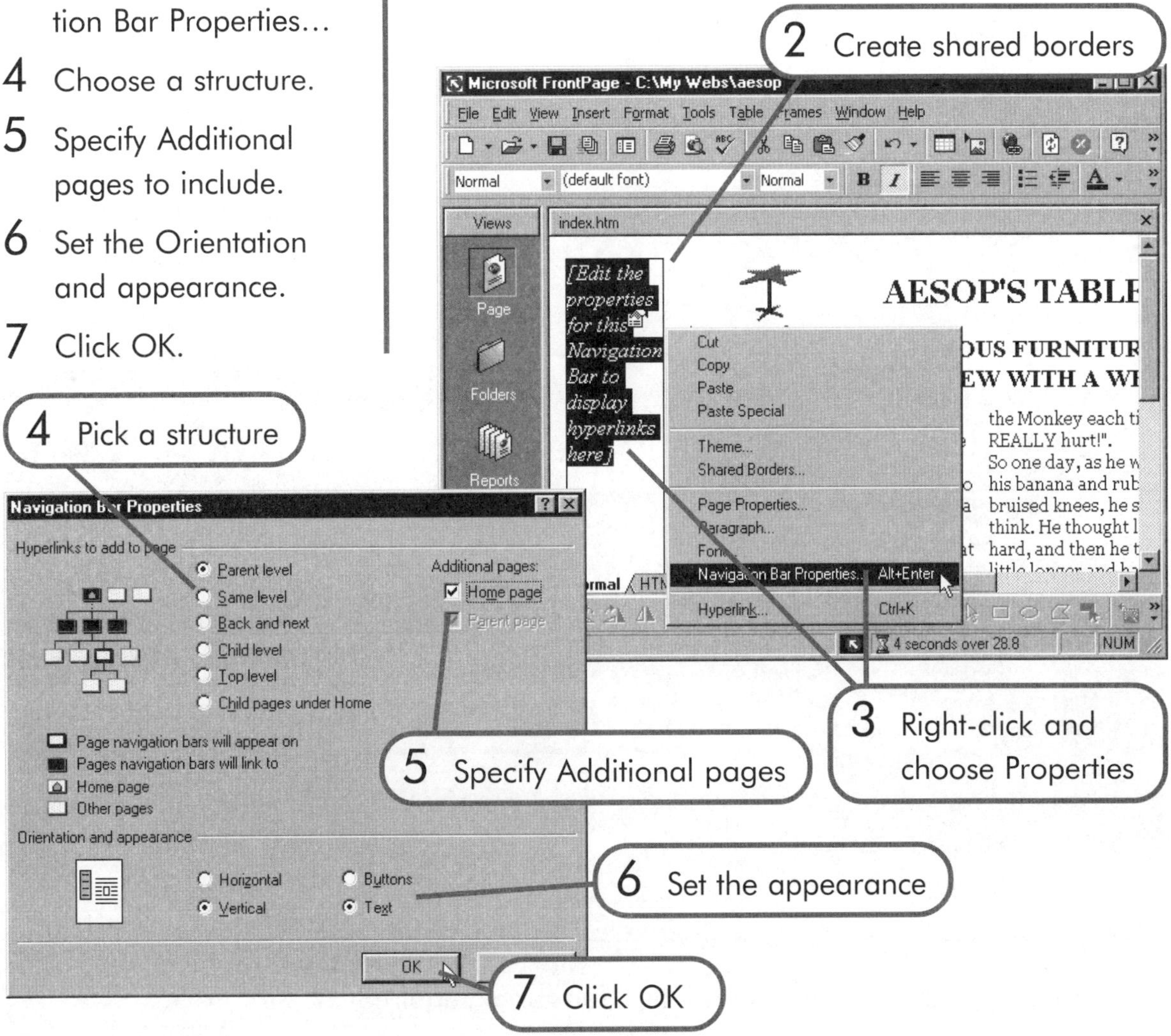

2 Create shared borders

3 Right-click and choose Properties

4 Pick a structure

5 Specify Additional pages

6 Set the appearance

7 Click OK

# Date and Time

## Basic steps

Your pages can have a small note which states when the page was last edited (and saved to the web) or automatically updated (i.e. a change was made to another page which affects this page because a component refers to it).

However, this Component only inserts a date and/or time – you will have to write some explanatory text around it, as in the example below.

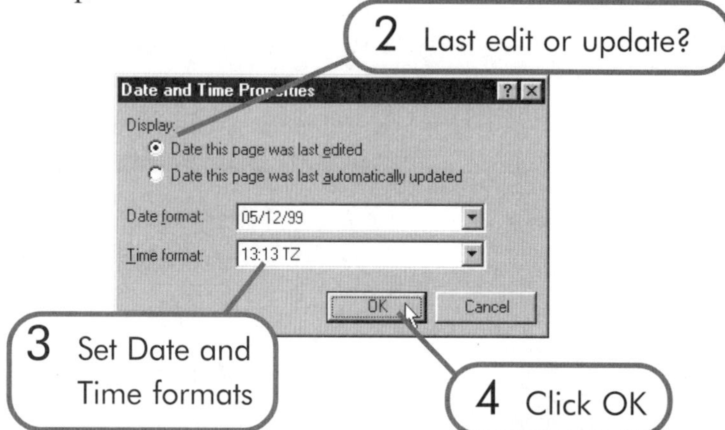
2 Last edit or update?
Date and Time Properties
Display:
Date this page was last edited
Date this page was last automatically updated
Date format:
05/12/99
Time format:
13:13 TZ
OK
Cancel
3 Set Date and Time formats
4 Click OK

1 From the Insert menu, select Date and Time...

2 Set it to display when it was last edited or updated by FrontPage.

3 Choose Date and/or Time display formats from the drop-down menus.

❑ If you choose a time display with TZ after it, this shows the time zone you are in.

4 Click OK.

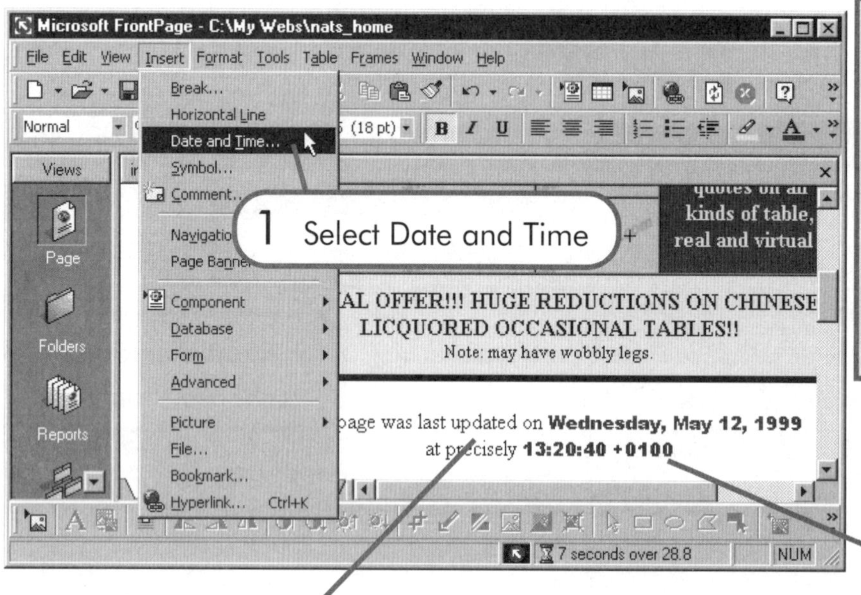
Microsoft FrontPage - C:\My Webs\nats_home
File Edit View Insert Format Tools Table Frames Window Help
Break...
Horizontal Line
Date and Time...
Symbol...
Comment...
Navigation
Page Banner
Component
Database
Form
Advanced
Picture
File...
Bookmark...
Hyperlink... Ctrl+K
1 Select Date and Time
kinds of table, real and virtual
AL OFFER!!! HUGE REDUCTIONS ON CHINESE LICQUORED OCCASIONAL TABLES!!
Note: may have wobbly legs.
page was last updated on Wednesday, May 12, 1999 at precisely 13:20:40 +0100
Views
Page
Folders
Reports
7 seconds over 28.8
NUM
This is GMT +1 hour

Add text around the Date and Time, and format as required

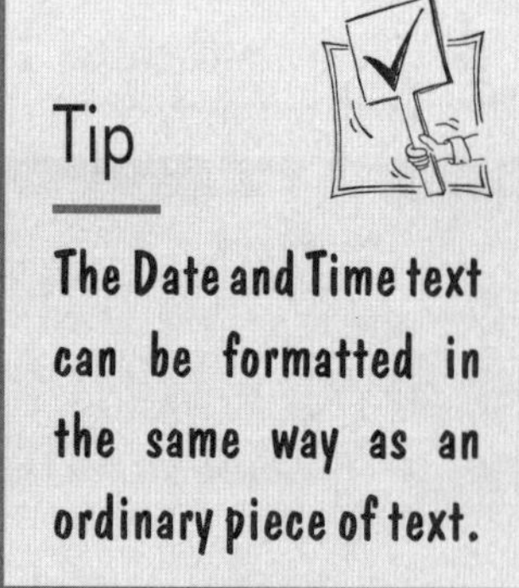

## Tip

**The Date and Time text can be formatted in the same way as an ordinary piece of text.**

# Search Form

1 Open the Insert – Component menu and select Search Form...

2 Type a prompt in the Label for Input field.

3 Specify the Width in characters of the field.

4 Type Labels for the Search and Clear buttons.

5 Click Search Results.

6 Tick the Display options if wanted.

7 Click OK.

The **Search Form** component allows visitors to search your web (excluding the **_private/** folder). The search returns the number of documents containing the keywords, with links to those pages. You can also choose to display extra information:

- **Score** – shows how close it matches the keywords.
- **File Date** – indicates when the page was last modified.
- **File Size** – gives the file size in kilobytes.

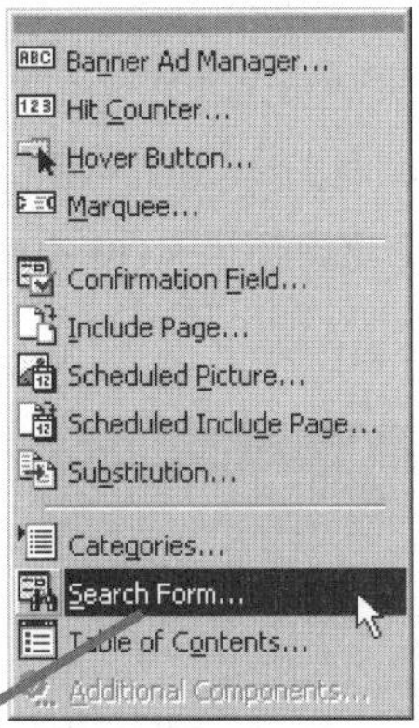

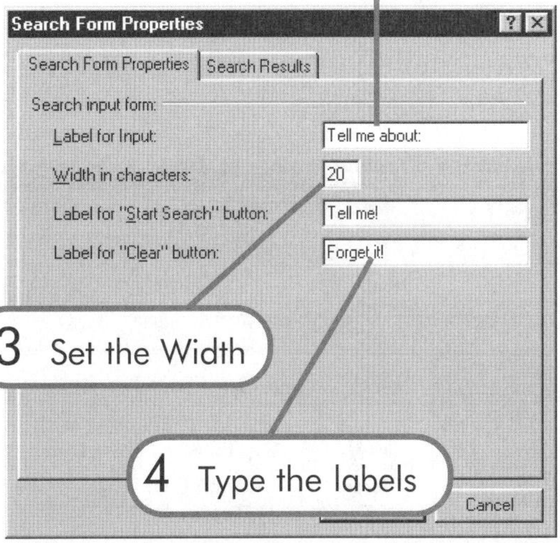

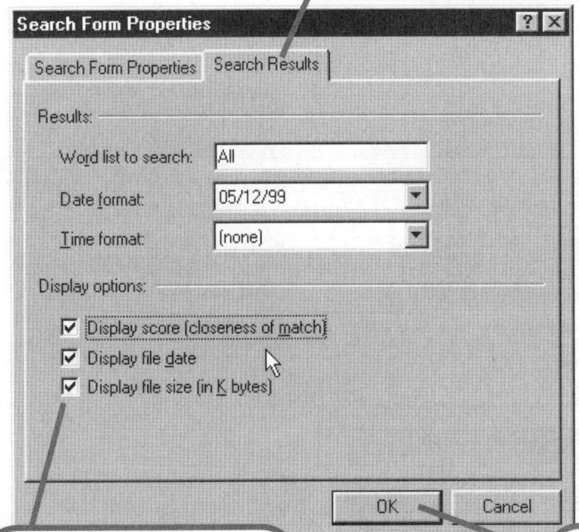

1 Select Search Form

2 Type a prompt

3 Set the Width

4 Type the labels

5 Go to Search Results

6 Display these?

7 Click OK

The Search Form, showing the prompt and button labels

# Confirmation fields

## Basic steps

When a form is submitted, you can opt to display a confirmation page, which might repeat the information for the visitor to double-check, or thank them for sending it. A confirmation field is associated with a named form field, and displays the value which the visitor has just submitted in that field. For example, where [Name] appears in the example below, the user who receives the confirmation page will read whatever he or she typed into the 'Name' field.

Confirmation fields can be inserted wherever you want; once they are there, you can change their size, font and colour – and with them the properties of the text which the user sees on the confirmation page.

1 Put the cursor where you want the field.

2 Open the Insert – Component menu and select Confirmation field…

3 Type the name of an existing form field.

4 Click OK.

5 When the page is complete, save it in the _private/ folder.

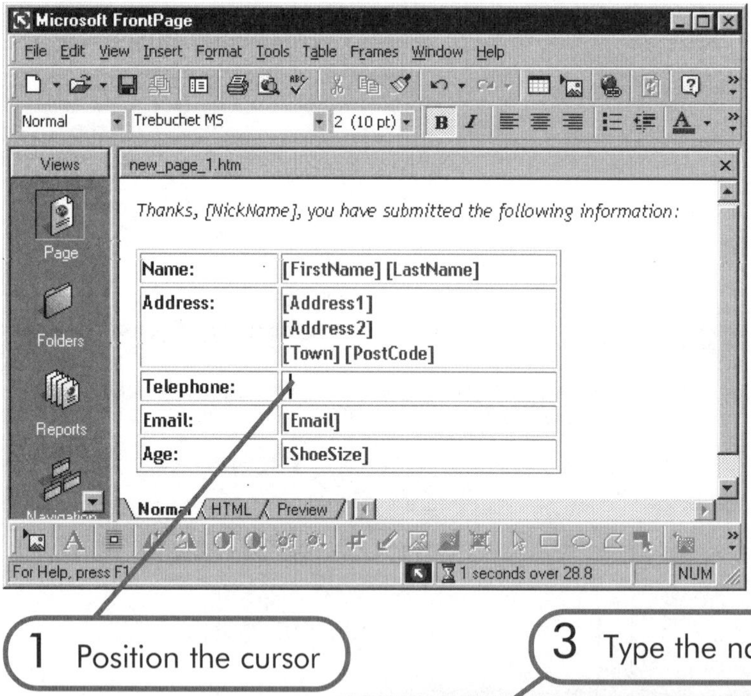

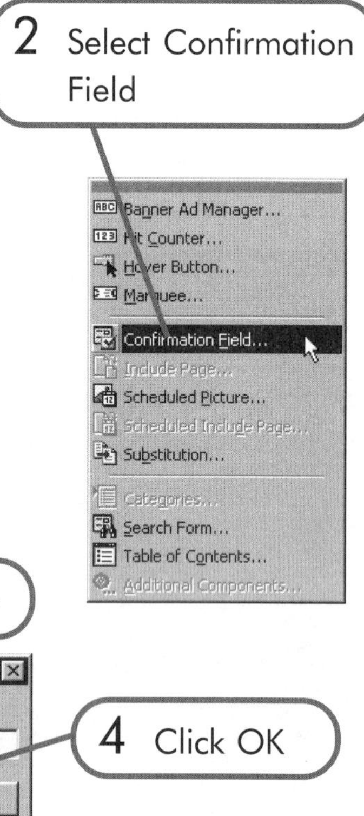
2 Select Confirmation Field
Banner Ad Manager...
Hit Counter...
Hover Button...
Marquee...
Confirmation Field...
Include Page...
Scheduled Picture...
Scheduled Include Page...
Substitution...
Categories...
Search Form...
Table of Contents...
Additional Components...

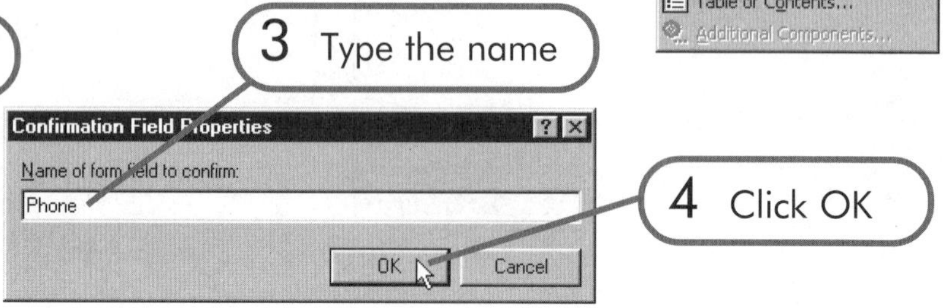

1 Position the cursor

3 Type the name

4 Click OK

## Basic steps

1. Right-click on the input form and choose Form Properties...
2. Click Options...
3. Switch to the Confirmation Page tab.
4. Browse... for the confirmation page.
5. Click OK.
6. Click OK again.

## Linking it to a form

Once you have a confirmation page, you will need to edit the appropriate input form to tell it to return a confirmation page to the user after they have submitted it.

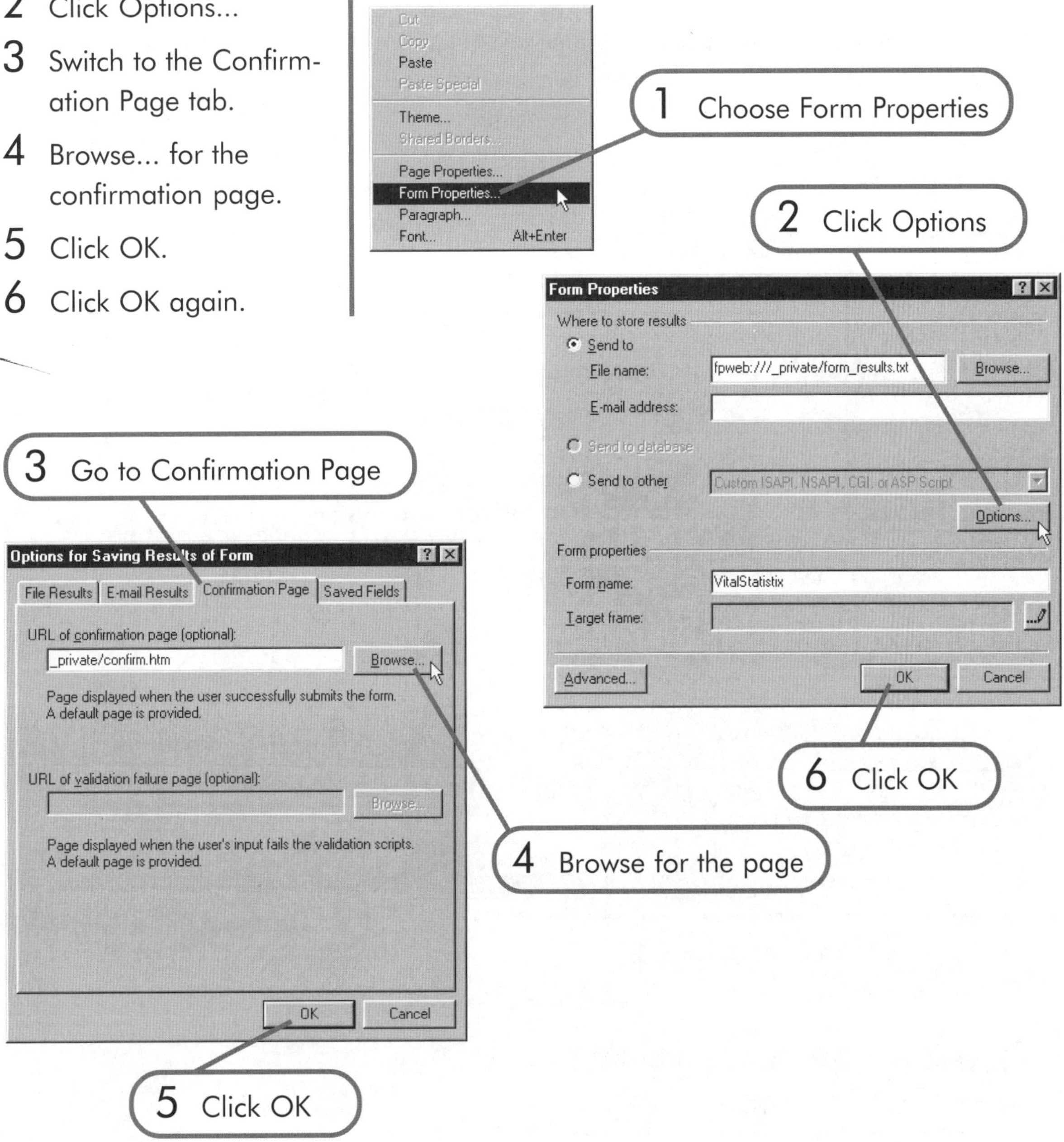

1 Choose Form Properties

2 Click Options

6 Click OK

4 Browse for the page

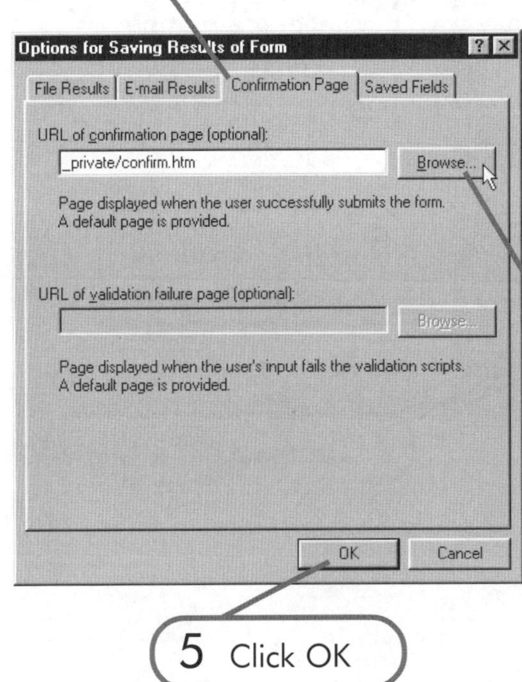
3 Go to Confirmation Page
Options for Saving Results of Form
File Results
E-mail Results
Confirmation Page
Saved Fields
URL of confirmation page (optional):
_private/confirm.htm
Browse...
Page displayed when the user successfully submits the form. A default page is provided.
URL of validation failure page (optional):
Browse...
Page displayed when the user's input fails the validation scripts. A default page is provided.
OK
Cancel
5 Click OK

# Hit Counter

## Basic steps

You can show visitors how popular your site is with a **Hit Counter**, which logs the number of times a page has been accessed by browsers.

You can either use one of the sample styles, or you can create an image of your own containing the digits 0–9. FrontPage will divide it into 9 equal segments and arrange the parts in the right order, so each of your digits must be the same width.

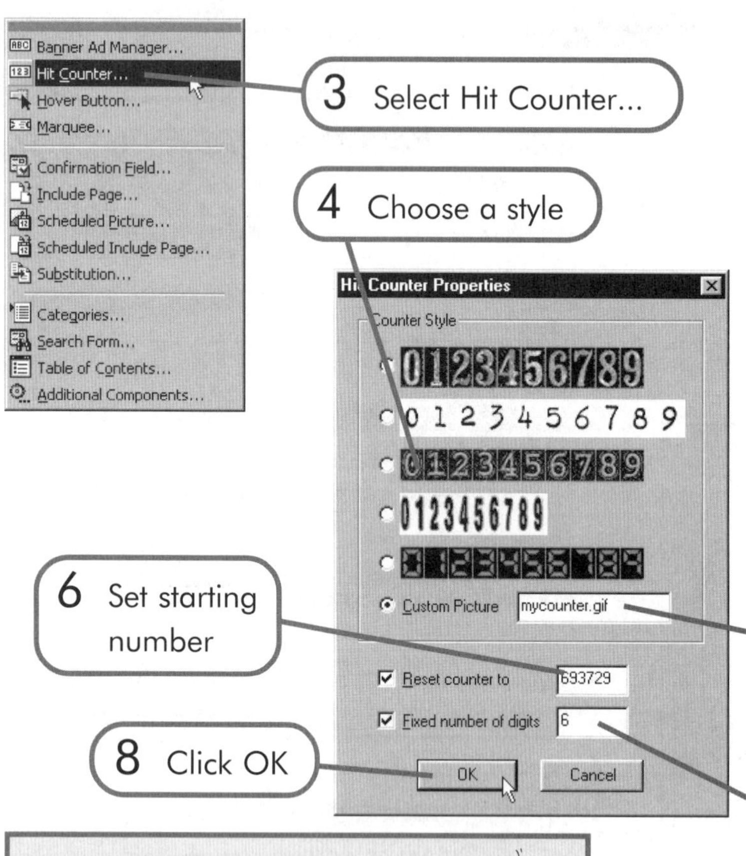

Banner Ad Manager...
Hit Counter...
Hover Button...
Marquee...
Confirmation Field...
Include Page...
Scheduled Picture...
Scheduled Include Page...
Substitution...
Categories...
Search Form...
Table of Contents...
Additional Components...
3 Select Hit Counter...
4 Choose a style
Hit Counter Properties
Counter Style
Custom Picture
mycounter.gif
Reset counter to
693729
Fixed number of digits
6
OK
Cancel
6 Set starting number
5 Type the counter image filename
8 Click OK
7 Set the digits to show


1 Position the cursor where you want the counter to appear.

2 Open the Insert – Component menu.

3 Select Hit Counter...

4 Choose a style.

*Or*

5 Type the filename of your own counter image.

6 Set the starting number (you terrible cheat, you!).

7 Set the number of digits to show.

8 Click OK.

### Take note

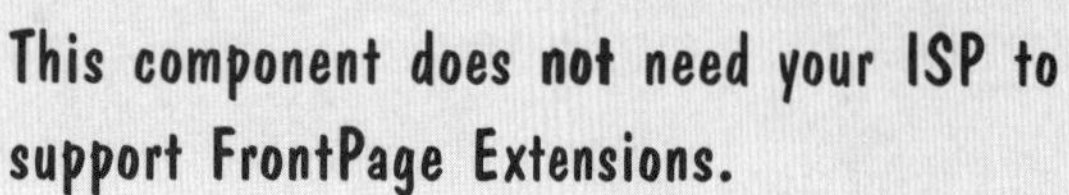

**This component does not need your ISP to support FrontPage Extensions.**

## Basic steps

1. Open the Insert – Component menu.
2. Select Banner Ad Manager…
3. Set the banner Width and Height.
4. Choose a Transition effect.
5. Set how long each image is displayed for.
6. Browse… for or type the name of the page to link to.
7. Click Add… and browse for each image.
8. Click Move Up and Down to sort the images (displayed in order from top to bottom).
9. Click OK.

# Banner Ad Manager

This is a Java applet which displays a number of images by timed rotation, and has some nice transition effects. You might use this if your page is sponsored by several people, or to display a selection of your own products.

The images can be used as a link to a page, but only to a single page, so if you want to link to several sponsors, you will need to create a page with a list of sponsors and links to each of them.

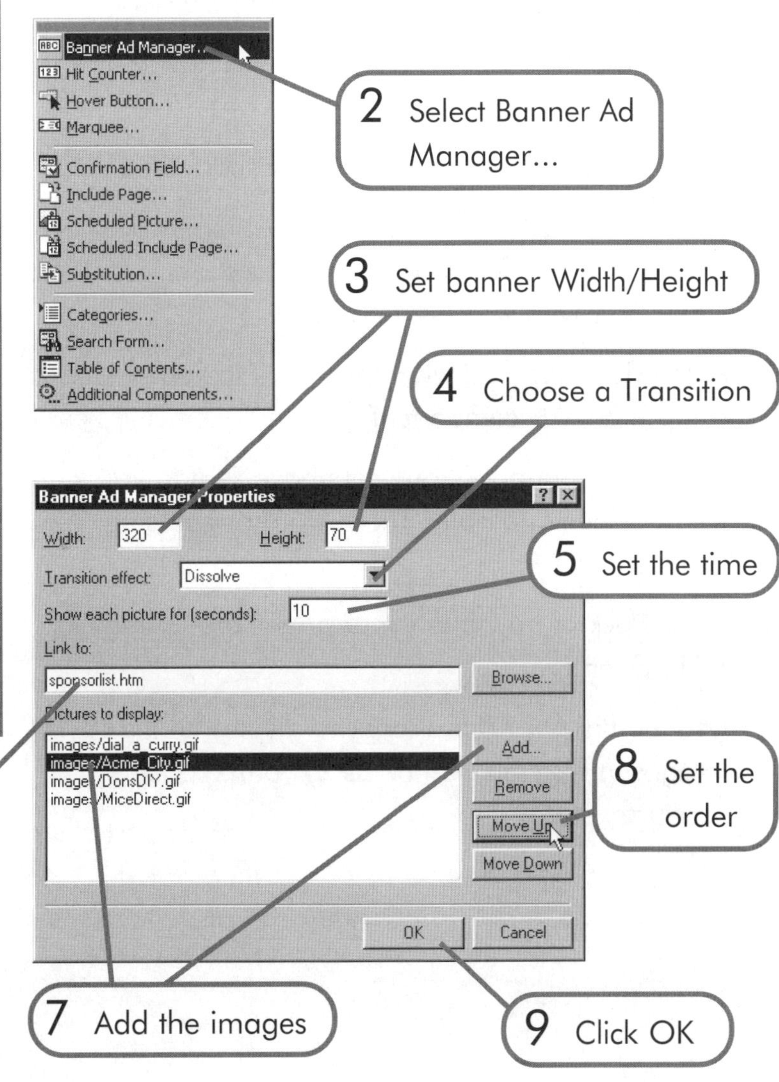

Banner Ad Manager...
Hit Counter...
Hover Button...
Marquee...
Confirmation Field...
Include Page...
Scheduled Picture...
Scheduled Include Page...
Substitution...
Categories...
Search Form...
Table of Contents...
Additional Components...
2 Select Banner Ad Manager...
3 Set banner Width/Height
4 Choose a Transition
Banner Ad Manager Properties
Width: 320
Height: 70
Transition effect: Dissolve
Show each picture for (seconds): 10
Link to:
sponsorlist.htm
Browse...
Pictures to display:
images/dial_a_curry.gif
images/Acme_City.gif
images/DonsDIY.gif
images/MiceDirect.gif
Add...
Remove
Move Up
Move Down
OK
Cancel
5 Set the time
6 Set the page to link to
7 Add the images
8 Set the order
9 Click OK

# Summary

- ❑ Use Include Page, Table of Contents and Substitution components to make your web-building a less tedious affair by getting FrontPage to perform routine tasks automatically.
- ❑ Insert Scheduled components to keep your web up to date.
- ❑ If you want the same material to be displayed on different pages, place it in a shared border.
- ❑ Use Navigation view to tell FrontPage how to link your web together.
- ❑ Add navigation bars to give your visitors an easy way to move between your pages.
- ❑ Use a Date and Time component to show visitors when your web was last updated.
- ❑ Allow visitors to find what they want in your web using a Search component.
- ❑ Confirm the information users have sent to you via a form, or personalise a 'Thank you' page using Confirmation fields.
- ❑ Keep track of how often your pages are visited with a Hit Counter.
- ❑ Use the Banner Ad Manager to display series of images in rotation with a link to your sponsors, products, etc.

# 9 Publishing your web

# Publishing your web

If your connection to the Internet is with a service provider who supports FrontPage Extensions, the process is very simple. In order to use them though, you may have to obtain a *sub-domain* (Web space which has a full http address of its own, rather than the */~username* format of personal space), so talk to your ISP even if you know that they support the Extensions.

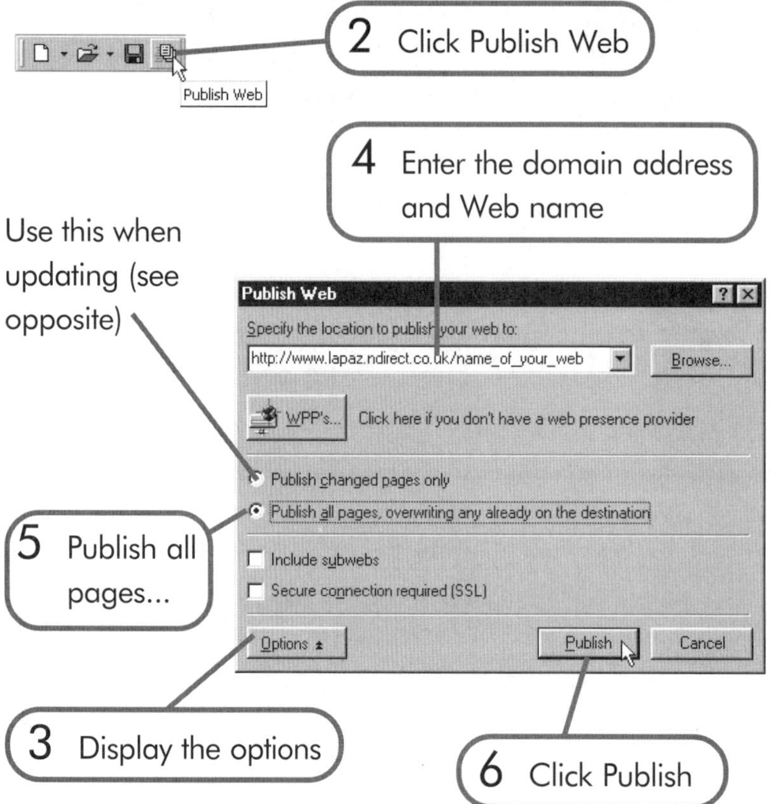

Publish Web
2 Click Publish Web
4 Enter the domain address and Web name
Use this when updating (see opposite)
Publish Web
Specify the location to publish your web to:
http://www.lapaz.ndirect.co.uk/name_of_your_web
Browse...
WPP's...
Click here if you don't have a web presence provider
Publish changed pages only
Publish all pages, overwriting any already on the destination
Include subwebs
Secure connection required (SSL)
Options
Publish
Cancel
5 Publish all pages...
3 Display the options
6 Click Publish


## Basic steps

1 Open the web you want to Publish.

2 Click the Publish Web button .

3 Click Options to open up the panel fully.

4 Type the address of the domain or sub-domain where your web will be published, including a forward slash and your web's name.

5 Select Publish all pages.

6 Click Publish.

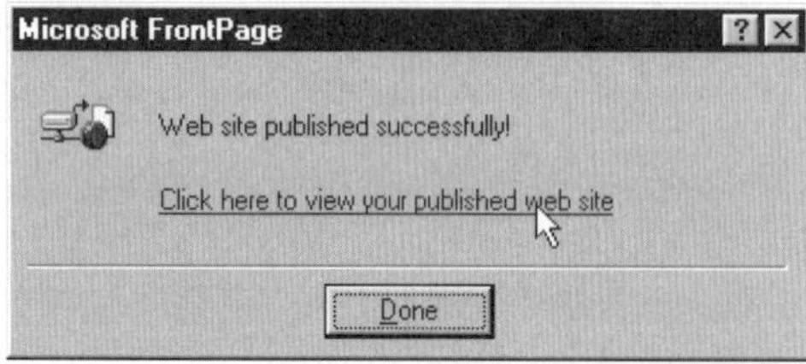

Microsoft FrontPage
Web site published successfully!
Click here to view your published web site
Done


You will be told when the upload is complete – and when it is, you can go straight off and view it online (which is when you'll find that really glaring mistake ...)

## Updating a web

**Tip**

**While you are working on your web at home, it is a good idea to keep track of any files you are deleting so that you can go on-line later and remove them from your Web server. But don't worry if you forget! You can use the Reports view to check for pages and files which are no longer linked into the web – see pages 16–17.**

Once you have a web up on the World Wide Web, you should update it on a regular basis – the Internet is so awash with information that a static, unchanging site is unlikely to inspire visitors to return to it time and again.

There are two ways of updating your web:

- Connect to the Internet and open your web on-line. Any changes you save to the web will then be effected immediately.
- Make changes on your PC and publish it as before, but this time checking the **Publish changed pages only** box.

If you edit your web at home and then publish it, the pages you have *changed* will be updated on the World Wide Web server, but any pages you *removed* will not be altered. Obsolete pages and images will not be accessible to visitors, but will sit on the server taking up space until you get rid of them. To remove files, you will have to go on-line and make the necessary changes directly on the server.

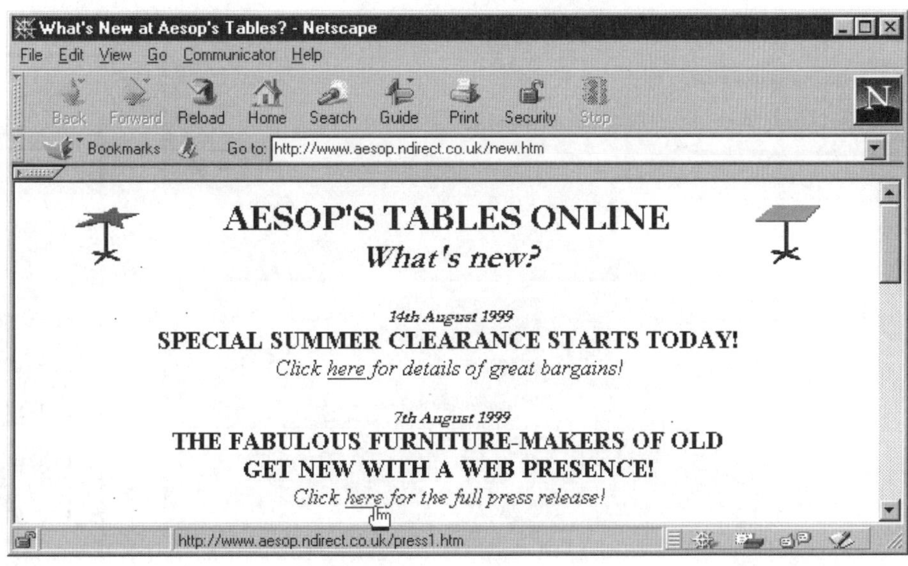
What's New at Aesop's Tables? - Netscape
File Edit View Go Communicator Help
Back Forward Reload Home Search Guide Print Security Stop
Bookmarks Go to: http://www.aesop.ndirect.co.uk/new.htm
AESOP'S TABLES ONLINE
What's new?
14th August 1999
SPECIAL SUMMER CLEARANCE STARTS TODAY!
Click here for details of great bargains!
7th August 1999
THE FABULOUS FURNITURE-MAKERS OF OLD
GET NEW WITH A WEB PRESENCE!
Click here for the full press release!
http://www.aesop.ndirect.co.uk/press1.htm

# Network connections

## Basic steps

Normally when you use the Internet, you are connected to the server's Unix network, but when you try to publish a web, you may well need to be connected to the server's Windows NT network as well. To set this up, you will need to configure your computer's **Network** properties.

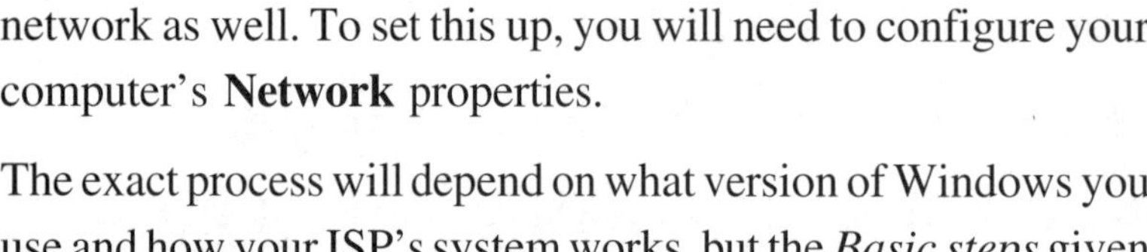

The exact process will depend on what version of Windows you use and how your ISP's system works, but the *Basic steps* given here for Windows 95/98 may well be useful.

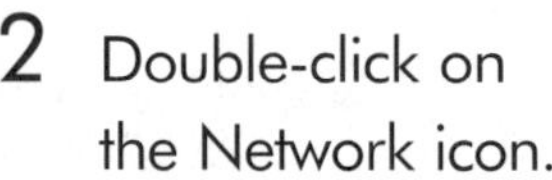

1 Open the Control Panel from the Start menu.

2 Double-click on the Network icon.

❑ If Client for Microsoft Networks is installed, go to step 7, otherwise:

3 Click Add…

4 Select Client and click Add…

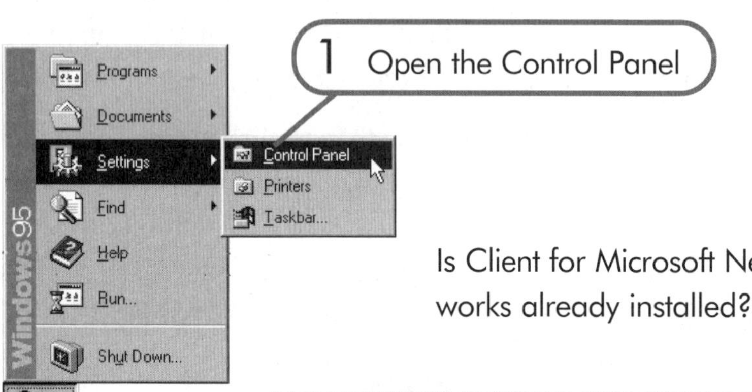

Programs
Documents
Settings
Control Panel
Printers
Taskbar...
Find
Help
Run...
Shut Down...
Windows95
Start


1 Open the Control Panel

Is Client for Microsoft Networks already installed?


Network
Configuration
Identification
Access Control
The following network components are installed:
Client for Microsoft Networks
Dial-Up Adapter
TCP/IP
Personal Web Server
Add...
Remove
Properties
Primary Network Logon:
Windows Logon
File and Print Sharing...
Description
The Client for Microsoft Networks enables you to connect to other Microsoft Windows computers and servers and use the files and printers shared on them.
OK
Cancel


3 Click Add

7 Select Client and click Properties

## Tip

**If you having difficulty publishing your web, the network connections are the most likely source of the problems.**

5 Select Microsoft in the Manufacturers pane, Client for Microsoft Networks in the Network Clients pane.

6 Click OK.

7 Highlight Client for Microsoft Networks and click Properties…

8 Turn on Log on to Windows NT domain and Quick logon (your ISP will tell you the name to enter in the Windows NT domain field).

9 Click OK.

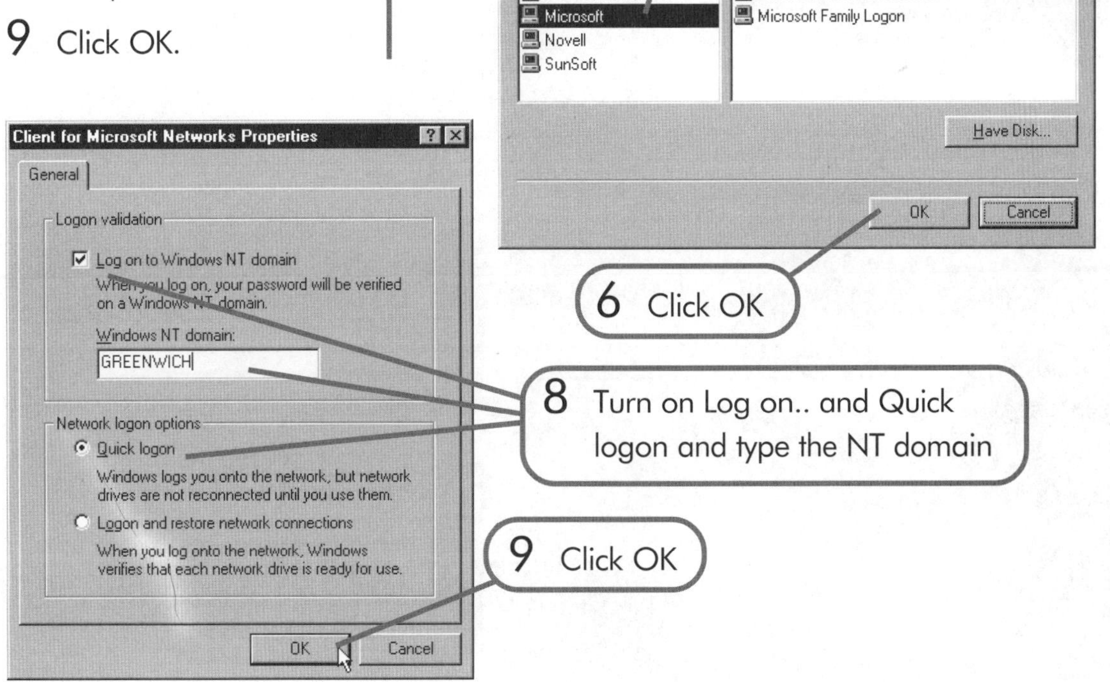

4 Select Client and click Add
Select Network Component Type
Click the type of network component you want to install:
Client
Adapter
Protocol
Service
Add...
Cancel
A client enables your computer to connect to other computers.
5 Select Microsoft then Client for Microsoft Networks
Select Network Client
Click the Network Client that you want to install, then click OK. If you have an installation disk for this device, click Have Disk.
Manufacturers:
Banyan
FTP Software, Inc.
Microsoft
Novell
SunSoft
Network Clients:
Client for Microsoft Networks
Client for NetWare Networks
Microsoft Family Logon
Have Disk...
OK
Cancel
6 Click OK
Client for Microsoft Networks Properties
General
Logon validation
Log on to Windows NT domain
When you log on, your password will be verified on a Windows NT domain.
Windows NT domain:
GREENWICH
Network logon options
Quick logon
Windows logs you onto the network, but network drives are not reconnected until you use them.
Logon and restore network connections
When you log onto the network, Windows verifies that each network drive is ready for use.
OK
Cancel
8 Turn on Log on.. and Quick logon and type the NT domain
9 Click OK

# Web Publishing Wizard

## Basic steps

There is a **Publishing Wizard** on the FrontPage CD-ROM which will guide you through the publishing process if your ISP does not support FrontPage Extensions.

If you have not already installed it, run the CD-ROM and click the **Web Publishing Wizard** icon to install it.

1 Open the Publishing Wizard from the Start menu.

2 Follow the instructions.

3 When you Browse Folders… for the web folder, it should be in C:\My Webs\

4 Type a name for your web space – this is the same even if you have several webs on it.

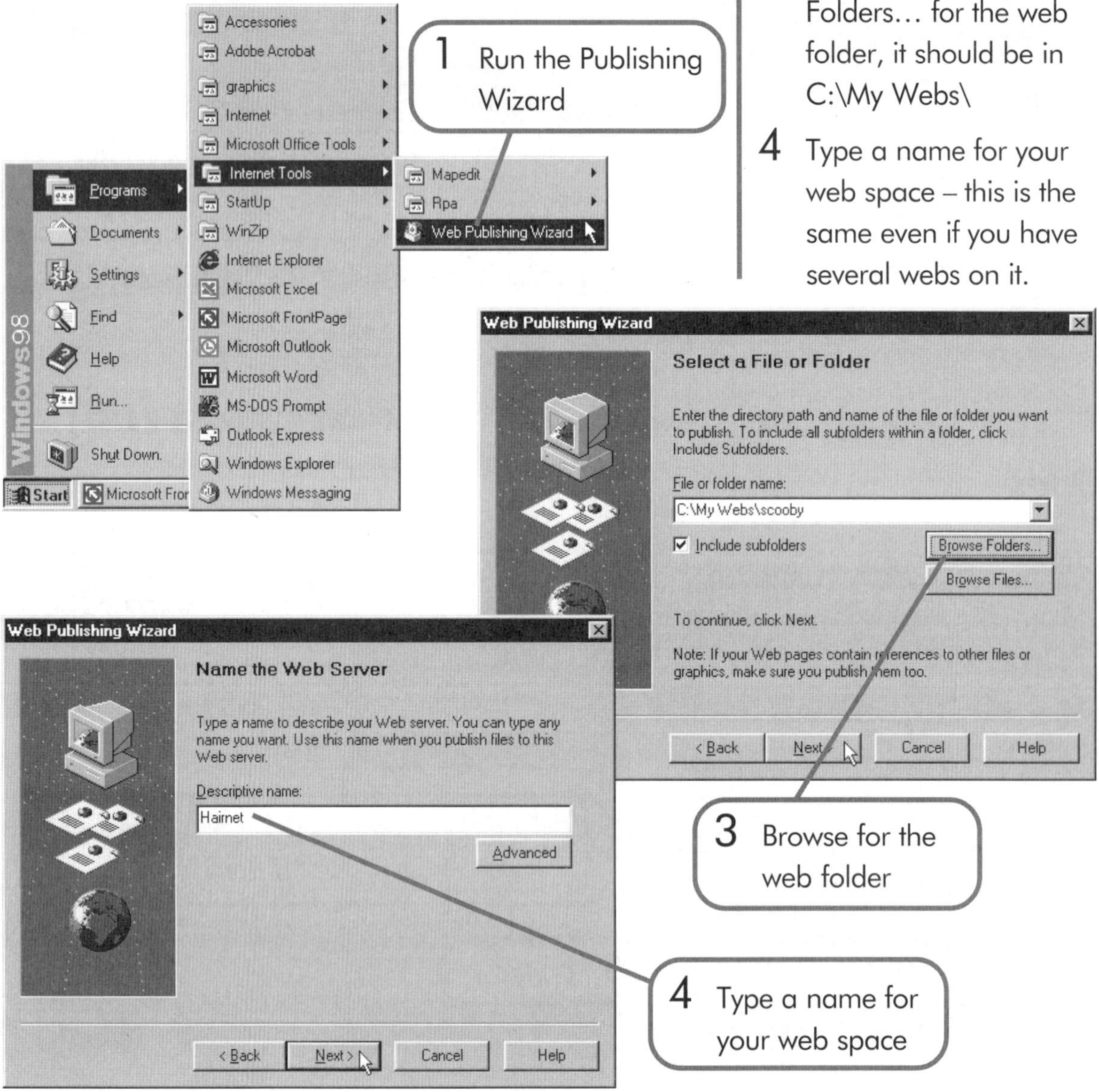

1 Run the Publishing Wizard

3 Browse for the web folder

4 Type a name for your web space

5 Enter the URL of your web space – ask your web host if you are not sure what it is.

6 The wizard will connect to the Internet and check your settings. You may be prompted for a username and password for your web space.

7 Click Finish.

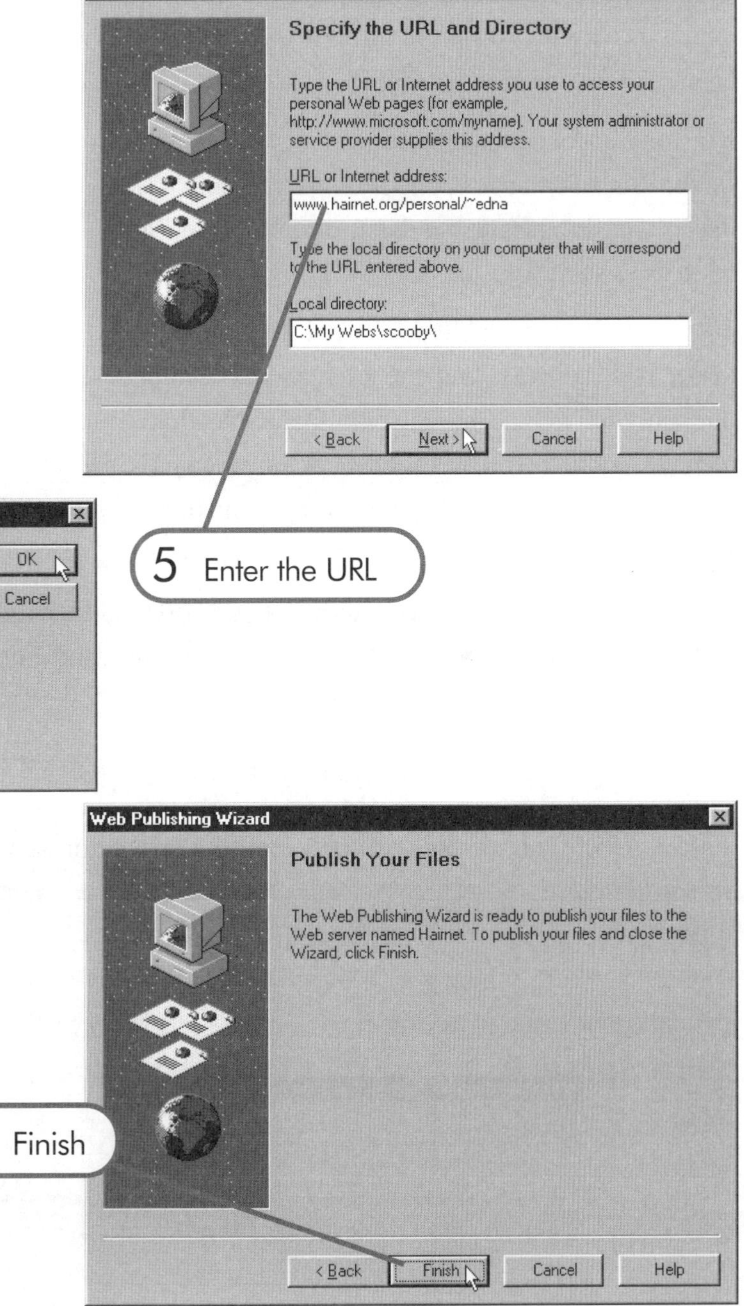
Web Publishing Wizard
Specify the URL and Directory
Type the URL or Internet address you use to access your personal Web pages (for example, http://www.microsoft.com/myname). Your system administrator or service provider supplies this address.
URL or Internet address:
www.hairnet.org/personal/~edna
Type the local directory on your computer that will correspond to the URL entered above.
Local directory:
C:\My Webs\scooby\
< Back
Next >
Cancel
Help
5 Enter the URL
Enter Network Password
Please enter your authentication information
OK
Cancel
Resource: www.acmecity.com
User name: bumpyjohnson
Password:
Save this password in your password list
6 Enter your username and password
Web Publishing Wizard
Publish Your Files
The Web Publishing Wizard is ready to publish your files to the Web server named Hairnet. To publish your files and close the Wizard, click Finish.
8 Click Finish
< Back
Finish
Cancel
Help

# Troubleshooting

## Basic steps

When the files of your web are transferred to a World Wide Web server, they are sent in a format called **File Transfer Protocol** (FTP). The information is received at the server's FTP address, which is slightly different to the http address which your browser visits to view web sites.

You may find when you try to publish your web onto your ISP's server that an error message is displayed, and a likely cause of this is that FrontPage has been unable to determine the FTP address to send files to.

To get around the problem, you will first need to find out your ISP's FTP address, and the directory to which you should publish your web. You may find this somewhere in the documentation sent to you by your ISP, or they may have a Help page on their Web site which deals with publishing or uploading problems.

If there is a section which explains how to upload your web from a DOS window, you will find two important command lines, which will look something like this:

```
Type: ftp ftp.ndirect.co.uk
Type: cd www
```

This is the ISP's FTP address

This is the directory to publish to

If you don't see anything which looks like the right information, just call your ISP and ask them.

1 Run through the Publishing Wizard's steps as before.

2 When the error message appears, click OK.

3 Ensure that FTP – File Transfer Protocol is selected.

4 Enter the FTP address of your ISP.

5 Enter the correct Subfolder.

❑ You should now get a message saying that FrontPage is ready to publish.

6 Click Finish.

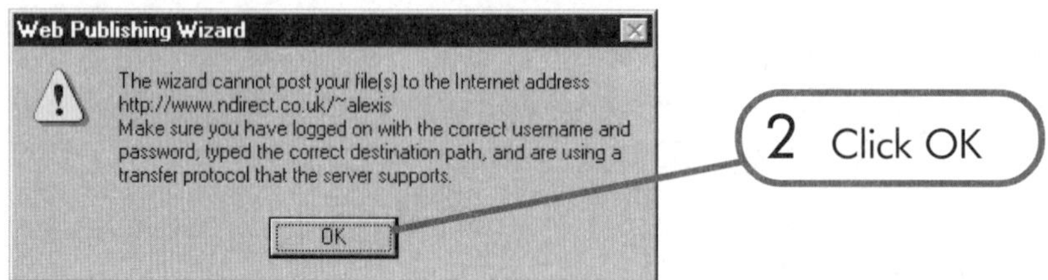
Web Publishing Wizard
The wizard cannot post your file(s) to the Internet address
http://www.ndirect.co.uk/~alexis
Make sure you have logged on with the correct username and password, typed the correct destination path, and are using a transfer protocol that the server supports.
OK
2 Click OK

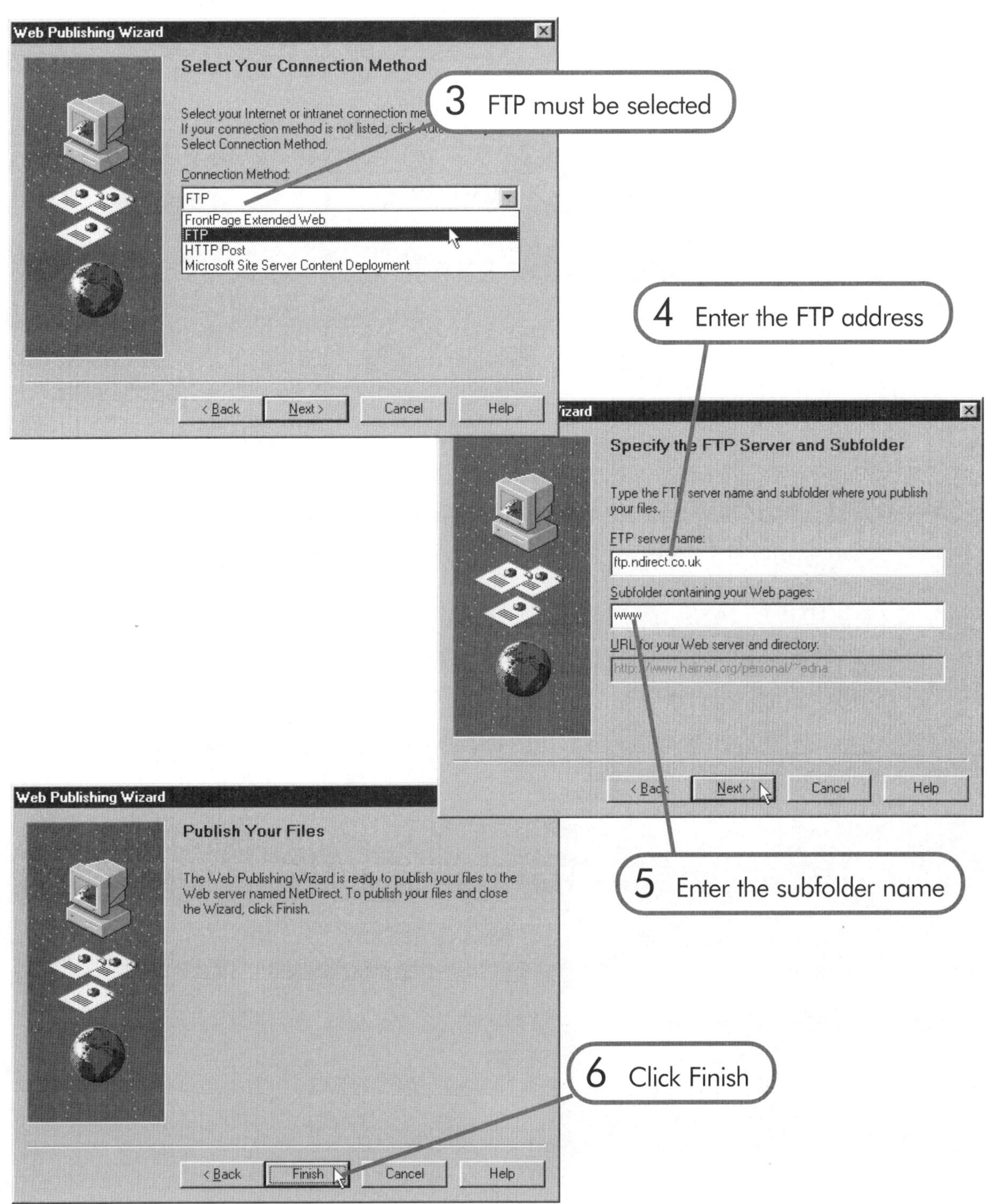
Web Publishing Wizard
Select Your Connection Method
Select your Internet or intranet connection me
If your connection method is not listed, click
Select Connection Method.
Connection Method:
FTP
FrontPage Extended Web
FTP
HTTP Post
Microsoft Site Server Content Deployment
< Back
Next >
Cancel
Help
3 FTP must be selected
4 Enter the FTP address
Specify the FTP Server and Subfolder
Type the FTP server name and subfolder where you publish your files.
FTP server name:
ftp.ndirect.co.uk
Subfolder containing your Web pages:
www
URL for your Web server and directory:
5 Enter the subfolder name
Web Publishing Wizard
Publish Your Files
The Web Publishing Wizard is ready to publish your files to the Web server named NetDirect. To publish your files and close the Wizard, click Finish.
< Back
Finish
Cancel
Help
6 Click Finish

# Summary

## If your ISP supports FrontPage Extensions:

- ❑ Publish a FrontPage Web from FrontPage, ensuring that the Publish all pages option is selected.
- ❑ Update a web by selecting Publish Changed pages only...
- ❑ ...or connect to the Internet to update a web in real time.
- ❑ Check your Network connections if you are having trouble.

## If it doesn't:

- ❑ Use the Web Publishing Wizard to guide you through the process (install it if necessary).
- ❑ Find your web in the \My Webs\ folder.
- ❑ If you are having trouble, ask your ISP for their FTP address and the directory you should publish to.
- ❑ You may also be able to find this information from the help pages at your ISP's Web site.

# Links and resources

support.microsoft.com/support/

The FrontPage section of Microsoft's home will keep you up-to-date with FrontPage development, but you will be lucky to get much help without having to pay for it.

news.microsoft.public.frontpage.client

The FrontPage newsgroup is an invaluable resource – if you have a problem, it is almost guaranteed that you will find a solution here.

www.alt-web.com

A handy gallery of web graphics, such as bullets, lines, etc.

www.gifs.net/animate/animate.htm

A nice library of animations, free for personal use.

www.jasc.com

Jasc produce Paint Shop Pro 5, a powerful but easy-to-use image editing program. It's shareware, which means you can use it free for a trial period before you have to pay for it.

www.jazzpiano.com/frontpage

Chris Calabrese's FrontPage Information Web is an unofficial FrontPage site which I have found much more useful than Microsoft. At the time of writing FrontPage 2000 was not commercially available, so the site was aimed at FrontPage 97 and FrontPage 98 users – but you will still find it useful.

www.real.com

RealAudio software allows you to create and hear streaming audio files.

www.thefreesite.com

You'll find all kinds of goodies here – and all for free!

www.jtucows.com

A good resource for downloading freeware and shareware programs for Windows systems.

www.worldwidemart.com/scripts

Matt's Script Archive has a huge downloadable range of program scripts for putting various clever tricks into your web.

# Index